EAT UP

THE NEXT LEVEL

EAT
UP

THE NEXT LEVEL

PERFORM AT YOUR BEST PHYSICALLY + MENTALLY EVERY DAY

DANIEL DAVEY

GILL BOOKS

Gill Books
Hume Avenue
Park West
Dublin 12
www.gillbooks.ie

Gill Books is an imprint of M.H. Gill and Co.

© Daniel Davey 2022

978 07171 9524 4

Designed by Graham Thew
Edited by Emma Dunne
Proofread by Esther Ní Dhonnacha
Indexed by Eileen O'Neill
Photography by Leo Byrne
Styling by Clare Wilkinson
Printed and bound by Printer Trento, Italy
This book is typeset in 10.5 pt Macho Light

This book is not intended as a substitute for the medical advice of a physician. The reader should consult a doctor or mental health professional if they feel it necessary.

This product is made of FSC®certified and other controlled material.

A CIP catalogue record for this book is available from the British Library.

5 4 3 2 1

DEDICATED TO MY FATHER, PETER DAVEY.

You gave me the confidence to find my own path. I am who I am, where I am and who I will be because of you, your love and your support – thank you.

ACKNOWLEDGEMENTS

The development of this book would not have been possible without the help of and excellent work by Heather Masterson and Dr Clíodhna McHugh, who worked incredibly hard to help me create a book that would be practical to use with great recipes but also built on a foundation of sound science. Thank you.

Thank you also to my mother, Eileen, and my wife, Sandra, who give me ongoing support and encouragement. To my daughter, Penny, thank you for eating 'most' of my food and not throwing it all over the floor! If you are happy with the meals, I have no doubt many more children will enjoy eating them with their parents.

CONTENTS

INTRODUCTION

This book contains 100 simple and delicious recipes and step-by-step actions you can take to create greater consistency in your food choices, mindset, relationship with food and lifestyle that can bring your health and performance to the next level. Why did I want to write it?

I could never have imagined the response to *Eat Up, Raise Your Game.* It was overwhelming, and to those who supported me, bought the book, sent kind messages and shared photos of what you cooked from it, I sincerely thank you. I was truly surprised and thrilled to learn that it was not just athletes and those who were competitive in sports that enjoyed the recipes and learned from the book, but also those looking for nutritious meals to suit the whole family. It was immensely fulfilling to hear and see.

The experience was so positive that I want to share what I have learned since then and, of course, bring new and even better-tasting recipes to you. I can honestly say that I am a better cook and a more experienced performance nutritionist today, and I believe this book will have a powerful impact on your nutrition, cooking and eating experience. Why? This book contains new information on topics related to sports nutrition and performance that I wasn't able to cover previously, and will enhance your understanding of them in a practical manner. I want to help grow your awareness of the connection between mindset

and achieving consistency in your nutrition, habits and behaviours. I have also created new recipes that I guarantee you will taste amazing. Above all, I've brought so much learning to this book from the feedback of those who have used *Eat Up, Raise Your Game.* And that's what it's all about: if you are willing, you can always make things better and find areas to improve.

THERE IS A KEY DIFFERENCE, HOWEVER, BETWEEN KNOWLEDGE AND IMPLEMENTATION OF KNOWLEDGE.

Never in our history have we had as much access to information but such confusion around what our behaviours should look like, evident from the growing prevalence of lifestyle-related illnesses. Food can have a tremendous positive influence on our bodies. Understanding how it can nourish, heal, support and energise the body helps us to be at our best each day. When I set out to write this book, the primary goal was to separate the noise in nutrition from the real science and present it in a way that would help to reduce the doubts, anxiety and often guilt associated with food. I believe when we invest in the key areas of our lifestyle, we can all perform better – not just athletes but everyone.

I have worked with high-performance athletes for most of my career and, subsequently, know what is required to win and to consistently perform at the top level in sport. In this book, I delve into not only the science of nutrition, but also the tools, strategies and mindset used by the best of the best, the top athletes, to maintain their consistency in high-performance sport. I address what I have found to be the critical aspects of an athlete's career and how making the right food choices in these circumstances will improve an athlete's performance, including:

1 **Exercise days**
2 **Rest days**
3 **Competition days**
4 **Recovering from injury**
5 **Supporting immunity**

My main message is to invest in your nutrition, your mindset and your physical and mental wellbeing for enhanced physical and mental performance.

CORE CONCEPTS

Over the course of this book, I will present many nutrition, mindset and performance strategies that you can implement for sustained success. A key element is mindset and how our mindset influences our behaviours and, subsequently, our food choices. While the value of nutrition for health and performance remains high, new challenges have evolved in our relationship with food. My principles around food have remained the same since *Eat Up, Raise Your Game*, where I focused on understanding the key determinants of a successful diet and my philosophy on food. In this book I am bringing

attention to mindset, behaviours and why we make the decisions we do in our eating habits.

UNDERSTAND, EXECUTE AND REFLECT

One thing that has become apparent from my years working with top athletes, clubs and high-performing individuals is that

THOSE WHO INTERNALISE, IMPLEMENT AND REFLECT ON KEY HABITS AND BEHAVIOURS ARE MOST SUCCESSFUL IN ACHIEVING THEIR GOALS.

It was this insight that led me to create the understand, execute and reflect (UER) system. If you take one thing from this book and implement it in your life, it should be to use this approach for the strategies and habits you'll learn about.

1 Understand
Have clarity on what you want to achieve. By establishing clear and precise goals you can understand the theory and principles surrounding them. This will help you to understand why I am recommending particular habits and processes. So as you read each chapter, become familiar with the concepts, strategies and recipes, and take your own notes.

2 Execute
Start to use this new system of planning and implementing in things like shopping, cooking, trying new skills, exploring new

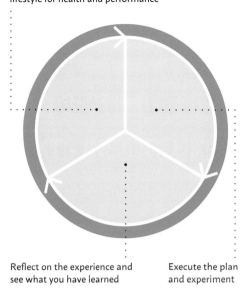

Understand and have clarity about the things that really work in your lifestyle for health and performance

Reflect on the experience and see what you have learned

Execute the plan and experiment

flavours and habits within your lifestyle. Don't be afraid to experiment and make mistakes – it's all part of the learning process.

3 Reflect

Check in and reflect on what you are doing in the plan – this will help you to really understand what is working well, what is not working and why. How did it feel to try new things and get a little out of your comfort zone? It is not just about what you learn from this book but what you teach yourself. The practice of reflection has become a major part of my life and approach when working with people.

AIM FOR CONSISTENT PERFORMANCE

The well-known past president of the American College of Lifestyle Medicine David Katz suggests that 'it's not what we know, it's what we do with what we know'.

The word 'performance' is often associated with artists or athletes executing spectacular actions in elite competitions.

HOWEVER, I BELIEVE THAT PERFORMANCE IS ABOUT PEOPLE BEING AT THEIR BEST IN THEIR DAILY ACTIONS, NO MATTER WHAT LEVEL THEY ARE COMPETING OR PERFORMING AT.

Performing at your best in your daily physical and mental activities is something we should all aspire to. Achieving your potential requires consistently making the correct choices in the key areas of exercise, lifestyle and performance. Nutrition is a vital component of this. Using this book and the 100 simple recipes will help you optimise your performance so you can achieve your goals. Performance is not a once-off activity. It requires consistency in practice, preparation and recovery. It takes time to perfect your performance strategies and, even then, there is always room for improvement. My vision for performance is based on a clear plan, executing that plan and reviewing progress along the way to see what's going well and what can be improved.

WHAT'S NEW?

Two years have passed since my first book, *Eat Up, Raise Your Game*, and quite a bit has changed in my life. I became a dad for the first time to a beautiful daughter, Penny, who has changed things in the most positive way – more than I ever could have imagined. She has brought great light, energy, focus and new purpose to everyday life. I want Penny to grow up in a loving, safe, fun, caring home that allows her to be whoever she chooses and challenges her to be as great as she can. I want her to have a positive relationship with food, full of great experiences, enjoyment, discovery and nourishment. That is something that my wife, Sandra, and I will work together on as a family each day.

WHAT ABOUT HEALTH?

The World Health Organization states, 'Health is a state of complete physical, mental and social wellbeing and not merely the absence of disease or infirmity'. My understanding of good health has changed as I have evolved in my career. I used to believe that to be in good health you needed to be rigid, seek perfection, be lean and engage in extreme levels of fitness. I didn't take account of having fun, happiness, being functionally fit and enjoying the benefits of a healthy lifestyle. I didn't realise that you could achieve good health and optimal performance without extreme discipline in nutrition and while enjoying life. What is fascinating is that my attitude to and relationship with food have completely changed over the past five years, but there has been little to no change in my weight and body composition. I had assumed that not only would there be changes, but also those changes would be considerable. I

have proved to myself that, while you do need to make mostly good choices with food, you can enjoy treats from time to time and a more relaxed approach to nutrition.

WE ALL NEED GUIDANCE, SUPPORT AND ENCOURAGEMENT

On a sad note, my dad, Peter, passed away in October 2021 at the age of 68, far sooner than he should have, but he made the most of every day of those 68 years. That was his motto: enjoy today. He was brought up on a small farm in Leitrim South, near Tubbercurry in Co. Sligo, before moving to care for an older relation at the age of just 12. There he tended the three cows on the farm, milking and working the land. While Peter farmed his whole life, his real passion was drama. He was an acclaimed actor and director and spent more than 50 years involved in amateur drama with the Phoenix Players in Tubbercurry. Some of his career highlights were winning an all-Ireland best actor award and acting professionally with the Blue Raincoats theatre company in Sligo town. That was a small part of what Peter did, but who he was to my family and to me was much more special.

Peter was my dad, my north star and the person I turned to for support and guidance. He had a huge influence on my life and a big impact on my interest in and relationship with food. He was a gifted listener; he would just sit and listen to me speak and then somehow always make sense of situations that I struggled with. In the aftermath of Peter's passing, I realised that I wasn't the only one who turned to him for advice, support and a friendly ear. We received countless letters and cards from people all across

Ireland and abroad, sharing their memories of when he had been there for them, just as he had been for me. That's just who he was.

Losing Peter has brought incredible pain and sadness. He has left a void that will never be filled, but there was light and hope too in all that we shared and experienced. The unity and love of our family and the support of friends and neighbours have allowed me to experience appreciation, gratitude and pride, feelings I wasn't expecting in the wake of such a loss. To have experienced that love during the hardest time in my life makes me incredibly proud. Peter was proud too. In the weeks prior to his passing, we had the chance to share our thoughts and words. While this wasn't easy, I will always be grateful we talked as openly as we did. They were special conversations that will stay with me forever.

In those weeks before my dad passed, we were fortunate to spend some really special time with him, caring for him and doing the little things that we often take for granted. In fact, I read many of the chapters from this book to him, which makes it all the more important to me. Food, optimum nutrition and cooking played a really important role in Peter's care at this time. We, as a family, cooked a nutritious meal in the evenings, and as the smells from the kitchen filled the house, the mood and morale in the house lifted. Peter would join us and have what he could. The nod of approval or seeing him enjoy the meal, no matter how small, gave us all a sense of comfort. That time at home helped me to cope with his passing.

PETER LEAVES A LEGACY IN SO MANY WAYS.

First and foremost, he was a loving father and husband. He was the person we all turned to for guidance and support. Much of who I am is influenced by him and many of the stories I share in this book are an acknowledgement of his wonderful influence. I will always be grateful for his love, support and everything I learned from him.

While there are too many variables to go into detail here about nutrition for someone with cancer – in particular the type of cancer, the treatment they are receiving and the stage of the illness – food can certainly play an important role in helping to maintain quality of life, function and a positive mindset. A few things are pretty universal:

- Getting adequate energy from a variety of foods and meals
- Getting a good source of protein at most meals – yoghurts, whey protein, eggs and milk are good options and easy to consume
- Smaller, more frequent meals are usually easier to manage than bigger meals
- Food enjoyment helps – ensuring the person has meals and foods they really like
- High-fibre foods are important for digestion and motility but need to be managed carefully if taking pain medication
- Keep meals varied and flavoursome – include the person in the planning of the meals
- Milk, soups, puddings and whey-enriched treats are a great way of getting in some extra protein and essential nutrients

IT'S ABOUT THE MESSAGE, NOT YOU!

Peter was never much of an early riser, but I would often go into his room on a Saturday morning to wake him with a coffee and have a chat. I remember once sitting on the edge of the bed and sharing some of my fears about writing *Eat Up, Raise Your Game* and the content I share on social media. What if I make a mistake? What if people don't like the recipes? And what will people think of me writing a book? He listened intently, as he always did, and then responded, 'If the positive message is about food, and to help others is your reason for sharing your information, then that's all that matters. Your thoughts are natural, you want to do a good job and you will do a good job.' I remember thinking how calming his words were, and in reality it's because he was speaking the truth. Such a simple but powerful perspective. That conversation gave me a great sense of calm among all my doubts and fears. I remind myself of those words as I share new messages in this book and each week when I share content on my online platforms. My intention is to help others, to improve people's health and performance. Maybe understanding his mindset and his simple message is something that can help you too.

HOW IT ALL STARTED

For those of you who don't know me, I grew up on a small farm in Chaffpool, Sligo, in the west of Ireland. It wasn't until I reached my late twenties that I realised the impact my upbringing had on the way I viewed food and my nutrition philosophy. My profound interest in farming, animals and caring for the land in a sustainable manner sparked an interest in food in me from a young age.

This was the beginning of my career path as a performance nutritionist.

I wasn't necessarily good at school, particularly in subjects like maths and Irish, and doing homework always felt like a punishment. I struggled to attend school at various stages, and I would do anything I could to get out of class. I preferred to be out driving tractors, milking cows or playing football. To say I didn't apply myself was an understatement. My parents did what they could to encourage me, but I just wasn't interested, and the more they tried, the more I would revolt. I did well in a few subjects, like agricultural science, home economics and English. That gave me hope that, while I didn't like school in general, I would get enough points to do science or agricultural science in University College Dublin (UCD).

I did the Leaving Cert and, while I knew I wasn't going to win any academic awards, I felt I did well in my favoured subjects. I was worried about maths, though, because even if I got the points for agricultural science, I wouldn't get in without passing maths.

On the day of the Leaving Cert results, I walked into the principal's office and he handed me the envelope. On the sheet were the exact points I needed for agricultural science in UCD, but I'd failed maths: 37.5 per cent. It was time to face the reality of my efforts, my actions and lack of commitment. The night after the results come out is supposed to be a celebration, but I was sick to my stomach and filled with regret. I found it difficult to look my classmates in the eye when they asked how I got on.

In the following weeks, I moved my focus to what I was going to do to get into college, and I stopped worrying about what I hadn't achieved. The plan was to repeat my Leaving Cert year with the aim of getting better results and passing maths. A few weeks later, just before I got up to do my best man's speech at my uncle Seamus's wedding, a text came from Michael Collins, the principal. In capital letters, it read, 'YOU GOT IT, 40%!' That was one of the best days of my life. Two weeks later I was starting agricultural science in UCD.

It felt like a new world opened up to me there, and studying things I liked with people who had similar interests was really enjoyable. The range of modules available opened my eyes to different aspects of food and food production. It gave me a detailed understanding of the journey of food from 'farm to fork'. During these studies, I not only made lifelong friends, but also decided that I wanted to pursue a career in nutrition.

A YEAR ACROSS THE POND

After my degree in UCD, I was accepted into a master's in nutrition, physical activity and public health at the University of Bristol, which confirmed that it was sports nutrition I wanted to specialise in. After gaining some experience working in sports nutrition, I went on to complete the International Olympic Committee (IOC) postgraduate diploma in sports nutrition.

While I was doing my master's, I played football with the London senior football team, doubling as their performance nutritionist. At the time I was very serious about two things: playing football and nutrition. I wasn't particularly tolerant of those who weren't fully committed to both. There were many robust conversations that year with various

players and coaches as I tried to gain buy-in to nutrition practice. As I saw it, athletes were making glaring mistakes with their nutrition and that was negatively impacting performance. Back then it wasn't unusual for players to go to McDonald's after a gym or pitch session. One of the conversations I look back on and now laugh about was with a really talented player on our team, John. After training, I was talking intensely about the importance of recovery and the potential damage of things like takeaways. John nodded as I was speaking, and when I took a breath, he asked me, 'You finished?' I said, 'No.' He said, 'Well, do you know what you need to do?' I said, 'What?' 'Relax ta fuck and drink more pints!' he said and walked off. I was left with my mouth open. Conversations like that left me frustrated and, in the early days of my nutrition career, even caused me to question the route I was taking. What I have realised many years later is that these conversations were teaching me a huge amount about communication, what motivates different people and the importance of building solid relationships with people before talking to them about what they should do!

A SLIGO MAN WORKING IN HURLING?

When I moved back to Ireland after my studies in Bristol, it was all about trying to get some real-life work experience. This was more of a challenge than I expected. For months, I did all kinds of jobs just to pay the bills – including standing on Leeson Street bridge, at around six in the morning, dressed in an orange suit and handing out fruit juice. But, just like all my other work experience up to that point, that was valuable too. I learned how to approach people in a friendly, nonthreatening manner – I also learned that jobs like that are not easy.

About 18 months after coming back to Ireland and working mostly in marketing jobs, my friend Brendan Egan told me about a job coming up with a supplement company. Although I never intended to work in the supplement industry, the three years I spent there learning how to formulate products, write nutrition labels and, most of all, see how a business was set up were invaluable. I gained great insight into the supplement industry, which was very useful to me as my career evolved, as it's always a topic of conversation with athletes and you need to know what works and what doesn't.

In 2011, I had the opportunity to join the Dublin senior hurling team as their performance nutritionist, when my very good friend Martin Kennedy asked me to be part of his performance team. Martin is an exceptional coach and a fantastic man. He supported me when I was just starting out; he encouraged me and believed in me when I needed it most. We all need an MK in our lives, and I do my best to help others the way Martin helped me. Working with the Dublin hurling team was my first real experience of high-performance sport, and I loved every minute of it. They were committed, motivated and had an incredible work ethic, which was really inspiring.

I continued to work full-time in the supplement industry during this time, which involved many early mornings, including being in the gym at 5 a.m. with the team sometimes, before going to work with the supplement company and meeting clients in the evenings. I gained a lot of great experience as well as new friendships within the team.

THE DREAM COMES TRUE

At the end of that year, a position came up with the Dublin senior football team, which I applied for. Following many reviews and meetings with Jim Gavin, I became their performance nutritionist from 2012 until the present day. Soon after this, in 2013, there was a job opportunity with Leinster Rugby and, following a lot of preparation and an extensive interview process, I was successful in my application for that role too. It was my dream to work in elite sport and in the space of two months I was working with the two teams I admired most. There have been many pinch-me moments over the past nine years but plenty of tough ones too. You need to continue to add value and evolve every season, which is one of the great things about the role but also comes with many challenges.

Being successful in the industry is not only about getting the necessary qualifications and ticking the boxes on your CV. It requires continuous growth, learning and reflection to be successful. If you are truly committed to working in this space, I recommend that you focus on building your knowledge, gaining experience, networking, becoming familiar with well-respected individuals in the field, making contacts, reading and being proactive in your learning. Instagram, TikTok, Twitter and so on have become saturated with 'nutrition experts', and it is very tempting to become part of that world, but in doing this, you may miss out on the fundamentals, such as gaining experience, building your knowledge and making real-life connections.

Everything I have experienced along the way, every unpaid job and challenging obstacle I have overcome, has taught me something valuable. All of these things that we pick up as we go accumulate and shape us into the person and, in this case, practitioner that we aspire to become.

ALTHOUGH I DIDN'T TAKE THE MOST STRAIGHTFORWARD ROUTE, I WOULD NOT CHANGE IT.

NAILING DOWN THE FUNDAMENTALS

Nutrition is an ever-evolving science, and even the most well-educated and -qualified scientists, researchers, dietitians and nutritionists are still learning. What is known and cannot be debated is that nutrition has an immeasurable influence on health, wellbeing and the risk for many diseases. To quote from the excellent article 'Emotions and Health Decision-Making' by Ferrer et al., 'the decisions that people make about their health significantly affect the quality, trajectory and length of human life'. The more consistent, positive and healthy your lifestyle habits, the better you feel, the better you look and the healthier you will be. While there is much we don't know about aspects of our body and mind, there are thankfully some sound nutritional principles that we do know. For example, there is a hierarchy of nutritional needs that every person can follow to determine their individual nutritional needs for health or performance. This determines the most important aspects of nutrition for a person and can prove invaluable when goal-setting for health and performance. Along with the elements of nutrition, of course, the psychology- and behaviour-related aspect also needs to be determined. This is what fascinates me most about nutrition: it cannot work in isolation from other lifestyle elements. We must understand how all aspects of our lifestyle impact our decision-making and our long-term health and performance.

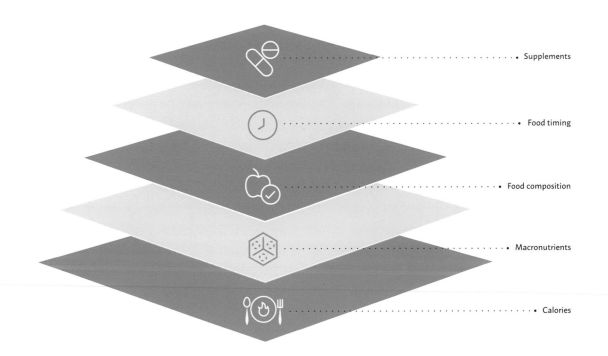

- Supplements
- Food timing
- Food composition
- Macronutrients
- Calories

1 Calories or energy
specifically suited to our personal needs is critical to optimally complete daily tasks and achieve various health or performance goals.

2 Macronutrients
– protein, carbohydrate and fat – are our primary sources of energy from food. Meeting our personal needs for each of these is critical for health, energy, body composition goals and, of course, athletic performance.

3 Food composition
relates to the nutrient density of the foods we eat day to day. Vitamins, minerals and antioxidants play a critical role in health, wellbeing and performance.

4 Food timing
relates to when food is consumed. This means at what point in the day you have your meals; in a performance context, it is specific to when food is consumed before or after exercise.

5 Supplements
are often what people want to discuss first when considering their dietary goals. While in specific cases supplements can offer an important solution for meeting the need for certain nutrients, supplements are the least important factor when it comes to the effectiveness of your diet.

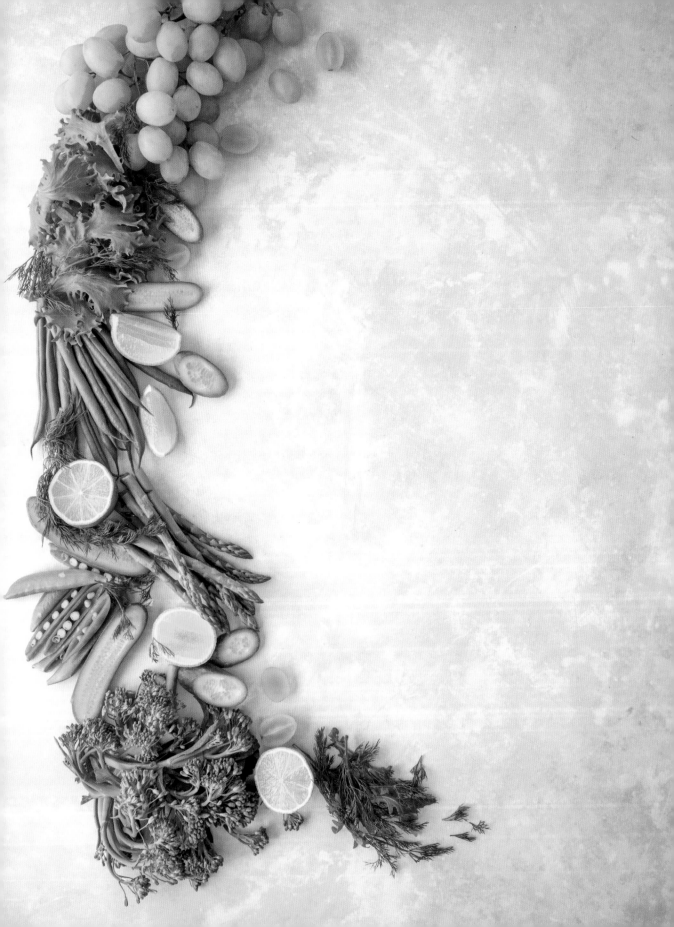

PART ONE: FOOD FOUNDATION

MY NUTRITION LESSONS

How many times have you heard the phrase 'it's about having the right mindset' when it comes to your nutrition or exercise? I would imagine many times. Unfortunately, it's not as simple as it sounds. There are many layers to having the right mindset with your nutrition and numerous things to consider when you are striving to build a consistent way of eating healthily. Firstly, you need to have excellent awareness about what works for you as an individual, and really understand what habits and decisions in your life allow you to be at your best.

Here are the top 10 lessons I have learned over the past 12 years from working with elite athletes, recreational athletes, those looking to improve their health and from my own personal journey with nutrition.

1 **Think about food and nutrition in a positive way.** Acknowledge your thoughts about food, and about how it makes you feel, and how this evolves as you continue to learn about what works best for you nutritionally.

2 **Knowledge does not necessarily translate into best practice.** Healthy eating is a habit. You have to put conscious effort into creating habits and routines in your daily life if you want to see consistent positive daily outcomes.

3 **Nutrition is one of many pieces of a jigsaw that fits together to make a healthy lifestyle.** No component works in isolation. Sleep, nutrition, exercise and the way you live your life; each have an impact on the other pillars of your performance.

4 **Building a positive relationship with food is essential for long-term, sustainable healthy eating habits.** A guilt-driven and negative relationship only creates a vicious cycle of negative emotions and a short-term focus on your goals.

5 **Create values within your home around food and cooking.** If you live with a partner, family or friends, try to get them involved and to buy in to these values. These can be based around:
   a Avoiding food wastage
   b Cooking your own meals
   c Eating together
   d Limiting takeaway meals
   e Eating seasonal foods

6 **Be patient!** We often underestimate how long it takes to create new habits or to make changes to our body composition. Meaningful change in your body and health is a by-product of patience, commitment and trust in the process.

7. **Expecting big changes too soon sets you up for disappointment when you fail.** Understanding your goals and aligning your expectations is critical for long-term success.

8. **Consistency, consistency and more consistency: understand it, embrace it and take pride in it.** Being consistent can result in extraordinary outcomes, but mastering it only comes with plenty of practice and reflection on what works in your personal routine.

9. **Good food choices are an investment in your health, your future and your family.** Think of each meal as an opportunity to make a small but positive investment in these things.

10. **Don't underestimate the power of reflection.** Reflection is giving careful consideration to your actions and behaviours in a manner that is honest, humbling and constructive for you. In high-performing environments, athletes regularly receive feedback on their performance and are expected to understand plans, details and practices that will allow them to consistently improve and strive towards being at their best. If we don't receive this type of feedback, we can achieve something similar through reflective practices. This can be just once a week thinking back over what went well and what you can do better, then dating and logging it in a journal (this is beneficial for all areas of our lives, not just nutritional habits).

INSIDE THE MINDS OF HIGH PERFORMERS

What differentiates elite athletes from those who never quite make it? This is a question that fascinates coaches, sports scientists, nutritionists and anyone who is interested in sport. The answer, of course, is not so straightforward. The roles of nature vs nurture, genetics and environmental exposure are all under considerable debate among the sports science community. In addition, the mindset of athletes is considered a critical factor for success. Successful elite athletes have commonalities in their psychological abilities, including sustaining high levels of motivation, thriving in high-pressure environments, coping with adversity and being resilient. These traits enable athletes to remain focused on achieving their goals. A quote I regularly use when speaking to groups is 'Doing the simple things consistently well can result in great outcomes, but doing things consistently well takes extraordinary discipline'. This quote epitomises the attitude of elite athletes and is what I see working with the most successful athletes in Ireland. They also strive for improvement no matter how small it may seem, they seek positive and negative feedback, and they never stop wanting to learn from those around them – from fellow athletes, teammates and coaching staff. Humility is a core trait that cannot be underestimated in these men and women.

EVERY DAY IS A LEARNING DAY

I'm extremely fortunate to work on a day-to-day basis with some of the most ambitious and driven individuals in the world. I have worked with teams that have won European Cups, All-Irelands and All-Stars, to name a few. Each team and athlete is different and presents an opportunity to learn. These athletes have to navigate challenges in their sports, including injury, losing matches, subpar performances or breakdowns in communications.

The most successful athletes always try to learn from these challenges. Mistakes happen, balls get dropped, games are lost and, from a nutrition perspective, there are periods of excessive eating and, let's be honest, alcohol comes into the equation too. When these adverse circumstances arise, it is the mindset to improve that matters most. These athletes never lose the desire for self-improvement and developing their knowledge of their sport. I have seen athletes reach the highest heights in their sport and get up the following week determined to improve and pursue even greater levels of performance. It's fascinating and infectious! In general, non-athletes, myself included, often become distracted and impatient with a lack of the results we think we should be achieving. Mental toughness has been described in research as the 'ability to sustain attention to the task-at-hand while under pressure, as well as in the face of distraction'. This really reflects my experience and I believe it's important to share the reality of how these men and women think. Too much emphasis is placed on the physical prowess of athletes and not enough on their mindset, attitude, work ethic and willingness to learn. If you truly want to learn from these athletes, look at how they build consistency and their mindset towards their goals. Just like a new sport-specific skill or gym technique, these too can be learned.

TEAM-FIRST MINDSET

From my experience, collaboration, teamwork, communication and a team-first approach are fundamental to building a successful team. In my jobs with Leinster Rugby and Dublin GAA, there was a huge backroom team involved, covering coaching, medical, athletic performance, analysis, sports psychology and nutrition. This team works collectively to ensure that all team members have both their on-field and off-field performance supported to the highest level. Only when each department is working in harmony will athletes fully achieve their potential. This is true for the backroom team too: they work and support each other in order to reach full potential in their work.

SUCCESS SIMPLY DOES NOT HAPPEN UNLESS YOU HAVE A COLLABORATIVE TEAM WITH A TEAM-FIRST MENTALITY.

If I look back at my own career playing football, the same can be said. Any team that performs consistently or is successful requires all players and backroom staff to be committed to the team with all the energy, effort and work directed towards helping the team succeed. Owen Eastwood, performance coach and author of the book *Belonging*, believes '70% of your behaviour is determined by the environment you happen to be in. So, you want to make it a positive place.'

Here are some of the common traits, behaviours and habits I have noted from working with incredible athletes.

1 They don't make excuses, such as 'I don't have time' or 'I don't know how'; they always find a way to get better.
2 They seek to learn and improve all the time.
3 They plan and organise their week and day as if every week is an important game week.
4 They compete with themselves to improve.
5 They accept when they make mistakes and want to learn from them.
6 They let their actions do the talking.
7 They are consistent in their execution of their lifestyle and training fundamentals.
8 They are curious, pleasant, humble, grateful and caring.

LIVING WITH SOB

When I started working with Leinster Rugby in 2013, I needed to find somewhere to live that didn't come with a daily traffic-ridden commute to work. Anyone who has lived in Dublin knows how difficult that search can be. Coincidentally, Seán O'Brien had just moved into a new apartment and, as luck would have it, was looking for a housemate. At the time, I didn't know Seán that well. But I did know he was a high-profile rugby player who was a former European player of the year, three-time Heineken Cup winner and Six Nations Championship winner, not to mention an out-and-out character. One day at training Seán approached me. 'I hear you're looking for a place at the moment – I could do you a good price?' I would be lying if I said the idea of living with Seán didn't excite me – it did! But I had to consider the obvious concerns associated with living with someone I worked with. I weighed up the pros and cons, but the possibility of building a really positive relationship with Seán as a friend while also having the opportunity to help him with his nutrition and his on-field performance swayed

my decision and I eventually accepted ... pending his idea of what a good price would be.

Seán was already a world-class athlete and a proven performer but was known to be inconsistent with his nutrition and lifestyle – he would admit that himself. For one of our first dinners together – it sounds like a date as I write it! – we cooked burgers with roast vegetables and a side of hummus. Seán's knife-skills, or lack thereof, were hilarious. He was chopping the vegetables with a bread knife and kept saying, 'This bloody knife is useless!' I smiled to myself but never said a word. In my defence, it wasn't because of who he was, but rather what he was: a 109-kg man, nicknamed the 'Tullow Tank', with a bread knife in his hand. I like burgers, but I wasn't prepared for them to be my last meal! We cooked the burgers in a nice tomato-based sauce with parsnip chips and roast peppers on the side. Seán cleaned his plate and relocated to the couch – he left me to tidy up, as his work was done. This was new territory for SOB, and I could feel it. I asked him what he thought.

He responded, 'Ya, lovely!'

I followed up with, 'That's good – you liked the peppers?'

'Ya,' said Seán, 'I actually don't eat peppers, but they were nice.'

Good start, I thought.

Living with Seán taught me a lot about elite athletes, behaviour change and what could be achieved over time with a subtle and progressive approach. I never once gave him a hard time or told him what he needed to do, but I always answered his questions and provided help when sought. We created a fun and enjoyable atmosphere in the house, with preparing and eating good food at the heart of it. As Seán's cooking skills and habits improved, he became a real ambassador for nutrition in Leinster. He talked to younger players about their habits and shared recipes and meals he had learned to cook. The benefits of peer-to-peer teaching are undeniable, especially when it is coming from someone of Seán's calibre. These younger players aspired to reach his level in rugby, and if he was telling them the benefits of developing cooking skills and focusing on their nutrition, they were going to do just that. He began to cook for his friends and family and took real pride when relaying back to me just how much they enjoyed it. The changes Seán had made to his nutrition and lifestyle became a huge asset when he had to battle injury and recovery. Seán was and is still known for his level of muscle mass – hence the nickname 'Tullow Tank' – strength and lean physique. But it was when he was getting back from his shoulder surgery that Seán achieved some of his greatest body-composition results, which he deserves great credit for. It really showed how his mindset about nutrition had changed and the power of his nutrition habits.

Seán and I became good friends over the time we lived together and continue to be. I often reference some of the stories of our time living together when working with athletes as real-life examples of how nutrition can play a huge role in performance and health. You can improve your nutrition at any point in your life, or indeed sports career. With Seán, it started with changing his mindset. He was competitive and wanted to continue to improve as a rugby player. He

could easily have just said, 'I have already achieved so much without being a good cook or developing good nutrition habits,' but he didn't. What is most gratifying about all my conversations about nutrition with Seán is that he will bring those skills and that knowledge with him, wherever he goes. I know he made a difference to those around him in London Irish and in his family, but it won't stop there. He enjoys his 'odd' pint or burger, but in the bigger picture, he is an ambassador for healthy eating and will feel the benefits for many years to come.

SOMETIMES LAUGHTER IS THE KEY

Paul Flynn, former Dublin footballer and All-Star, is another athlete who I formed an excellent working relationship with and also a great friendship. I admired Paul for many reasons beyond his natural and brilliant football abilities. He is one of the hardest-working athletes I have ever worked with. But what was extraordinary about Paul was his mindset and ability to be so relaxed and often humorous in some of the most pressing circumstances. His positive energy was infectious to not only the players but also the coaching staff. He was a team player by definition, completely committed to the team goal and performance, all while having a smile on his face and enjoying the experience. Jack McCaffrey is another man who comes to mind when I think of being relaxed under pressure. Although I'm not sure if that will come as any surprise to GAA followers. Being around Paul, Jack and many other Dublin players while preparing for the biggest games of their lives and seeing them bop around the dressing room was so refreshing and, for me, inspirational. It epitomises what sport, at its heart, is supposed to be about: fun! Paul, and many other athletes like him who I have worked with, understood that the work was done, the effort was put in and the best way to get your best performance was with a relaxed body and mind. Over-analysing, fixating on the outcome or fearing a mistake can cripple you and create tension in your body and doubt in your mind.

Jonny Wilkinson, former England Rugby out-half, has talked about the pressure he used to put himself under to perform. He said that, when he was younger, 'half of me was loving the game and half was worrying about what would happen if it went wrong. And as I got older that ratio became 70–30, then 85–15, and it left so little space for joy.' He went on to say, 'I lived a huge amount of my career thinking I was going to achieve joy through suffering, but all I did was create a habit of suffering. I lived for those beautiful moments of being in the zone during the games, and I told myself they were the result of the ridiculous suffering I went through and the sacrifices I made. So, I told myself I had to suffer more, because that was the way I was going to get back into the zone.'

I wish I had learned this sooner, and when I was playing football all those years ago, in the biggest moments, that I smiled more. What I can say is that, while I didn't have the chance to bring it into my competitive sporting life, I have consciously implemented it in many other situations in my life, like playing golf, public speaking, media events or simply sharing information on my social media. Making things more fun and allowing myself to feel relaxed have been instrumental to finding a better flow to the things that are important to me.

Do you think it's something you could work on?

MICHAEL JOHNSON

Over the past few years, I have listened to some of the most successful sportspeople talk about what drives them to not only achieve a high level of performance in their sport, but also continue to strive to improve. Similar to many Irish athletes like Roy Keane, Brian O'Driscoll and Johnny Sexton, a man I greatly admire is Michael Johnson. For those of you who don't know him, Michael Duane Johnson (born 13 September 1967) is an American retired sprinter who won four Olympic gold medals and eight World Championship gold medals over his career. He formerly held the world and Olympic records in the 200-metre and 400-metre, as well as the world record in the indoor 400-metre sprint. In 2018, at the age of fifty, he suffered a stroke, rendering him unable to walk. He talked about the anger he experienced when it happened. But that anger soon changed to determination and to a proactive mindset which focused on positive self-talk. He said to himself, 'If anyone can do this, I can!' Listening to a former world and Olympic sprinting champion describe the struggles he endured while learning how to walk again was even more admirable than his sporting achievements. I found his words about what he believes is required to reach your goals so impactful that I had to include some of my favourite examples here.

1 Your goals and ambitions should be personal and internal to you and not heavily influenced by what others expect of you.

2 You can always learn from disappointments in life – there is always something that will make you stronger and more resilient.

3 There is a difference between arrogance and confidence. Confidence is respecting your opposition by preparing as best you can, while believing in yourself and the hard work in your preparation. Arrogance is not doing the work, not respecting your competition and expecting that your talent alone is enough to achieve your performance goals.

4 Do you really want to improve? Understanding our weaknesses gives us clarity on the areas to prioritise but you must be willing to reflect to recognise those weaknesses. Once you're aware of them, you can work to improve them.

5 Don't shy away from the difficult jobs, and don't leave the hard part till last – doing the hard work first is fundamental to you reaching your potential. 'You will learn it sooner or you will learn it later, but you will learn it.'

WIN THE LITTLE MOMENTS

There is a saying that coaches and athletes often use: 'win the little moments'. This is usually in reference to situations where there are two options or a minor consequence of failure. In sport the outcome of a game or a scenario in training can often magnify particular little moments, lending them greater significance in our heads than they deserve. Looking back at a moment that may not have gone as well as you wanted distracts you from the overall process and the next action, which is what you should be focusing on. In daily life, we all have little moments that can be won from the minute we open our eyes in the morning: the time you get out of bed, your dental hygiene, the breakfast

you choose to have, hydrating with a glass of water, planning your day and the manner in which you deliver on your commitments.

YOU CAN CREATE INCREDIBLE MOMENTUM BY WINNING THESE MOMENTS, AND THEY CAN HAVE AN IMMEASURABLE IMPACT ON OTHER EVENTS IN YOUR DAY – BUT IT'S MORE IMPORTANT NOT TO LET A MOMENTARY DIP DISTRACT YOU FROM WINNING THE NEXT LITTLE MOMENT.

The book *The Power of Habit* by Charles Duhigg has had a significant impact on the way I approach my day and the habits I have built, as well as how I help others with their decision-making. If you don't know why you do something, it's very difficult to change it. According to Duhigg, 'small wins are exactly what they sound like and are part of how keystone habits create widespread changes. A huge body of research has shown that small wins have enormous power, an influence disproportionate to the accomplishments of the victories themselves. Small wins are a steady application of a small advantage … once a small win has been accomplished, forces are set in motion that favour another small win.' For me, this is very powerful, and it helps me build a better understanding of how things are connected.

WHAT IS REFLECTION AND WHY IS IT IMPORTANT?

Habit reflection is a tool to produce a change in practice or behaviours to bring about an improvement. This improvement comes ultimately from understanding what works and what doesn't work in your routine, and why you make the decisions you do. The more you understand why you do certain things, the easier it is to change a behaviour. Essentially, habit reflection involves thinking back on and acknowledging your previous habits and then applying those lessons to the new habit you want to create. It is described in the book *Reflective Practice in the Sport and Exercise Sciences* as experiences being converted into learning.

In my work with clients, I often ask them to reflect on their habits and behaviours and then connect each behaviour they have identified to positive or negative decisions they have made. This is to help them understand how some decisions we make are the consequences of repeated patterns of behaviour that have built up over years. This eventually results in sequences of conditioned responses and decisions. Reflection is about the power of self-awareness and learning about yourself in a holistic way. It is a wonderful feeling when a person who is practising reflections says, 'I realised this' or 'I made the connection between a habit and a decision.' In simple terms, for an athlete it is often the impact of eating sufficient calories and carbohydrate to fuel an intense match. The athlete begins to feel the difference in energy levels by having followed the right fuel-up plan!

Reflection does not have to follow a strict format. However, I have found that creating a roadmap of sorts to include a big-picture view and a small-picture view is helpful. Some well-known public speakers call this 'bird's eye' and 'worm's eye'. Your strategy for achieving your health goals is your bird's eye view, and the tactics of how you will achieve these health goals is your worm's eye view.

Here are some practical tips for effective reflective practice that have helped me to change my own habits and that I have used with clients and athletes to help change theirs.

1 **Purchase a journal you really like.** Why would having a nice journal make a difference? In my experience, the more I value or like the thing I am using, the more likely I will be to look after it and engage with it.

2 **Don't rush it.** Make your reflection time part of your daily routine. If daily routine feels unrealistic then try weekly reflection, but be specific about the most suitable time in your week. Reflective practice should become a habit; it shouldn't feel like a chore. Try to allocate some time straight after your training, matches, work or focused session to review things, and write down the main points when they are fresh in your head.

3 **Use a simple structure.** Don't over-complicate it. Using a simple format to structure your reflective practice will help to make it manageable. For example: what went well? What didn't go well? Changes for next time? Structure your reflections into logical segments that will reveal the story of what happened and why, and what might need to be changed or kept the same for next time.

4 **Find a mentor or someone to discuss your reflections with.** Mentors are people we can trust and who encourage us in our strengths and challenge us in our areas of development. Choose someone who you respect and trust and who understands your development needs.

5 **Find a system that works for you and suits your learning style.** If you don't have your own approach, it makes the practice harder to sustain and it will revert to being a chore. So if writing in a journal doesn't work for you, try something else. For example, if you prefer to talk and share your reflections then speak to someone; if you're more of a visual learner then use imagery or even video or voice record yourself and watch or listen to it back. You will find through practice something that works for you.

6 **Recognise your emotions and feelings.** Consider the timing and your state of mind when you reflect. Be aware that our feelings are constantly changing; therefore the timing often influences our reflective assumptions. Try to evaluate your progress at a time when you are objective – that is, not stressed, tired or too emotionally involved in your activities. Think about how you felt first, then break down the facts of what actually happened, alleviating some of the emotional factors involved, such as anxiety or your expectations.

7 **Reflect on positives and negatives.** Most often, it is the negative experiences that we mull over the most. Make sure you reflect on both the positives and the negatives. Reflecting on positive experiences can be very uplifting and motivating. It encourages you to see what you have been doing well and how you can use this to your advantage in the future. It is natural to want to repeat our successes, and by reflecting on the things we did well we can form a plan to make this happen again and again. And while we do want to see progress, reminding ourselves why we do what we do is important when things are not going exactly to plan.

8 **Share your learning.** I am fortunate to have a platform in daveynutrition where I can share my thoughts and experiences. Your sharing does not need to be with a mentor or coach; it can be online, in group sessions or simply with friends or family. Sharing your experience can enhance the depth and scope of your learning and will benefit you and others.

9 **Make it fun.** Enjoy the process of reflection. View the difficult experiences as learning curves that contribute to sharpening your skills and help you fulfil your goals. In my experience, the embarrassing and cringe moments are the ones I remember most because of the emotions attached to them. For example, I once went on morning television to demonstrate how to make pancakes. I gathered all my equipment together the night before, but just as I was about to go on air, I realised I had no spatula to turn the pancakes – and flipping them was way too risky. By chance, one of the backstage staff lived nearby and was able to run home and get me one just in time. Ironically, I still ended up burning the pancakes live on TV because I got distracted talking – but needless to say, I've made a utensil and ingredient checklist ever since!

YOUR RELATIONSHIP WITH FOOD

A topic that I believe needs more attention and discussion is our relationship with food. A worrying trend I am seeing in my conversations with clients and athletes about nutrition is an increase in negative emotions, anxiety and guilt with various types of eating – in short, an unhealthy relationship with food. I am now seeing more anxiety, obsessive eating behaviour and stress in people's relationship with food, even though access to information has never been easier. For instance, I'm seeing people not knowing how to eat a healthy diet without tracking their calories or following a rigid structure of eating. This can also be a result of negative self-talk and a cyclical experience of extreme behaviours which can often compound into more serious health issues. These can be mental or physical health issues and, despite what some may think, this is common with athletes as well as the general population.

SCIENCE VS OPINION?

I said in *Eat Up, Raise Your Game* that I was not interested in debating the science of nutrition; that remains unchanged. Unfortunately, though, I am seeing non-evidence-based guidance gaining greater attraction and people's opinions being a major source of attention and reference. The accuracy and relevance of this information is not only highly debatable, but it can be extremely damaging for people who are vulnerable to unhealthy eating practices. I believe that opinion and anecdotal evidence are becoming frequently used as references for many positions on food choices. I believe we must continue to use scientific evidence as our primary basis for dietary recommendations.

If we don't, then what are we basing our choices and practices on?

Opinions are not only subjective but can be dangerous when shared without evidence by those with influential positions. Opinion has been referred to as 'the medium between knowledge and ignorance' by the Greek philosopher Plato and science as 'the father of knowledge' by the great Greek physician Hippocrates, considered one of the greatest figures in the history of medicine. This is why I aim to keep my position on food embedded in a foundation of science: while opinions can be interesting and entertaining, it is crucial that we use science to guide our focus and practice.

PERSONAL REFLECTION

This may come as a surprise, but I didn't always have a positive relationship with food, even though I thought I did at the time. Through my own personal reflection, I now recognise that some of the habits and practices I thought helped me perform better and to be more consistent with my nutrition were actually misplaced and damaging to my relationship with food. This was even following the completion of my master's degree in nutrition, which you would expect to provide me with adequate knowledge to feel comfortable with my food choices. But it really doesn't work like that. Knowledge is only part of the solution. I found myself having rigid approaches to things like treats or desserts and never allowed myself to enjoy a break from eating consistently healthy foods. This was particularly evident in social situations, like weddings or parties, where I would always order the healthiest food choices and never have dessert. It didn't help that people often felt the need to comment on my choices at social occasions, drawing unwelcome attention to them.

Then two major things happened to change my mindset around what I thought it meant to be really disciplined with food.

MISPLACED FOCUS

The first was that I realised I was fooling myself – not having that dessert was only creating an unnecessary pressure and it always took from the social occasion. In reality, I was only eating out from time to time, so the choices I made in those situations made no difference to the bigger picture with my goals. The phrase 'there is no perfect diet' is an old one, but it took considerable time for me to understand what this meant. It was a significant change in mindset, moving from one of guilt to constructive reflection. I realised that I was often projecting what might happen and how I would feel rather than that being the reality of the situation. My misplaced focus was that I believed that my inherent discipline, which I get from my father, Peter, was something I needed to double down on. The enjoyment of food was always secondary.

MATURITY

The second was that I stopped caring about what people thought of my menu choices and my eating habits in general. I decided to be true to myself – 90 per cent of the food choices I made in my own time were good ones, so why care about the perception of my diet by others?

THAT CHANGE IN MINDSET TOOK A HUGE WEIGHT OFF MY SHOULDERS, AND I REALLY BEGAN TO ENJOY MY FOOD MORE.

An unexpected outcome of these two changes was that not only did my own relationship with food start to improve, but so did the quality of the conversations with those I was eating with: they relaxed too – even though I was never judging others' plates, they didn't know that! That relaxation included the athletes I work with; I noticed a change in our relationship and an openness began to develop. They saw me much more as a person rather than the performance nutritionist. It was some of these changes to my own mindset and behaviours that allowed me to build some of the most special and valuable friendships in my life.

ACCEPTANCE

I am delighted to say that my relationship with food continues to improve, even now. Negative emotions are rarely associated with food choices. It's not that they don't happen: it's that they don't build into irrational and harmful thoughts. The aim is to make as many good food choices over the course of the week as I can, and when I make a choice that I didn't plan to, the next one will be better. That's how I aim to coach my clients and athletes to achieve their goals. I believe that finding a positive, happy place with food starts with acceptance and understanding in a number of critical areas:

1 Your personal vision
2 Self-talk
3 The principles of nutrition
4 Building emotional control

You might wonder why those areas are so important, but the more you accept all aspects of yourself and appreciate them as the things that make you who you are, the easier it is to prevent negative emotions hijacking your decisions around food or other aspects of your lifestyle. It is also vital to understand some scientific principles related to nutrition.

WHO AM I AND WHAT'S MY VISION?

Having a vision in any aspect of your life is immensely powerful. My primary experience of this is the vision of the great teams that I have been a part of over the past 10 years, who have striven for various types of success on the field of play and off it too! One of the most critical aspects I have learned is that a vision must have clarity and purpose, and success is measured in the impact you have on the group, not just in medals or trophies.

How people stay connected to that vision is immensely important. Staying connected means that you have values and a set of behaviours that you agree upon as a group and you are accountable to those values and standards over the course of time. Being part of teams and groups that have been successful and having a clear vision have made me reflect on the importance of a vision for my own personal health and the health of my family and those I care for. When I was creating a personal vision for my own habits and rituals, I realised that it didn't have to be an exact blueprint – it could have

an element of flexibility – but there were key things I needed to commit and hold myself accountable to. These are the pillars of health and performance:

- Lifestyle
- Exercise
- Nutrition
- Sleep
- Mental health

When I think of my personal vision for health and wellness, acceptance plays an important role: I am not striving for perfection, but I am striving for a high-performing, sustainable, enjoyable level of fitness and health. I accept I am not perfect. I don't have a perfect diet; I don't always exercise consistently; and I don't have the perfect body. I eat nourishing food most of the time; I enjoy cooking; I enjoy sharing recipes and eating with my family and friends. It took time to accept who I am, what my values are and the life I want to live, but once I understood these things and accepted my imperfect self, I found a level of contentment that I had never achieved before. It's a peaceful place in my mind, and by not straying far from my rituals and values, things stay consistent.

Building your personal vision can help in any aspect of your life. In sport, athletes use their strongest attributes and those of the best athletes from their sport to build a picture of what they want to achieve for themselves. It is very different from comparing yourself to or wanting to be like someone: it is searching for ways to grow by modelling certain behaviours of other high-performing individuals. It can be motivational and exciting and bring clarity to an aspect of themselves that they strive to improve. It doesn't mean that you copy anyone else, and it's important that you are realistic in your approach. Do you really know yourself, and have you thought about what is best for you?

WHAT IS YOUR VISION?

I now ask all my clients and the athletes I work with what their vision for themselves is. What are their health values? How do they view their habits, routines and decisions about food? What's really important to them? Once that is established, you can progressively build towards it and set targets or goals around what you want to achieve. It is very difficult to set realistic goals unless you know what type of lifestyle you are working towards. That means focusing on the process, rituals and behaviours of eating well rather than the outcome. Awareness of these behaviours and having a clear vision for yourself and regular reflection helps you to remain consistent, especially when life is difficult. If you find yourself moving away from good habits and a solid routine, having a clear vision and knowing what has worked effectively for you in the past will help you to find your way back to better health and performance when you periodically lose your way.

I often look at the behaviour of friends for inspiration. For example, my good friend Cillian Reardon, former senior strength coach in Leinster rugby and now head of performance in Glasgow Warriors rugby, was excellent at creating a really good structure to his day. He would get up early, do some stretching and mindfulness in the morning, exercise, identify his key tasks for the day and come to work ready to help others. We would often train together after work in the evening, and Cillian would bring great clarity and

purpose to the session. He would write the exercises on a whiteboard and say how long we would do each component of the session and why. I always felt better for each session and, from just being around him, I found that I was more effective in how I completed them. I try to build really positive relationships in my work and personal life, connecting with people who inspire me, support me, help me and are fun and open-minded. I try to do the same for them where I can and in the most supportive and appropriate way I can.

Below is a simple example of my personal vision around health. It breaks down my behaviour for each pillar of health into the things that I intend to do – my goals – and the non-negotiables that I absolutely *must* do.

BUILDING YOUR VISION BASED ON NON-NEGOTIABLE HEALTH BEHAVIOURS

PILLAR OF HEALTH	INTENTIONS	NON-NEGOTIABLES
Nutrition	• I eat as many nutritious meals as I can • I eat seven portions of vegetables each day • I enjoy meals out with friends at the weekends • I cook most of the meals for me and my family • I sit and eat my food • I enjoy alcohol but drink socially and in moderate amounts	• I cook most of my meals • I only drink alcohol on average two to three days per week • I eat three main meals per day and have two snacks
Mindset	• Food is a positive investment in my health; it's not a chore to make nourishing meals • I reflect on my eating behaviours to see what is working well and what isn't • I avoid the negative emotions associated with food that may result from a poor decision	• I avoid the negative emotions associated with food that may result from a poor decision
Movement	• I try to limit sitting for long periods of time • I meet friends for walks • I train intensely twice a week • I go running a couple of times a week • I complete two resistance sessions a week	• I complete two resistance sessions a week • I run twice a week, even if only for 15 minutes each time
Sleep	• I aim to be in bed before 23:00 on weekdays • I get up at the same time most mornings • If I have a bad night's sleep, I go to bed earlier the next night	• If I have a bad night's sleep, I go to bed earlier the next night

Of course, as you build habits and good decisions into your life, the goalposts for your intentions will naturally move. Something that was once hard work will become second nature, and you should re-evaluate your intentions to reflect that. The fantastic thing about this exercise is that the reflective process can continue to evolve as you reach different stages; here's an example of such a phased approach.

PILLAR OF HEALTH	PHASE 1	PHASE 2	PHASE 3
Nutrition	• I aim to eat as many nutritious meals as I can • I eat two portions of vegetables daily • I eat three portions of fruit daily • I use smoothies and soups to eat sufficient fruit and vegetables • I enjoy meals out with friends at the weekends but plan around the occasion to ensure I keep myself in a good headspace • I aim to improve my relationship with alcohol and manage my habits around it	• I don't always eat balanced meals and nutritious meals but I have a better understanding of what the right meals look like • I am spending a bit more time at the table enjoying my food	• I cook most of my meals • I only drink alcohol on average two days per week – some weeks I don't drink at all • Drinking alcohol is more about the experience with friends and having fun than becoming intoxicated • I eat three main meals per day and aim for a protein source with each meal • I sit and eat my food • I eat seven portions of fruit and vegetables each day
Mindset	• Food is a positive investment in my health; it's becoming less of a chore to make nourishing meals • I aim to limit the negative emotions associated with food that may result from a poor decision	• Food is a positive investment in my health; it's not a chore to make nourishing meals • I reflect on my eating behaviours to see what is working well and what isn't	• I limit the negative emotions associated with food that may result from a poor decision
Movement	• I try to limit sitting for long periods of time • I meet friends for social activities such as walks, golf or a cycle • I train intensely twice week • I complete two resistance sessions a week	• I am getting better at planning my exercise routine • I meet friends to exercise • I really feel the difference when I exercise regularly	• I complete two resistance sessions per week • I run twice a week, even if only for 15 minutes each time
Sleep	• I aim to be in bed before 23:00 on weekdays • I get up at the same time most mornings	• I am using my phone less close to bedtime and building a better sleep routine	• If I have a bad night's sleep, I go to bed earlier the next night

SELF-TALK

'I just can't be consistent; I go through phases of really high levels of motivation, but I seem to find myself back exactly where I was in the beginning every time – one step forward and two steps back.' These are the words I hear from people over and over again. It brings mixed emotions because I know how frustrating it has been for them, but I also know I can help if the person focuses their attention and efforts in the right area. The important thing is that the person is not only ready to change but also open to the process of changing the focus to building better habits and behaviours and a more positive relationship with food. Self-talk has an important role to play in all this because, as you talk to yourself more than anyone, your words and thoughts can have a dramatic impact on your potential to achieve your goals. In the words of the legendary Roman emperor Marcus Aurelius: 'The happiness of your life depends upon the quality of your thoughts: therefore, guard accordingly, and take care that you entertain no notions unsuitable to virtue and reasonable nature.'

Self-talk could be described as your inner voice and the ongoing conversation in your head. It can have a significant impact on your mood, confidence, mental health and, without question, relationship with food.

Nobel Prize winner and author of *Thinking, Fast and Slow,* Daniel Kahneman describes self-talk as two different systems. System 1 self-talk brings current experiences into awareness in an 'emotionally-charged reaction to a situation'. System 2 self-talk is 'logical, positive and motivational self-talk'.

Here's an example of system 1 self-talk that is heavily emotionally led. You decide to have a biscuit with your cup of tea, but one turns into two and in a short space of time you have eaten six or seven biscuits. You say to yourself, 'You glutton – you're a greedy pig. Why didn't you stop after one or two? Now you've blown your good day of eating. You have no self-control.'

In contrast, here is an example of how system 2 self-talk could develop, which is logical, constructive and reflective. 'I ate too many biscuits. It didn't feel good and, on reflection, my energy levels weren't sustained. My next food decision will be a good one, and in the bigger picture it can be managed with other good decisions. On reflection, I wasn't even hungry when I ate all of those biscuits – it was more from boredom. I will learn from that and assess next time if I really want the treat.'

Since exploring the concept of mindfulness and mindful eating, one powerful technique that I have adopted and shared is *pause, breathe and proceed.* The 'pause' is the most difficult part of the process, but it allows you to think about your habits and assess your decisions before committing to them. There are no simple and drastic results, but if you are looking for better long-term decision-making, these are the tools to get you there.

Positive self-talk can be powerful and transform our thinking with the right mindset and approach, but it doesn't always come naturally. You must practise it and be willing to learn from your own reflective practice. It takes honesty and repetition, but you will unblock so many answers and begin to learn so much about your own emotions and how they impact your decision-making.

NEGATIVE SELF-TALK	CONSTRUCTIVE SELF-TALK
• I am just not able to commit to good habits consistently	• Here are three things I am going to commit to … • This is an exciting new challenge for me
• I don't have the cooking skills to make a complex recipe	• I am going to pick two simple recipes with ingredients I recognise to cook this week • I am going to learn a lot through trying new things
• I don't like many fruits and vegetables and feel there are very few meals I like	• Here are the fruits and vegetables I like; I'll find suitable recipes for them to make tasty meals
• I just can't say no when I am offered a treat or foods, even though I know I shouldn't be eating in excess	• Treats are OK but when I have enough and I am satisfied, I don't eat them mindlessly
• I am so confused about nutrition and really don't know what to eat	• This is what I understand about nutrition: fruits and vegetables are important, and I feel good when I eat nourishing meals

Something that I learned over time was the importance of emotional control. This is an awareness of your emotional state that can influence your decision-making. In Bill Biswick's book *20 Life Lessons Drawn from Elite Sport*, it's a key strategy for athletes to build the skills to make better decisions.

Bill teaches his athletes to check their emotional state against the acronym HATED:

H – Hungry
A – Angry (or Alcohol)
T – Tired
E – Emotional
D – Dehydrated

He says 'the first step in building emotional control is to check for any underlying conditions that might be stressing you'. If you have a better understanding of what's stressing you, you can evolve coping mechanisms to manage. From my experience of working with athletes and clients, drawing attention to things that can influence your decisions around food or lifestyle is one of the most powerful tools for behaviour change.

BIG PICTURE ON HEALTH AND RISK FOR DISEASE

Many of the emotions that people develop around unhealthy eating behaviours can manifest from predicting the future or fear of the consequences of those behaviours. It can lead to extreme behaviours, habits and routines around food that are often short-term solutions with potential long-term consequences. Yo-yo dieting, food obsession, extreme restriction and elimination of food groups, like extreme low-carbohydrate diets or extreme high-fat diets, are just a few of the dietary approaches used for fat loss and sometimes even performance-related goals. This was a trap I fell into myself at times. Through solid and robust conversations with my good friend Dr Brendan Egan about the subjective nature of some of my nutrition predictions and becoming aware of the work of David L. Katz, the former president of the American College of Lifestyle Medicine, I became clearer on what really matters for long-term health and reduced risk of disease.

Dr Katz was part of a study that looked at the influence of lifestyle on health and risk for various lifestyle-related diseases. A key finding from their research is that 'approximately 80% of chronic disease and premature death could be prevented by not smoking, being optimally physically active, and adhering to a healthful dietary pattern'. This is a fascinating statistic, but it wasn't how compelling the science was that really struck me. It was that there was no specific requirement for 'super foods', the elimination of food groups or even extreme forms of exercise. It was simply following the general guidelines for lifestyle, nutrition and physical activity. I draw incredible comfort from that.

A large longitudinal study of German and Chinese students has also highlighted the strong relationship between a healthy lifestyle and 'better psychological wellbeing and fewer mental health difficulties'. Much of the confusion around nutrition, and indeed lifestyle in general, comes from sources that try to convince us that we must have a specific pattern of eating or movement, which just

isn't the case. A particular method of nutrition practice that has gained huge traction in recent years is macro counting and tracking calories. We'll take a closer look at the pros and cons of that type of approach in the next section.

MOVE, EAT PLENTY OF VEGETABLES, EAT A WIDE VARIETY OF FOODS AND DON'T SMOKE, AND YOU GIVE YOURSELF A HELL OF A CHANCE OF LIVING A LONG, HEALTHY LIFE.

HEALTHY CONNECTIONS FOR HEALTHY HABITS

What makes us happy?

I have thought a lot about this question. When I was young and aspirational, I certainly pursued the wrong things for fulfilment. Like many young, impressionable kids, I fell into the trap of aspiring to be popular, whether it was being a well-respected athlete, being friends with the popular girls and boys in my school or surrounding myself with the most ambitious and talented players on the teams I played with.

As you mature, you begin to think differently and connect with people in a deeper way. Relationships change and you gravitate towards those who share your values and mindset. This often leads to you surrounding yourself with a smaller group of people – in particular, your family. These are the people who really care about you, your health, your career and your aspirations in all aspects of your life. These relationships are fundamental to your health, wellbeing and happiness. I have been lucky enough to have been brought up in a loving home, have experienced loving relationships and have good friends. This support network has enabled me to become successful in a job that I love. This doesn't mean that life always runs smoothly. There are good times and challenging periods, but the people I rely on are there when I need them. I can trust them to tell me the truth when I make a mistake; they are the first to congratulate me when I succeed; and they are the ones I want to celebrate the special moments in my life with.

I would ask you to think about your current relationships and support system. Are they positive, caring and supportive? Do these people encourage you? Do these people help you when you need it? Do they challenge you to strive for more? If they do, then that is wonderful. But if they don't, you shouldn't be afraid to look for friends who fully value you and share in your best interests.

If your family or support system has strong values around love, wellbeing and lifestyle then achieving your goals can be easier. I feel privileged to be the son of Eileen and Peter Davey. They allowed me to carve my own path and learn from my mistakes while always being there when I needed to talk or sought their advice and guidance. They have always been my soft place to land when things weren't going my way. There is a tremendous peace of mind and security that comes from having a non-judgemental home that allows for open conversation and freedom of thought. You are certainly challenged and kept grounded but always from a loving perspective.

BUILDING YOUR OWN SUPPORT TEAM

The idea of building a support network to help achieve goals is something that I really began to focus on about five years ago. I recognised that having pillars of support helps create accountability, motivation and inspiration. This is so important if you are trying to adopt new behaviours, sustain success and ultimately achieve your goals. A study hit the headlines in 2014 about the barriers to maintaining fat loss. This study found that the most important factors in achieving and maintaining fat loss were perceived accountability to others, social support, planning ahead, awareness and mindfulness of food choices, basic nutrition education, portion control, exercise and self-motivation.

My mother, Eileen, has a close friend called Mary who she walks with every morning before work. They walk, have a chat and are back in time for breakfast, ready for a good day ahead. I know when my mother is walking with Mary her wellbeing and health are generally in a better place. Mary is accountable to my mum and vice versa. A daily walk with a close friend seems simple, but it brings enjoyment, support and accountability into your life. Not only are you benefitting from the physical exercise, but the opportunity to talk through things that are on your mind also provides additional psychological support, which in itself is a form of therapy.

Who are those people in your life?

I want you to think of the people you can count on to share your health or performance journey with. If you already have a support system or team, then great. But if not, create one. It can be a husband, wife, friend or partner. The lead researcher from the study above highlighted that the women involved didn't find that 'accountability to themselves was so important, but having support from others was – just having that social support from someone who was going through the same experience'. If you can find that one friend or family member who shares your goals or can just hold you accountable, it is really helpful.

The idea of building your team is not to detract from the importance of inner reflection or the personal responsibilities required for good health and consistent habits. It is about adding another layer to your environment and fitness lifestyle. Having a sense of belonging is part of our DNA, stemming all the way back to hunter-gatherer times when teamwork was the key to survival. The world has changed significantly in recent years. We live in a world where we compare ourselves to others, are consumed by status and seek instant gratification, all of which has been heavily driven by social media. The worrying thing is that this mindset sets us up for failure, creating an endless pursuit of materialistic things that ends in frustration and greed. In an abundance of research on all aspects of health and wellness, one study stands out to me. The Harvard Study for Adult Development was conducted more than 75 years ago and looked at variables of long-term health and happiness. The study found that the men who lived longer, happier and healthier lives considered strong positive relationships to family, loved ones and people in the community as the most important variable for happiness. In fact, this correlated to longer lives with better mental and physical health. Wealth and status didn't feature as drivers for happiness, yet in today's society they are what drives many of our behaviours. I don't know about you, but that makes me want to

focus on continuing to strengthen relationships with the people I care about.

WHAT I AM REALLY TRYING TO GET ACROSS IS THAT CONNECTION AND SUPPORT ARE IMPORTANT.

You don't need to be part of an elite team to create accountability, support or comradery. It can be as simple as a daily walk with a close friend, just like my mother does with her friend Mary. Of course, it takes effort and commitment, but if you want to create something that lasts, then being a part of something active with others makes it fun and enjoyable. If you don't have that person or those people in your life already, then think about who that person could be and reach out to them. Since I stopped playing Gaelic football, I have taken up golf and soccer, trained with colleagues after work and even set up online running challenges with close friends. Training or exercising with people is always more fun. And if you are competitive by nature, like me, seeking that little bit of competitiveness can help to keep your body and mind fit and healthy.

Here are a few things to think about:

- Who is important in your life? Have you told them?
- What kinds of things are important to you in your connections?
- Could your connections have a positive influence on your current health or fitness goal?
- Could you support each other?

GET YOUR KITCHEN READY

If you have a well-organised kitchen stocked with essential cooking equipment and utensils and a simple process to follow, then cooking and food preparation will be less stressful and more enjoyable. It may seem like a simple concept, but the simplest concepts are often the most effective. It's similar to when you wear a comfortable training kit that's matched to your session: you are more likely to do that session with a smile on your face. 'Look good, feel good, train good,' as the saying goes.

WHERE TO START?

Your kitchen can be a place of great enjoyment, adventure and fun. I can't think of anything better to do with family and friends than creating meals and memories together. If your cooking and eating experiences are enjoyable, it makes it easier for you to stay on track with your nutrition and lifestyle goals – while a negative relationship with cooking or being in your kitchen can create frustration and stress and negatively impact your nutrition and lifestyle goals.

Firstly, keep things simple and practical. Do a quick review and inventory of your current kitchen set-up, cooking equipment and utensils. Then assess what changes you can make to improve your kitchen efficiency. Small and practical changes now will help your efficiency in the kitchen and your experience. You will be able to look back and see the investment in planning as something that was really beneficial for supporting better, more sustainable nutrition habits.

1 Does the flow of your kitchen make sense? Are your kitchen equipment and utensils placed according to frequency of use and accessibility? The aim should be to position each appliance according to function and have your food items close to where you prepare meals.

2 Keep your knives and chopping board near your main preparation area and pots and pans near your hob.

3 Do you have a good waste-management system – for example, a countertop compost bin with compost bags? This was a game-changer for me! It created a simple system for disposing of waste and cleaning up was so much easier.

4 Place your bins together for ease of waste disposal. If you are house-sharing, make sure to label where each item goes – for example, compost for food items and tins and paper in recycling.

5 Assign specific cupboards and areas for specific food items and keep them there! If you know where things are and you don't have to go looking for them, it makes life so much easier. For example, keep spices high up and near the hob for ease of finding.

ESSENTIAL KITCHEN ITEMS

If you have poor-quality cooking utensils like blunt knives and pots that are constantly burning, then cooking is going to become a stressful chore. Sharp knives and a good set of pots and pans will ensure your meal preparation and cooking will run smoother, making it a much more enjoyable experience to prepare your own meals.

Here are the main utensils you should consider for your kitchen:

Essential kitchen items

- Sharp knife
- Non-stick pan
- Non-stick pot
- Robust peeler
- Solid chopping board
- Salad bowl
- Glass measuring jug
- Powerful blender (>1000 watts)
- Wooden spoon
- Spatula
- Stainless steel baking trays and tins
- Serving dishes
- Tin opener

Cooking tips

1 Plan your meals for the week ahead and save your shopping list of required ingredients from your meal plan on your phone.

2 Buy dry ingredients like rice, quinoa, lentils, nuts and seeds in bulk to reduce shopping trips.

3 Cook an extra portion of dinner in the evening that can be used as lunch the next day or frozen for future use.

4 Bulk cook your carbs and use them the next day for lunch or even dinner. A real winner is cooking precooked rice with onions, garlic, and an egg for lunch the next day! Make sure you:
- Keep rice in the fridge for no more than one day before reheating.
- Always check that rice is steaming hot all the way through when you reheat.
- Do not reheat rice more than once.

5 Buy frozen fruits and vegetables to ensure that you always have options in the freezer to help you make nutritious main meals.

6 Make soups, fruit salads and snacks that can be stored as easy options for when you need something quickly.

7 Get creative and try new recipes, spices and foods. This will not only expand your cooking skills but will also improve the variety in your diet and prevent boredom.

8 Cook with your kids! Children mimic adults and showing them cooking skills early in life has been shown to be extremely beneficial for their later development and food choices.

TIME MANAGEMENT

Poor management of your time, being disorganised and a lack of investment in your kitchen skills results in bad decisions and potentially a negative experience with cooking. You will always have time to do things you prioritise and enjoy doing. Quite often the issues that arise around lack of consistency with nutrition or a bad relationship with cooking can be traced back to poor time management and a lack of planning, not a lack of time or nutrition knowledge. Simply, if eating healthy food is a priority for you and you value your health the way you should, then you need to think ahead, plan and prepare your meals. If you don't do this, you may rush your food choices or pick something that is convenient but unhealthy.

Here are some simple things you can do for a more mindful and enjoyable cooking experience.

1 Create accessibility and flow in your food prep area. For example, place the ingredients you use the most, such as spices, nearest to the cooking area.

2 Efficiency is key, so keep your kitchen clean and tidy with appropriate bins for waste management, including general waste, recycling and compost. Keep your fridge clean, tidy and organised. Designate shelves for different food groups, such as meats, vegetables and dairy products.

3 Regularly clean your oven and have a tray at the bottom of it to catch any spills. This will help to prevent your oven smoking and makes cleaning it easier.

4 Have a system for how you arrange your cookware and kitchen essentials.

5 Create a cooking playlist or even a go-to podcast that you can put on while cooking.

6 Keep nourishing, nutritious foods in sight; wrap treats up and keep them out of sight.

A MINDFUL KITCHEN

Mindset is often an underappreciated concept when goal-setting or trying to bring about change in eating behaviours. A positive mindset is so important for achieving success, particularly in a task-led approach from beginning to end. The same can be said for cooking, how you view your kitchen and the time spent there. If you have the right mindset about cooking, it can have a positive effect on your behaviour, your creativity, your experience and of course your health.

Your mindset will be shaped by your previous experiences. Therefore, how you view the process of preparing meals will influence your experiences. For example, cooking dinner in the evening can be the first step in winding down from a difficult day at work or college. If you have a positive view, whether that it's an enjoyable experience or an investment in your health, this can have a positive knock-on effect on your overall relationship with food.

Focusing on each simple task can help you stay present and in the moment. Engaging in the cooking experience, noticing the evolving delicious aromas and listening to the sounds and background music can bring a wonderful sense of calm and relaxation. It is not easy to create a mindful experience in the kitchen if it's messy or disorganised. Organising your kitchen, keeping it clean and tidy, enhancing your cooking skills, improving your cooking experience and refining your understanding of what ingredients go well together can be extremely rewarding and can benefit your and your family's health.

The wonderful thing is that the journey never ends – your knowledge, skills and experience will continue to evolve and so will your consistency!

PART TWO: THE SCIENCE OF OPTIMAL PERFORMANCE

STRATEGICALLY FUELLING FOR COMPETITION – WHY, WHAT AND WHEN?

In this section, I will discuss nutrition for competition. This information can be tailored to athletes from any sport – from team sports, such as GAA, soccer, basketball or hockey, to individual sports, such as athletics, boxing or high-intensity sports that exceed 60 minutes.

'AFTER NATURAL TALENT AND APPROPRIATE TRAINING, AN ADEQUATE DIET IS KNOWN TO BE THE NEXT MOST IMPORTANT ELEMENT FOR ENHANCING THE TRAINING AND PERFORMANCE OF SPORTS PEOPLE'
WILLIAMS, 1996

At the most basic level, nutrition is important as it provides a source of energy for athletes to train and perform. It enables athletes to train longer and harder, delays the onset of fatigue, improves recovery, improves body composition, reduces potential for injury, maintains a healthy immune system and enhances focus and concentration. Now that you understand the multifaceted nature of nutrition and its importance in performance, I want you to ask yourself, do you have a nutritional plan, and if so, does that plan adequately prepare you for performance?

CHOOSING THE RIGHT FUEL TYPE

Carbohydrates that provide fuel for high-intensity movement and are stored in the body (muscles and the liver) are called 'glycogen'. Carbohydrate is the primary source of fuel for athletes, particularly those engaged in regular bouts of high-intensity exercise and high volumes of intense exercise, such as field sports, CrossFit or triathlons. Research supports that a minimum of 50 per cent of an athlete's energy should be consumed through carbohydrate food sources – ideally, complex carbohydrate sources. Examples of complex carbohydrate foods include whole grains, pasta, rice, some fruits and root vegetables. Athletes can use simple carbohydrate foods, such as dried fruits and fruit juices, to help meet their carbohydrate targets in the fuel-up period before competition. Dried fruits and fruit juices are often criticised for their high sugar content. But remember, sugar is a carbohydrate, and if an athlete is preparing for intense exercise, these foods will contribute to their energy needs. Athletes need to apply caution when selecting highly refined sources of carbohydrate foods if the level of exercise being performed is low to moderate intensity.

The role of carbohydrate during high-intensity exercise is to help the athlete to:

1 Sustain energy levels for maximum performance
2 Perform harder for longer
3 Execute skills and decision-making under pressure
4 Limit the risk of fatigue or injury

Remember, high-intensity exercise consists of running, cycling, swimming at or above 70 per cent of your total exercise capacity. At this intensity, your heart rate will be approximately 70 per cent of your maximum heart rate (HR max). A simple method for calculating your maximum heart rate is by subtracting your age from 220.

What I hope you take from this chapter is that, despite what we may see and read on social media, anyone who engages in regular physical activity (not just athletes) has no reason to avoid carbohydrate foods.

DIFFERENT EXERCISE INTENSITY EQUALS DIFFERENT ENERGY NEEDS

Fat is an efficient source of energy that the body stores in abundance. Fat is the primary source of fuel used during low or moderate intensities of exercise, such as walking, slow-jogging, light-intensity cycling or swimming. During low to moderate intensities of exercise, the body's energy system relies much more on our fat stores rather than circulating sugar or glycogen (the body's carbohydrate stores).

Recreational athletes need considerably less carbohydrate than those engaging in high

volumes of high-intensity exercise. In fact, people who are mainly recreationally active may benefit more from eating carbohydrate-rich foods only on exercise days and implementing a lower-carbohydrate diet on rest days. This allows the body to utilise its fat stores as a source of energy, and also allows for more efficient use of carbohydrate when consumed. This doesn't mean that carbohydrates are not necessary for performance. Think of it from the perspective of fuelling the work required. An individual doing manual labour, for example block-laying, requires much more energy than an individual whose job is more sedentary, such as sitting at a desk. In simple nutritional terms, consume more carbohydrates on days you are completing moderate or high-intensity exercise compared to days when you are predominantly inactive.

TARGET AMOUNTS OF CARBOHYDRATE FOODS

The amount of carbohydrates that you need to consume will depend on the length and intensity of the competition. Carbohydrate (CHO) loading for team-sport athletes is typically >8g of carbohydrate per kg of body mass. This equates to 640–800g in the 36 hours pre-competition for an 80kg athlete. For endurance events such as a marathon or triathlon, the target is even more – approximately 10–12g of carbohydrate per kg of body mass. A simple way of applying this would be to add three to four extra carbohydrate meals on top of your typical intake (likely three meals and two snacks) in the run-up to competition. For example, two extra meals could be a bowl of porridge with some chopped banana and a fruit smoothie with honey. You could also choose fruit juices as an easy way to add carbohydrates to your meal plan – apple juice works effectively.

TIMING

Did you know that what you eat in the days before competition is potentially more important than what you eat on competition day? This is not always appreciated by athletes.

TO ACHIEVE OPTIMUM PERFORMANCE NUTRITION, PREPARATION MUST TAKE PLACE IN THE DAYS AND WEEKS PRIOR TO COMPETITION.

For an athlete to start their competition, be it a game or a race, with maximum fuel stored and available (also known as saturated), nutritional preparation begins at least 36 hours prior. Although your pre-competition meal is important, it does not equate to adequate nutritional preparation to supply sufficient fuel, no matter how enormous the pre-competition meal is (and you would be surprised how many times I have seen this happen!). In fact, this is more likely to have negative impacts on performance, as your digestive system will not have time to process and absorb the large amount of food consumed. This can result in bloating and discomfort during your competition. Timing is everything; therefore, having a nutritional plan that includes timing for the lead-up to competition is essential if you want to achieve optimum performance.

CARBOHYDRATE GUIDE – RECOMMENDED GRAMS OF CARBOHYDRATE PER KG BODYWEIGHT

ACTIVITY	GRAMS
Extreme high-intensity and high-volume exercise (3–5 hours)	10–12g per kg
High-intensity endurance exercise (1–3 hours)	6–10g per kg
Light to moderate-intensity exercise (45–60 minutes)	4–5g per kg
Light physical activity (walking, cycling, yoga, etc.)	2–3g per kg
Minimal physical activity	2–3g per kg

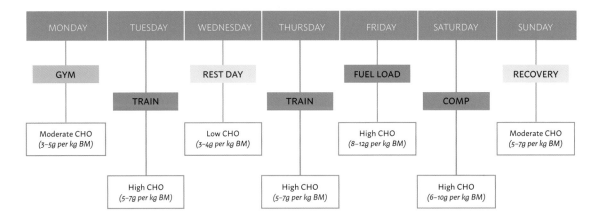

The aim should be to plan your nutrition strategy based on your competition's start time. For most sports, competitions take place during the weekend. If a competition is on a Saturday evening you will more than likely train two days before, on the Thursday evening. In this case, you should increase your energy intake, in particular your carbohydrate intake, immediately after training. Your first post-training meal (within 45 minutes) should include a rapidly digesting source of carbohydrate and protein – a flavoured milk, for example – followed by a nutritionally balanced meal such as homemade shepherd's pie with root vegetables. The day before the competition is particularly important for maximising carbohydrate stores. Therefore, this is the day when you need to consume energy and carbohydrate-based meals. You can of course space these meals out over 36 hours; you don't need to eat the full 8g of carbohydrate per kg in 24 hours. A simple way of looking at it would be the total number of meals and foods that help you hit that target. This could be 10–12 meals with a rich source of carbohydrate. Practice what works well for

you and adapt as you need to. The table on page 45 outlines the amount of carbohydrate needed in grams depending on the level of physical activity being completed over time.

CARBOHYDRATE TARGETS FOR TRAINING

As I have outlined above, when training regularly, you should consume foods that provide the body with a steady supply of energy. Carbohydrates are the main macronutrient that athletes need to consume in the lead-up to competition, as they are the primary and most efficient source of energy used during high-intensity exercise. While you may have heard recent reports about the potential benefits of low-carbohydrate diets for health and training, **there is still no compelling evidence that such approaches are appropriate for performance in high-intensity sports.**

Carbohydrate needs can easily be met from eating whole foods, such as oats, root vegetables and fruits. For example, on training days, you could have porridge for breakfast, fruit and nuts as a snack and some sweet potato or quinoa with lunch and dinner. Athletes should eat their last meal at least two to three hours before they train. The quantity of these foods does not have to be large – small portions will more often than not adequately meet your energy needs for training. After exercise, a small snack of a fruit smoothie or a meal with vegetables and lean meat will promote optimum recovery.

CARBOHYDRATE PRE-COMPETITION

It is widely accepted that athletes should maximise their carbohydrate stores in the lead-up to competitions. However, in my experience, many athletes do not eat sufficient amounts or the right types of carbohydrate foods in their preparation for competition. Research has continuously shown that consuming a high-carbohydrate diet improves exercise performance by sustaining energy levels and delaying the onset of fatigue. Glycogen, the body's stored source of carbohydrate, is limited in supply and therefore must be replaced after each training session.

COMPETITION DAY

If you have applied the above recommendations, the majority of your fuelling should already be taken care of by the time competition day arrives. On the day of the competition your nutritional plan should be focused on topping up your fuel stores with light and easy to digest meals.

For competitions in the early afternoon: get up early to have a medium to large breakfast based around carbohydrate foods. The meal should be low in fat, low in fibre and contain a slow-digesting source of carbohydrate. A bowl of porridge, cereal or even some whole-grain pancakes fit the bill nicely here.

For competitions in the late afternoon: your breakfast should be your largest meal, as you want to have your stomach more or less empty at the start of the competition. Therefore, your last meal should be three to four hours before the competition and should be easy to digest. So fat, high amounts of protein and high-fibre foods like vegetables should be limited. Chicken and pasta is a common choice, but rice, noodles, potatoes and even something like pancakes can also work well.

WHAT ABOUT SNACKS CLOSER TO THE EVENT?

If an athlete has adequately prepared through carbohydrate loading in the days prior to competition and their carbohydrate stores are saturated, consuming snacks closer to the competition isn't necessary. However, if an athlete feels hungry or if they habitually consume a specific light snack one to two hours before a competition then it is perfectly fine to continue to do so. Examples of snacks that athletes commonly use include jellies, energy drinks and high-energy snacks like Jaffa Cakes.

DURING COMPETITION

Consuming fuel in the form of carbohydrates during a competition can help to delay the onset of fatigue during high-intensity exercise. Although there are many carbohydrate foods to choose from, like sports gels, glucose sweets and energy snacks, the preferred form is a sports drink. Sports drinks are designed to provide a source of carbohydrate that is easily absorbed. Sports drinks have the added benefit of providing electrolytes that replace those lost through sweat and assist with a better uptake of fluid to offset fluid losses.

The recommended consumption of carbohydrates during competition is 30–60g in the form of one to two 6 per cent carbohydrate sports drinks per hour. Any more than this and you may risk stomach distress. Six per cent carbohydrate means 6g of carbohydrate per 100ml. So, if you were to consume a 500ml sports drink that is 6 per cent concentrated, this would provide you with 30g of carbohydrates.

MEAL TIMING: COUNTING DOWN TO YOUR COMPETITION START TIME

48 HOURS	36 HOURS	24 HOURS	12 HOURS	6 HOURS	4-2 HOURS	60 MINUTES
The majority of your fuel is consumed in this phase			Large or medium sized meals		Medium sized meals or light snacks	Mainly fluids or sports foods
During competition						
50–60 g of carbohydrate per hour using sports drinks or gels						

STAY HYDRATED

Water is essential for life and optimal physical wellbeing. We know that most people need to drink more water and that dehydration has implications for our health, but how much more do we need to be drinking, and what is our body's requirement for fluid?

Water is required for countless functions in our body. Some of the primary functions include the transport of nutrients to cells, to control body temperature and to facilitate the transit of toxins and waste products from the body. Fluid is lost from the body through urine, respiration (breathing) and perspiration (sweating). If fluid losses exceed fluid intake, an imbalance occurs, resulting in a signal being sent to the brain (i.e. thirst) that encourages us to drink. If we don't consume fluids when this imbalance occurs, dehydration can develop. Dehydration can impair physical and mental function, which has implications in many walks of life and therefore is best avoided through appropriate daily fluid intake.

Symptoms of dehydration are:

- Thirst
- Nausea
- Dry skin
- Poor concentration
- Fatigue and weakness

- Increased body temperature
- Muscle cramping
- Dark-coloured urine (dark yellow or orange)

Daily fluid requirements can tend to be overstated and over-hyped by the media and the ever-expanding number of bottled-water and drinks companies. That's not to say that regular fluid intake throughout the day is not essential – it certainly is. But our bodies have the capacity to manage fluid balance better than we are sometimes led to believe. When we are in good physical health, a normal individual will become thirsty when they require fluids. It is a normal homeostatic response – those responses that naturally keep the body's functions in check. By then drinking fluids, you will restore or maintain your fluid balance. It is true that if you feel thirsty, then you are likely to already be slightly dehydrated, but this is readily recovered in the space of a couple of hours. So you don't need a water bottle in your hand every half hour of the day...

However, there is an important distinction when it comes to athletes or those who exercise regularly, as these people have much greater requirements for fluid due to significant fluid losses from sweating and heavy breathing during exercise. Numerous studies have shown that athletic performance can be hindered by even relatively mild dehydration, so athletes should not rely solely on thirst to monitor hydration. Instead, athletes must aim to maintain fluid balance before exercise and limit the extent of dehydration during exercise to achieve optimal physical performance. For this reason, athletes must follow a strict hydration strategy to minimise the risk and effects of dehydration.

DAILY FLUID REQUIREMENTS

A general fluid guideline for the average-sized person who is not involved in heavy physical labour or regular intense exercise would be approximately 2 to 2½ litres daily. Appropriate fluids for optimal daily hydration include water, milk, tea, coffee (if you are a regular consumer) and fresh homemade juices. You may be surprised about a couple of things. Firstly, all fluids contribute to daily intake – it doesn't have to be pure water. Secondly, fresh whole fruit and vegetables also contribute fluid to the body, but that's assuming you eat a good amount of fresh fruit and vegetables! Fluid requirements will, of course, significantly increase if your work involves manual labour, if you have larger body mass or if you are working in a warm, humid or air-conditioned environment.

Typical intake providing enough fluid on a daily basis might be:

- A large glass of water with breakfast – 400ml
- A large mug of black tea – 300ml
- A pint of water with lunch – 500ml
- A mug of green tea in the afternoon – 300ml
- A glass of fresh vegetable juice – 300ml
- A pint of water with or after dinner – 500ml
- **Total fluid intake – 2.3 litres**

FLUID REQUIREMENTS FOR EXERCISE

The guideline above is for someone who is not exercising on that day. If you regularly exercise your fluid requirements are much higher – probably about 1 litre extra per hour of exercise, and more if exercising in the heat. If you are preparing for a race or competition, or if you are going to complete a high-intensity training session, you should follow the hydration protocol below.

Optimal hydration protocol*

1 Drink 500ml the evening before the event (two hours before you go to bed).
2 Drink 500ml of water with breakfast.
3 Drink 500ml of water every two hours leading up to your training or event.
4 You may need a little more depending on environmental conditions, or if your urine is not a clear/straw colour each time you pass water.
5 Sip on 300ml of fluid as you warm up.
6 During intense exercise, consume three to four mouthfuls of fluid every 10–15 minutes.
7 After exercise, replace fluid lost until thirst is satisfied and urine is a clear/straw colour.

If you have the opportunity to weigh yourself before and after training, a good rule of thumb is to consume 1.5 litres of fluid for every 1kg lost in body mass.

This is a general recommendation. Fluid requirements may vary depending on body size, level of hydration and environmental conditions.

I DON'T LIKE WATER!

I regularly hear 'I don't like drinking water, so can I drink juice or add something to sweeten it?' I don't recommend the vast majority of commercially available fruit juices or juice-based drinks. Exceptions to this rule would be if they are freshly made or are being used to add carbohydrate to the diet in the lead-up to or after exercise. If you don't like the taste of water alone, you can flavour it by adding

slices of fresh fruit like oranges and lemons or berries. Cooling water with ice is always a good way of making it more palatable and refreshing, especially in the summer months. Adding a pinch (roughly one-eighth of a teaspoon) of salt to the drink is a good way of improving the absorption of fluid and offsetting sweat losses. It is also an alternative to buying a sugar-sweetened and flavour-enhanced sports drink.

ARE YOU HYDRATED?

There is no doubt that water is a vital component of your diet. Regular fluid intake is essential for optimal physical function and should be recognised in your daily habits, but what this means in practical terms is a lot simpler than you might believe. Satisfying your thirst with water is common sense, but drinking a large glass of water on the hour, every hour (or perpetually carrying a large bottle of water) leading to numerous toilet trips is not!

As an athlete, monitoring your hydration status on a regular basis is advised, but particularly important the day before and the morning of a competition. The simplest way to do this is by checking the colour of your urine – a light, pale colour will suggest you are hydrated, and a dark-yellow/orange colour will suggest you are dehydrated. The recommended fluid intake during exercise is 150–250ml every 15 minutes. This works out as three to four mouthfuls.

Sports drinks provide an added benefit of replacing electrolytes lost in the form of sweat during bouts of high-intensity exercise, which enables a better uptake of fluid, preventing dehydration. If you engage in bouts of high-intensity exercise and sports drinks have not been a part of your nutritional plan, I recommend you consider including them. If you choose to, try using them during training over a few weeks to see which drink suits you best.

MACRO COUNTING: PROS AND CONS

Our understanding of nutrition has changed significantly over the past 10 years, leading to the development of new nutrition practices. One practice that has become increasingly popular is macronutrient (macro) counting – or, as many athletes say, 'if it fits your macros'. This popularity is partly due to the increased use of smartphones and health- and nutrition-related apps. We do a large number of daily tasks with our phones and their role in health monitoring and assessment is certainly expanding. A survey of mobile phone users in the United States by Krebbs and Duncan in 2015 reported that over 58 per cent of mobile phone users have health and fitness apps on their phones, which is likely to be similar in Ireland and the United Kingdom.

WHAT IS MACRONUTRIENT TRACKING?

In simple terms, macro counting is the splitting of your macronutrients, including carbohydrate, fat and protein, into daily targets or percentages to meet a daily calorie target. As your daily calorie intake from food will most likely include a combination of carbohydrate, protein and fat, macro counting provides a method for managing your calorie intake in a healthy manner. The calorie target can be used

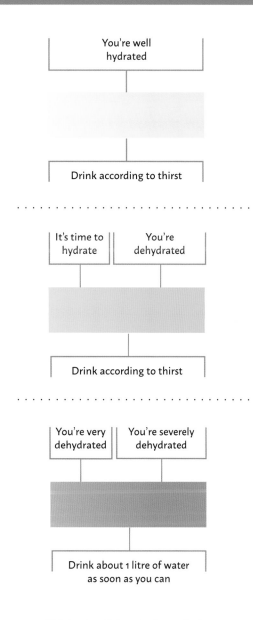

YOUR URINE COLOUR IS AN INDICATION OF YOUR HYDRATION LEVEL

You're well hydrated

Drink according to thirst

It's time to hydrate | You're dehydrated

Drink according to thirst

You're very dehydrated | You're severely dehydrated

Drink about 1 litre of water as soon as you can

Toilet water dilutes urine by 1–2 shades

for three main purposes: to create a deficit for fat loss, to achieve a calorie surplus for building lean mass or to maintain a calorie balance. Macro counting is not just used by athletes – many non-athletes who are simply interested in learning more about their food-intake patterns also use this approach. The detailed example below shows how macro counting manages calorie intake and macronutrient needs.

An example of a macronutrient split

- Carbohydrate: 300g = 1,200 calories
- Fat: 80g = 720 calories
- Protein: 200g = 800 calories
- Total calories = 2,720

THE ADVANTAGES OF TRACKING YOUR MACROS

The main advantages include:

1 Enhanced understanding of calories and macronutrients in food

2 Improved individual accountability and helps you to stay on track with your specific nutrition plan

3 Can help you achieve your body composition goals in a more efficient and effective manner

4 Provides a simple format for you to follow

WHAT TO CONSIDER WHEN COUNTING YOUR MACROS

Although there are many benefits associated with macro counting, there are also some potential drawbacks.

1 Macro counting doesn't focus on habit formation, food quality, micronutrients or how food makes you feel.

2 Calorie counting is often unreliable due to human error and inaccuracies associated with digital apps.

3 You might be choosing foods that are traditionally unhealthy just because they fit into your macros. You can achieve a calorie deficit, balance or surplus from any type of food. However, choosing nutritious foods like fruit, vegetables, nuts and seeds will provide high nutritional value and will benefit your long-term health; while ultra-processed foods won't contribute many nutrients to your body or keep you feeling energised. Eating a nourishing meal should always be your first priority, with the second being whether it includes sufficient protein and appropriate carbohydrate and fats.

THE IMPORTANCE OF ENJOYING YOUR FOOD

Optimum nutrition is not just about reaching a macro or calorie target. Optimum nutrition incorporates variety, contributes to a resilient immune system, includes taste preferences and takes account of how vibrant and energetic we feel from eating foods that we enjoy. These things are all fundamental to lifestyle and nutrition and relate directly to our health and happiness.

If you are meticulously counting your macros, you can become frustrated and miss out on the potential enjoyment you can get from food preparation and eating. From my experience, when people only focus on macro or calorie counting, they miss the big picture of nutrition and fail to address the broader aspects of their relationship with food, particularly their habits and behaviours. We must be conscious of why we are eating and how that food makes us feel. *Am I full, was that meal satisfying and how are my energy levels after eating it?* Becoming overly focused on specific nutrients can potentially damage your relationship with food and may even develop into an obsession or disorder. With the right expert support and a holistic view of your nutrition, macro counting can have tremendous benefits as a component in your overall nutrition strategy. However, becoming over-reliant on it is not beneficial. You should be able to enjoy a meal without having to estimate the nutritional elements on the plate.

FOOD IS SO MUCH MORE THAN A NUMBER.

NUTRITION INFORMATION IS IMPORTANT

If you have read my first book, you will have noticed that calories, macros and other nutrition information are provided with each recipe. This is not necessarily for macro counting purposes but rather providing an education opportunity.

It helps you understand your daily energy and macro needs, how each recipe fits your goal and what types and how much of each food you need to achieve a goal. There are many benefits to this approach, including:

- Flexibility to choose recipes that you like and are nutrient dense

- Encourages sound habit formation, as you prepare and cook your own meals
- Generates personal investment in your overall nutrition and not just the numbers associated with the food you are eating

If a person wants to assess the number of calories and specific nutrients they are consuming then periodic tracking using apps, such as MyFitnessPal, can offer an excellent way of understanding whether you are meeting the targets set out in your goals. As long as you still enjoy your food experience, and you don't become over-reliant and dependent on macro counting or using these apps, then they can add benefit to your nutrition strategy.

MACROS IN ELITE SPORT

In my experience of working with elite athletes, I use macronutrient counting intermittently as an evaluation tool, to ensure that the athletes are meeting their needs for energy, carbohydrates, protein and fats on a daily basis or in preparation for training or competition. Macro counting can also be used when an athlete needs to know that they are eating enough calories to support muscle growth, or indeed appropriate calories to create a calorie deficit for fat loss. This isn't something I would recommend for athletes to do consistently, however, as it can lead to too much focus on the numbers rather than on habits and behaviours around eating.

If an athlete wants to self-educate or keep themselves accountable, journaling or tracking is a great exercise to practise. Using a journal to plan your week and review your nutrition is also an effective way to reflect on your overall lifestyle and help you to consider the whole picture for sustainable health and performance practice.

THE BOTTOM LINE ON TRACKING

If you are reaching the recommended levels of physical activity, are at an optimum weight, eating a sufficient variety of nutritious foods and are in good health then you certainly don't need to obsess about tracking your food. However, if you want to improve your understanding of macros, understand how foods provide you with different nutrients or create a level of accountability, then tracking can be used, particularly for a short- to medium-term period. It is important to focus on developing the essential habits associated with achieving long-term health and wellbeing like nutrition education, food preparation, cooking, and not just on the numbers. You can achieve your health or performance goals by eating delicious and easy-to-prepare meals while being calorie aware rather than obsessed.

NUTRITION STRATEGIES FOR INJURY RECOVERY

Did you know that:

1 Injury results in both physical and psychological impacts.

2 Nutrition can play a vital role in injury recovery.

3 After an injury, soft tissue structures undergo a natural healing process through three specific phases of healing: inflammation, proliferation and remodelling.

4 When an injury occurs that results in immobilisation (joint or bone is fixed in a cast), muscle disuse atrophy (muscle loss) occurs, often at a rate of 0.5 per cent per day! For example, muscle loss can be up to 400g from a leg during the early stages of immobilisation.

5 There can be significant muscle strength loss during an injury – this can be as much as 40 per cent.

6 Appetite reduction can occur during injury recovery, which is not correlated with an actual need for calories.

NUTRITION AND INJURY RECOVERY

Nutrition for recovery from injury is probably the area that has evolved most in the past 10 years. Historically, nutritional interventions for injury recovery were never a central part of the recovery plan, even in elite sport. We now know that nutrition plays a multifaceted role in the mental and physical healing process. The aim for any athlete who gets injured is to return to full function in the fastest possible time. For this to happen, close attention to nutrition is paramount.

When an injury occurs during competition season, particularly in the run-up to a big game or competition, athletes will try almost anything to recover in time for selection. I have seen it countless times. The majority of information online that claims to increase the speed of recovery from an injury has no scientific basis. Although it would be great if there was a quick fix, unfortunately there is no magic cure or potion. However, there are numerous evidence-based strategies you can proactively implement to support recovery from an injury. When aiming to maximise the rate of recovery from an injury, athletes should consider the following:

- Do not restrict calories to create a calorie deficit during the various stages of recovery.
- As energy demands change due to trauma and volume of movement, you need to match energy intake to remain in energy balance.
- Your body requires sufficient energy and nutrients to facilitate the repair and regeneration of new tissue while minimising the loss of muscle mass due to under-nutrition, immobilisation and reduced levels of training.
- Include a wide range of foods in your diet to avoid deficiencies in certain micronutrients. In particular, deficiencies in calcium, vitamin C and vitamin D and the minerals zinc, copper and manganese can potentially impair the healing process.

THE STAGES OF INJURY

The three main stages of injury are:

1 Inflammation: this begins at the time of injury and lasts up to four days.
2 Proliferation: this starts about three days after injury and overlaps with the inflammatory phase.
3 Remodelling: this can continue for six months to one year after injury.

When an injury occurs, an inflammatory response is triggered. Inflammation has a bad reputation, but acute inflammation is actually essential for tissue repair. The degree of inflammation will depend on the severity of the injury and whether there's any bleeding in the injured area. This typically results in

pain, redness and swelling and is due to the vascular and cellular response that releases the chemicals required for the healing process and allows for an increase in blood flow to the area. As the inflammation stage subsides, your body begins to repair the damaged tissue through proliferation. New collagen fibres are formed, known as scar tissue. As scar tissue is less flexible than normal tissue, applying excess stress or returning to training too soon can result in re-injury. As healing progresses into the remodelling stage, tissues improve in quality, organisation and strength. During this stage, cellular organisation of the collagen fibres is increased along with the strength between the bonds.

LEAN MASS – YOUR CURRENCY FOR PERFORMANCE

As a consequence of injury, loss of lean muscle mass will occur, predominantly in the affected limb. In the case of significant injuries, bone demineralisation and even tendon atrophy can occur in the one-to-two-week period immediately following the injury. This can result in a substantial reduction in the volume of exercise that can be completed compared to that previous to the injury. As the first two weeks are when loss of lean muscle mass is most significant, implementing nutrition strategies during this period is critical to recovery. You can lose vital lean muscle mass two to three times faster during these weeks than you can build it at the end of the rehabilitation period. Hence, the more you can retain, the less you need to rebuild. Interestingly, in 2021 the UEFA expert group, the leading organisation in professional football, released a statement on nutrition in elite football indicating that the impact of nutrition during rehabilitation was the area with the greatest potential significance for injury recovery.

CHANGES TO EATING BEHAVIOUR

All athletes, whether recreational or elite, injured or healthy, can benefit from good nutrition planning to enable consistency in meeting their specific needs for energy and nutrients. While adequate energy and nutrient intake are important to facilitate repair and regeneration of injured tissue, avoiding overeating and poor food choices is also relevant. When an injury occurs, athletes often feel a loss of motivation to maintain good eating habits and may underestimate the influence nutrition can have on the rate of recovery. Being injured is not a good time to try and comfort yourself with ice-cream, although the odd treat certainly won't hurt!

When planning meals, there should be a modification in carbohydrate foods and a greater focus on quality protein sources and healthy fats. This is because the athlete is not as active, which in turn reduces the requirement for carbohydrate as a source of fuel. In contrast, a slightly higher protein intake (2–2.4g of protein per kg body mass) can help to retain muscle that otherwise may be lost with inactivity.

ANTIOXIDANT-RICH FOODS

The role of antioxidant supplements in recovery and how they can speed up the healing process is a common query from athletes. As stated previously, the post-injury inflammatory process is responsible for activating the healing process. For this reason, a significant reduction in inflammation may

not be optimal for recovery, especially in the early stages of the injury. Antioxidants have the potential to impede the inflammatory process and, for this reason, large doses of antioxidants are not encouraged.

Minimising the impact of the injury, managing inflammation and supplying the body with necessary nutrients and building blocks for new tissue are crucial for athletes to return to play as soon as possible. There are specific foods that have some evidence to support their potential to speed up the recovery process. For example, essential fatty acids reduce levels of inflammation, whereas fresh vegetables, herbs and spices support the healing process. You need to make sure that you get the bulk of your omega-3 fatty acids from animal, fish or seafood sources. Certain plant sources and a combination of nuts and seeds are a viable omega source, but do not provide the strength of omega-3s or bioavailability of something like salmon or mackerel. Having a range of recipes that focus on these antioxidant and anti-inflammatory nutrients during the injury phase has the potential to play an important role in the nutrition strategy for recovery.

Facial injuries, specifically, are more likely to occur in contact sports. Not only are such injuries painful and uncomfortable, they also have significant implications for meeting nutrition targets. To limit the loss of lean mass, support recovery and maintain physical and mental wellbeing, a soft food/liquid diet strategy that contains adequate calories and a mix of essential nutrients may be necessary. Recipes that are suitable for this include smoothies, soups, puddings and smooth porridge. There are plenty of great options in the breakfast and snack sections of this book.

	VITAMIN C	VITAMIN A	VITAMIN E
Main functions	• Stimulates collagen synthesis • Facilitates wound healing • Maintains bone health	• Increases collagen deposition • Proliferation of epithelial cells • Helps to manage inflammation	• Modulates muscle proteolysis genes • Functions as an antioxidant • Enhances immune function
Good sources	• Kiwi 131mg • Grapefruit 94mg • Orange 93mg • Strawberries 85mg • Broccoli 51mg	• Sweet potato 961µg • Pumpkin 953µg • Squash 572µg • Carrots 534µg • Spinach 472µg	• Sunflower seeds 7.4mg • Almonds 7.3mg • Apricots 2.8mg • Whole avocado 2.7mg • Spinach 1.9mg
Recommended daily amount	• Men: 90mg • Women: 75mg	• Men: 90mg • Women: 75mg	• Men: 15mg • Women: 15mg

MINDSET

Coming to terms with being injured is not easy for any athlete. But having an appropriate nutrition plan and routine helps to provide structure and combat the frustration associated with being injured. Setting goals and targets that are both interesting and motivational are critical in the early stages. For example, aim to improve non-sport-related aspects of your lifestyle, such as sleep, mindfulness, cooking skills and nutrition knowledge, that will make you a better off-field athlete. Although they are not directly related to performance, taking time to improve these areas will certainly enhance performance upon return to full activity. It will also give an injured athlete a sense of 'control' over their recovery that they lack due to the absence of normal training.

HYDRATION

Hydration is always important, and even more so during periods of injury. Regular consumption of water during the recovery period helps to remove waste products from the injured tissue and maintain fluid balance. In fact, some injuries can lead to a significant loss of fluid, and thus greater fluid intake is required to replace it.

ENERGY BALANCE AND ENERGY REQUIREMENTS

Meeting your energy needs is a key variable during recovery from injury. While many people may think that calorie requirements will drop due to inactivity, there is often an increase in the resting requirement for calories that needs to be considered. Basal Metabolic Rate (BMR) refers to the minimum daily calories that your body needs. This can rise due to stress and an increase in metabolic processes. It is essential that an athlete remains in energy balance during the injured phase of their recovery. Sufficient energy is needed for repair of the injured site;

however, if energy intake is too high, leading to a calorie surplus, large fat deposition can occur. Although energy demands are higher than when sedentary, they are not as high as when training. If rapid healing is a priority, an increase of 10 to 15 per cent of the estimated energy requirement (EER), from 200 to 500 kcal maximum, could be beneficial in the recovery process from a muscle injury. The recovery period from an injury is not the time to try and reduce body fat, as this may impact the healing process, hence caloric restrictions are not advised. This recommendation can differ based on the size and magnitude of the injury. For the most part, recovery from the injury should be the priority, and to do this, one must consume enough, but not too much, energy.

A typical 5 foot 10 male athlete requires a daily average of 2,200 kcal when sedentary, >3,000 kcal during training and roughly 2,700 kcal during the early stages of injury. This may be further increased if an athlete is using crutches for mobility for extended periods.

MEAL TIMING

A steady supply of energy and nutrients is hugely important for injured athletes. The aim should be to eat every two to four hours and each meal should contain a protein source of sufficient quantity. Fasting or skipping meals is not recommended during injury. Having adequate energy and appropriate nutrients to support the rehabilitation process is of paramount importance. Having a clear mindset around this is beneficial for the athlete: this is not the time to be distracted by other goals like getting lean.

CARBOHYDRATE REQUIREMENT

Carbohydrate intake is essential during periods of heavy training and competition. However, carbohydrate requirements are lower during injury. Athletes should avoid refined and starchy carbohydrates, as this is the easiest and most effective way to meet your appropriate energy intake and will help to manage body composition. Carbohydrates should be sourced from unprocessed foods, such as fruits and high-fibre vegetables. There is a reduced requirement for cereals, bread, pasta and potatoes, and very limited space for junk foods, including sweet drinks, chocolate or refined carbohydrates. These foods are simply not going to support your recovery.

PROTEIN

Protein is critical for optimum healing from injury and the requirement for protein is increased during injury. Increasing daily protein intake by focusing on the amount, type and timing of intake can help prevent the loss of muscle mass and strength during the injury period. In general, ~2.4g of protein per kilogram of body weight, per day, is required for optimum recovery. Good protein sources include lean red meats, fish, eggs, nuts and seeds, pea protein, whey protein and natural yoghurt.

HOW SHOULD I PREPARE FOR SURGERY?

Nutrition in the preparation for surgery and post-operative recovery is a highly specific area. This generally refers to the 24 hours pre-surgery and 1–2 days after, depending on the duration of the surgery. Working with athletes in a contact sport like rugby, where serious injuries that require surgery occur, I became aware of how little information was provided to athletes regarding their pre- and post-operative nutrition. Apart from following a protocol that involved fasting for long periods of time before the surgery, athletes often had no idea what foods to bring with them. When I began to read about nutrition, surgery and healing, some literature pointed to a specific nutrition plan. This included an increase in carbohydrate foods pre-surgery that could reduce surgical catabolic stress and improve post-operative outcomes. In practical terms, feedback from athletes going through the experience offered the greatest insights to the benefits of having a plan.

Athletes who I have worked with have all embraced the concept of pre- and post-operative nutrition plans. Not only does a plan give them something to focus on during a period of stress, disappointment and frustration, but it also helps them to feel they were able to positively contribute to the outcome of their surgery.

Here are some simple food ideas for pre- and post-op nutrition. They're likely to be particularly helpful after surgery, to ensure that the athlete isn't reliant on hospital meals and has food available that will help aid his or her recovery:

- Whey protein added to smoothies, breakfasts and snacks
- Cow's milk or flavoured milk
- High-protein plant-based milk
- Protein milk
- Protein bars
- Homemade protein balls and bars
- Meat-based sandwiches
- Milk-based smoothies

The potential benefits:

1 Increased energy availability
2 Reduced stress response to the surgery
3 Helps to maintain lean mass
4 Assists wound healing

Key nutrition elements pre-operation:

- Ensure optimal levels of hydration.
- Increase the intake of low-fibre carbohydrate-based foods to increase energy availability post-operation.
- Ensure adequate intake of protein – 1.7g protein per kg – consumed from a whey protein or milk protein drink.

Key nutrition elements post-operation:

- Meet the body's energy requirements.
- Achieve sufficient protein to support healing and repair.

This chart shows how you should tailor your meals in the run-up to surgery: increase the carbohydrates in your diet in the days before; eat a moderate, well-rounded meal with a good source of carbohydrate the evening before; and take a protein shake or protein milk that is rich in essential amino acids (EAA) in the hours before your surgery.

COLLAGEN PROTEIN FOR JOINTS AND TENDON REPAIR

The role of collagen and gelatin protein in joint, tendon and bone healing has garnered significant attention due to the increasing prevalence of long-term joint injuries and osteoarthritis from sport participation. The benefits of vitamin-C-enriched dietary gelatin

WEEK BEFORE	EVENING BEFORE	MORNING OF	

| Meals
Protein and complex
carbohydrates | Light,
carbohydrate-rich meal
(6–12 hours before) | Supplement
(2–4 hours before)
HMS and EAA | SURGERY |

and hydrolysed collagen proteins to support healing and repair offer a promising strategy to support recovery from tendon and joint injuries. However, it's in combination with a progressive rehabilitation programme that collagen has been shown to provide a potential benefit. Eating bowls of jelly and ice-cream while not following an appropriate rehabilitation programme is not going to get you back fitter and stronger than before!

WHAT IS COLLAGEN?

Collagen makes up one-third of all protein in the body and is the most abundant form of structural protein in tendons, cartilage and bones. As collagen is the principal component of the extracellular matrix (ECM), it is vital for the strength and regeneration of this tissue. Collagen is made up of three amino acids – glycine, proline and hydroxyproline. The protein is hydrolysed enzymatically, degrading into smaller bioactive peptides that are easily absorbed within the digestive tract before entering circulation and reaching the bones and tendons. Research supports using a dose of 10–15g collagen once a day for several months in conjunction with an appropriate rehabilitation programme. Appropriate exercise provides the key loading stimulus for healing of the injury in combination with

appropriate nutrition and the collagen. It is important to note that to achieve the benefits from collagen supplementation, it needs to be taken over a prolonged period of time – months rather than weeks. Those taking it as part of their recovery need to be patient and not expect any instant results. If you want to include this as part of your nutrition strategy, I recommend including it in some of my smoothies or smoothie-bowl recipes – something palatable that you'll enjoy eating regularly, as from my experience, compliance with the long-term protocol is the biggest challenge. Other supplements like creatine or caffeine can show acute or certainly shorter-term benefits, which provides affirmation to effort involved. Unfortunately, this is not the case with collagen supplements. Still, despite the research being in its infancy, there are no known side effects or downsides (apart from the cost, of course), so it has become an important part of the nutrition strategy I recommend to athletes who suffer a joint or tendon injury. While hydrolysed collagen protein will have a greater bioavailability and superior amino acid profile, using gelatin as part of your recovery process is certainly a good second option. You can make flavoured gelatin shots and bites and have them an hour before your rehabilitation session. Just make sure you consume at least 15g.

SUPPLEMENT	INJURY	DOSE
Whey protein may be used to help an injured athlete achieve their daily protein needs	Any injury that results in reduced mobility	1–2 scoops daily, about 50g
Omega-3 oils may help to manage inflammation	Trauma injuries, such as bone breaks and muscle tears	1–2g daily
Probiotics may offer benefits to an injured athlete by supporting optimal gut health and immune function	Injuries that require ingestion of antibiotics	1–2 tablets providing 10–20 million live active bacteria
HMB (short for β-Hydroxy β-Methylbutyrate) may help to limit muscle wasting	Any injury that results in reduced mobility	3g daily
Collagen may support tendon, joint and ligament healing	Tendon, bone or joint injuries	15g daily
Creatine may support the recovery process by limiting loss of lean mass	Any injury that results in reduced mobility	3g daily

SUMMARY OF NUTRITION RECOMMENDATIONS FOR INJURED ATHLETES

1 It is vital to meet energy demands to support the healing process.

2 Adequate protein intake is essential for the generation of new tissue and maintenance of muscle mass.

3 Food intake must be altered during each stage of recovery from injury to match changing energy demands.

4 Herbs and phytochemicals (antioxidants and plant compounds) can be used for two to four weeks after the injury to manage inflammation.

5 Appropriate supplements can support recovery and help control inflammation.

NUTRITION STRATEGIES TO SUPPORT YOUR IMMUNE SYSTEM

An abundance of research shows that a healthy lifestyle, including nutrition, boosts our immune system and helps to fight off sickness. We all go through periods where we become sick or unwell due to being run down, whether it is due to the stress of exams, excessive workloads or overtraining. Our lifestyle – including sleep patterns, environmental stressors, physical activity levels and, of course, nutrition – has the potential to negatively or positively influence our immunity and risk for illness.

There is a tremendous amount of information available online relating to nutrition and the immune system. If you type 'nutrition' and 'immunity' into Google, you'll receive in excess of 120 million hits. However, not all of this information is supported by science, so we must be cautious where we source our information. If you look in the wrong places for nutrition guidance to support immunity, you could spend unnecessary amounts of money, negatively impact your performance and potentially put yourself at risk. Fortunately, there are multiple evidence-based and practical ways that you can boost your immune system and reduce your chances of getting sick. These can be implemented into your daily life in conjunction with public health advice regarding hand washing, physical distancing and sneezing and coughing etiquette.

THE IMPORTANCE OF SLEEP

Yes, lack of sleep and lack of quality sleep negatively impact your immune function! There is surprisingly strong evidence to support that sleep and the circadian system exert a strong governing influence on immune functions and enhance immune defence. So the saying that 'sleep helps healing' isn't just an old tale. It is important to check that you are getting sufficient and quality sleep. One particular study that looked at sleep habits and susceptibility to the common cold found that people who sleep less than seven hours on average were almost three times more likely to develop a cold compared to those who averaged eight hours of sleep per night.

Not only is sleep necessary for a healthy immune system, but it is also critical for athletic performance. Elite athletes are

particularly susceptible to sleep inadequacies, characterised by habitual short sleep (less than seven hours per night) and poor sleep quality (sleep fragmentation). Therefore, if you want to be able to achieve optimum performance, developing a good sleep routine and habits is a must. Aim for seven to nine hours per night of good quality sleep. It can be helpful to keep a sleep diary and note any particular triggers which disrupt your sleep or make it more difficult for you to fall asleep.

GENERAL NUTRITION AND IMMUNITY

A balanced, nutrient-rich diet which provides you with your daily need for energy is undoubtedly the most important factor in helping to prevent frequent occurrences of colds, flu and other infections. Neil Walsh, a professor of physiology, reported in his review 'Nutrition and Athlete Immune Health' that 'nutrient availability influences immunity because macro- and micronutrients are involved in a multitude of immune processes, e.g. macronutrients are involved in immune cell metabolism and protein synthesis and micronutrients in antioxidant defences'.

Nutrient-rich foods (fresh fruit and vegetables) have the ability to support your immune system and help fight off pathogens that can lead to the development of a cold or infection. On those occasions that you do catch a cold, certain vegetables, fruits and supplements have been found to support immune defences and reduce the symptoms and duration.

ATHLETES AND IMMUNE FUNCTION

While being physically active is known to help to support immune function, athletes who engage in a high volume of high-intensity training with sub-optimal recovery and nutrition are known to have higher instances of illnesses like upper respiratory tract infections. This can be extremely frustrating, particularly when it results in missing training. For example, a study found that during the summer and winter Olympics, illness – primarily respiratory, but also gastrointestinal – was second only to injury as the most common reason for an elite athlete to seek medical attention. This further highlights how nutrition can play an integral role in preventing athletes becoming fatigued or immunocompromised, and has enabled me to further my understanding of the importance of implementing these strategies in my day-to-day work with elite athletes.

The current daily recommendation for vitamin C intake for an adult is 75mg. This increases to 1g when sick. This increased intake is only recommended for the period of the illness, not on an ongoing basis.

FOODS RICH IN VITAMIN C

VEGETABLES	FRUIT
• Red bell peppers • Broccoli • Brussels sprouts • Kale • Snow peas • Sweet potatoes	• Cantaloupe • Grapefruit • Strawberries • Kiwi • Mangoes • Nectarines • Oranges • Papaya • Tomatoes

VITAMIN C

Vitamin C supplementation is perhaps the most well-known nutritional strategy associated with combating colds and flus. Ironically, vitamin C has not been conclusively shown to reduce either the incidence or symptoms of a cold or flu. Although some studies found positive effects on the treatment of colds in people under short-term stress, such as those who were exercising at high volumes or intensities, others found no evidence to support its benefit in the prevention or treatment of colds. Alternatively, research on 11,000 people in Helsinki reported that male teenage swimmers with colds treated with vitamin C supplementation recovered twice as quickly as those who were not. Interestingly, the same study reported that children appeared to be more responsive to vitamin C supplementation than adults.

ZINC

Zinc is an essential nutrient and appears to play an important role in the immune system, although exactly how it works is not entirely clear. There is some research to suggest that ingesting zinc within 24 hours of the onset of symptoms can reduce the duration of a cold by one to three days, and reduce coughing episodes from five to two days, while also reducing the severity of symptoms. Although there are no set recommendations, the general recommended daily dose is a minimum of 75mg daily. Seafood, meat, nuts and seeds are particularly good sources of zinc.

OMEGA-3 FATTY ACIDS

Omega-3 fatty acids play an important role in managing inflammation as well as supporting the body's immune system. Research has shown that EPA and DHA (the most abundant omega-3 fats found in fish) can boost the level and activity of immune cells in the body. Foods rich in omega-3 include oily fish, nuts, seeds and some plant oils, such as flaxseed and rapeseed oil.

VITAMIN D

The exact role vitamin D plays in the immune system is complex but primarily it helps to keep our immune system balanced, particularly during the cold and flu season. Most immune cells in our body contain a vitamin D receptor, which is believed to be an activator of sorts for these cells, including our fighter T and B cells. However, it is known to stimulate the activity of cells that support an important immune respsonse in the body. This is called an autocrine response.

Recently, researchers in Trinity College Dublin have encouraged people to increase their intake of foods rich in vitamin D and to consider taking a vitamin D supplement containing a minimum of 400 IU (10µg) of vitamin D per day. They also noted that higher intakes, up to 20µg per day, may provide additional benefits. Aside from this, several European countries include vitamin D supplementation in their national recommendations. Some good sources of vitamin D include liver, oily fish, eggs and fortified foods like dairy products and cereals.

GREEN TEA OR HERBAL TEA

Tea has been used for generations by people all around the world when wanting to warm up or when feeling sick. Anecdotally, tea is known to be a comforting drink, but it may also offer some genuine benefits to the immune system and help prevent and fight off infections. All tea (black, green or white) contains a group of antioxidants known as catechins, which are known to have a positive effect on inflammation in the body. There are no guidelines as to how much you should drink, but in the case of green tea, several cups per day have been shown to be associated with potential health benefits. Matcha tea, which has soared in popularity in recent years, is made from the same plant as green tea, but while the latter is made by soaking the leaves, matcha is made up of the leaves and stem of the plant. It is usually mixed into hot water as a powder. Both are sources of natural caffeine and provide an abundance of the powerful catechin antioxidants.

HYDRATION

Staying hydrated is hugely important when you have a cold or an upper respiratory tract infection. Our body is so reliant on water to carry out basic bodily functions and deliver vital nutrients to the body's cells. But in the context of our immune system, it also maintains body temperature and transports waste products and toxins out of the body. High body temperature, sweating and coughing are typical symptoms of the common cold or flu, and each results in increased fluid losses. Therefore, it is essential that you are replacing lost fluids. It is recommended that you consume at least three litres of fluid per day through water and teas of choice while you are recovering from a cold or flu.

GINGER

Fresh ginger root not only tastes great, but also contains a variety of naturally occurring molecules that have been linked to reducing pain and inflammation and may help with your cold symptoms. Fresh ginger can be used in many ways, but to gain the greatest benefits, slice, grate or chop it into dishes. One of the best ways to consume it when suffering from a cold is by grating it into a herbal tea with some lemon and a little squeeze of honey.

GARLIC

These pungent cloves potentially offer more than just great flavour to your food. Garlic contains allicin, a sulphuric compound that produces potent antioxidants. So there is no harm in adding some extra garlic to your cooking if you are feeling under the weather. Don't worry about the smell – you should be keeping your distance from friends and family anyway!

LET'S SUMMARISE

The old cliché 'prevention is better than cure' is certainly true when it comes to colds and similar illnesses. Adequate sleep, managing stress, being physically active and eating a balanced diet that provides your body with sufficient energy, fluids and essential nutrients are vital for keeping your immune system strong and preventing colds. If you do develop a cold, take a systematic approach: use more natural anti-inflammatory and nutrient-rich foods, such as ginger, garlic, green vegetables and citrus fruits. Increasing your intake of these foods will only help your body's immune system. In the case of supplements, only take those that have been scientifically shown to help. Vitamin C, vitamin D, probiotics and zinc have all been shown to at least reduce the symptoms and duration of colds. So, although they won't cure you, there is certainly no harm in taking them, and they potentially offer some help in getting you back to feeling yourself.

FEEDING THE GUT: PROBIOTICS AND PREBIOTICS

Gut flora and their role in general health and wellbeing are a hugely exciting area of research. Having a healthy gut requires good bacteria, which have been linked with a host of health benefits. Some of these include improvements in health through reductions in inflammation and symptoms of asthma and rheumatoid arthritis, and improvements in body composition, immune function, energy levels and digestive health.

Although probiotics and prebiotics sound similar, they are different and, yes, you need both in your diet for a healthy gut. Probiotics are bacteria that help maintain the natural balance of organisms (microflora) in the gut and intestine. Prebiotics are the food for the bacteria in our intestinal tract and they consist of different plant fibres (we get them through fruit and vegetables). Some foods can be both pre- and probiotic, such as artichokes and kimchi. We call these synbiotics. Simply put, prebiotics are foods that promote the growth of beneficial gut bacteria, but probiotics are edible sources that actually contain health-promoting microbes.

WHAT ARE PREBIOTICS?

Prebiotics are found mostly in plant-based foods and provide nourishment for the beneficial bacteria in your gut. The body isn't able to break down these substances, so they are passed on to the microbiota where your gut microbes turn them into useful metabolites, such as short-chain fatty acids and vitamins. Prebiotics nourish your gut microbiome, boost the growth of beneficial bacteria and promote the production of health-promoting substances. The most stable sources of prebiotics are specific types of dietary fibre. However, just because many fibres are prebiotics doesn't mean that all fibre is prebiotic. Some insoluble fibres can't be broken down by gut microbes.

Inulin, oligofructose, fructooligosaccharides (FOS) and galactooligosaccharides (GOS) are all examples of prebiotics. Pectin, which is most commonly used for jam making, and β-glucan, a fibre found in oats, also appear to have some prebiotic potential, but inulin, oligofructose and FOS are the main fibres generating interest in research for improving gut health.

WHERE DO YOU GET PREBIOTIC FIBRE FROM?

Numerous foods contain prebiotic fibre, such as raw onions, garlic, banana, leeks, asparagus, chicory and artichokes. You might notice that the main sources of prebiotic fibre are natural, whole foods. Making a consistent effort to eat a balanced diet with a wide variety of fruits and vegetables will help to ensure you are getting sufficient prebiotic fibre for gut health. The supplement form of prebiotic fibre is an option for anyone who really struggles to consume a balanced diet, or who has issues with their digestive health when eating fibre-rich foods.

Antibiotics used to treat bacterial infections kill off both the bad bacteria and some of the good bacteria in the gut. So when taking antibiotics, it may be beneficial to use a prebiotic supplement that allows the good bacteria to recover and reduces the risk of the bad bacteria becoming dominant.

If you feel that you are not getting a sufficient supply of fibre in your diet, start by introducing more plant-based meals and snacks into your diet. If that is a major struggle, then a prebiotic fibre supplement is definitely worth considering.

WHAT ABOUT PROBIOTICS?

The potential health benefits of food sources of probiotics, or fermented foods, in the diet have been strongly debated in the science community, with Stanford Medicine publishing a study in 2021 that was one of the first pieces of research to really add credibility to the potential benefits of foods like kombucha and fermented vegetables in the diet.

The aim with taking probiotics, of course, is to help to build or maintain a diverse microbiome that supports digestive health and a robust immune system. The gut microbiome has been shown to be heavily connected to the physiological functions of immunity and protection from pathogens. While our microbiome is most heavily influenced by dietary food selection, research suggests that supplementing with probiotics can help prevent upper respiratory infections,

which include the common cold. Probiotics have also been shown to reduce the severity of colds, symptoms of irritable bowel syndrome (IBS) and even some autoimmune conditions.

Despite growing research in this field, it's important to state that the European Food Safety Authority (EFSA) and the US FDA do not currently attribute the ability to prevent or treat diseases to probiotic administration. It's beyond the scope of this book to dig further into the science of this, but it's certainly a space in which we're going to see further research. Briefly, most of the analysis has focused on the bacteria lactobacilli and bifidobacteria – suggested to be the two most important forms of probiotic for promoting an optimal balance of good bacteria.

Based on my reading and experience of fermented foods and probiotics, I will certainly be continuing to enjoy a glass of kombucha and recommend a wide mix of fermented foods in the diets of those I work with. The latter includes diverse vegetables, fruit and products such as kombucha, kimchi, kefir and other foods labelled with 'live cultures'. If you are planning to purchase a probiotic, I would suggest firstly consulting an expert nutritionist or dietitian, as our digestive systems are highly individual and can respond differently to various nutrition or supplement interventions.

WHAT ARE GUT FLORA?

Gut flora (also known as intestinal microbiota) are the bacteria that colonise your intestines. Intestinal microbiota is composed of about 100 *trillion* bacteria and encompasses as many as 1,000 different species – hard to believe we could be a host to that much life, isn't it? In real terms, these bacteria account for up to

3 per cent of your overall body mass – that's about 4–5lbs of bacteria in the average person!

These bacteria inhabiting your gut consist of both 'good bacteria', which help to keep us healthy, and 'bad bacteria', which can lead to increased risk of disease and sub-optimal health. A healthy gut should obviously contain plenty of good bacteria and a low level of bad bacteria. These essential good bacteria provide vital defences against pathogens (infectious molecules) and forms of bad bacteria by colonising the gut and creating a barrier effect that limits the development of bacteria and fungi that can cause illness and digestive disorders. Good bacteria also support the immune system by helping to develop immune cells that fight off infections throughout the body.

Additionally, gut flora produce certain vitamins such as biotin (vitamin B7), which is a water-soluble vitamin that helps the body metabolise proteins, fats and carbohydrates. These good bacteria are also responsible for the fermentation and breakdown of unused energy or indigestible food, which has made its way through the gut, into molecules known as short-chain fatty acids. These fats are important in the function of cells within the colon, and also play a positive role in limiting fat storage elsewhere. These are just some of the essential functions of gut flora – research suggests that there are numerous other roles for the colonies of gut bacteria within our bodies.

FAT LOSS WITH FIBRE

One of the most important factors for successfully reducing body weight is appetite control. Simply put, if you have good appetite control, you are less likely to overeat and more likely to consume an appropriate amount of calories and the types of foods needed to achieve your goal. Fibre intake, and in this case prebiotic fibre intake, has been suggested to suppress the hormone (ghrelin) that increases the feeling of hunger and additionally increases the hormones (peptide YY) linked with feeling full and satisfied. Additionally, prebiotic fibre binds to unhealthy fats and toxins in the diet and in turn promotes their excretion, which may also aid fat loss.

From the moment a person is born, the food they eat directly impacts the type of bacteria that colonise their gut. The modern Western diet tends to be high in refined sugars and processed fats, coupled with a low intake of fibre-rich (plant-based) foods. This can result in the development of an imbalance of bacteria in the gut and a greater level of unwanted bad bacteria with adverse implications for long-term health. This pattern of an energy-dense but nutrient-poor diet leads to significant changes in intestinal ecology over time and is likely to be one of the contributing factors to chronic diseases, such as obesity and type 2 diabetes. For this reason, it is incredibly important to eat food that promotes an optimal balance of good to bad bacteria in the gut.

KEY POINTS ON PREBIOTIC FIBRE

1 Gut flora (also known as intestinal microbiota) are the bacteria that colonise your intestines.

2 Prebiotics are substances (fibre) found mostly in plant-based foods that provide nourishment for the beneficial bacteria in your gut.

3 Prebiotics nourish your gut microbiome, boost the growth of beneficial bacteria and promote the production of health-promoting substances.

4 The bacteria inhabiting your gut consist of both 'good bacteria', which help to keep us healthy, and 'bad bacteria'.

5 A healthy gut should obviously contain plenty of good bacteria and a low level of bad bacteria.

6 A varied diet with lots of plant-based meals and wholegrains will provide your gut with sufficient prebiotic fibre.

PART THREE: THE RECIPES

THE FRAMEWORK

While all recipes can be enjoyed on any day once they meet a person's need for appropriate energy and nutrients, the following strategy has been implemented to categorise the recipes. Macronutrient information, not calories, predominantly determines the exercise category for each recipe; there are three, depending on the level of activity you plan to undertake on any given day. The micronutrient information, meanwhile, determines the suitability of the recipes for either injury recovery or immune support.

CATEGORY		ACTIVITY OR PURPOSE	NUTRITION	OBJECTIVE
Rest day recipes	Zz	Low and moderate levels of exercise	• Lower carbohydrate • High protein • Higher fibre	• Stable energy • Wellbeing • Health
Exercise day recipes	»	Moderate and high-intensity exercise	• Higher carbohydrate • High/moderate protein • Lower fibre	• Energise • Perform • Restore • Recover
Intense exercise day recipes	»»	Intense exercise such as competition	• Higher carbohydrate • Moderate protein • Lower fibre • Lower fat	• Energise • Performance • Fuel • Restore • Recover
Immune support	⊘	Supporting immunity and building your defence against illness	• Fibre • Vitamin C • Zinc • Vitamin D • Probiotics	• Revitalise • Recover • Protect
Injury recovery	⊕	Healing from injury and restoring function and strength	• Protein • Omega-3 • Antioxidants • Vitamin D • Iron • Gelatin	• Limit loss of muscle • Heal • Repair • Regenerate

BREAKFAST

ALMOND BREAKFAST SMOOTHIE

CALORIES PER SERVING	CARBS (G)	PROTEIN (G)	FAT (G)	FIBRE (G)
355KCAL	26	23	16	5.3

Zz REST DAY

⊕ INJURY RECOVERY

INGREDIENTS

250ml almond milk

2 tbsp almond butter

1 tbsp porridge oats

¼ tbsp coconut oil

1 scoop vanilla whey
   protein powder

1 banana

1 tbsp Greek yoghurt

1 tbsp honey

3 ice cubes

1 tsp cinnamon

SERVES: 2

PREPARATION TIME: 5 MINUTES

TOTAL TIME: 5 MINUTES

EQUIPMENT: BLENDER

This is an ideal smoothie for anyone who is in a rush in the morning and wants a quick healthy breakfast. The almond butter gives a lovely nutty taste to this delicious and satisfying smoothie. Use a frozen banana for a creamier, milkshake-like breakfast!

1 Blend all ingredients together. You can alter the thickness of your smoothie by adjusting the amount of milk and ice cubes.
2 Serve and enjoy.

Each portion provides:
- **vitamin E 115%** RI (13.82mg)
- **magnesium 49%** RI (185.26mg)
- **calcium 33%** RI (266.90mg)

Vitamin E is an antioxidant; calcium and magnesium have essential roles in bone formation and density, muscle contraction, protein synthesis and heart health.

BAKED EGG SHAKSHUKA

CALORIES PER SERVING	CARBS (G)	PROTEIN (G)	FAT (G)	FIBRE (G)
436KCAL	22	26	26	6

Zz **REST DAY**

✓ **IMMUNE SUPPORT**

INGREDIENTS

1 tsp olive oil

75g chorizo (chopped)

1 onion (chopped)

1 red bell pepper (chopped)

pinch of salt

pinch of pepper

3 cloves of garlic (crushed)

1 tsp cumin

1 tsp smoked paprika

½ tsp chilli flakes

2 tins of chopped tomatoes

6 eggs

30g feta cheese (chopped)

1 tbsp fresh parsley

1 tbsp honey

⅓ green chilli (finely sliced)

SERVES: 3

PREPARATION TIME: 5 MINUTES

COOKING TIME: 30 MINUTES

TOTAL TIME: 35 MINUTES

EQUIPMENT: LARGE PAN WITH A LID

A simple, filling and delicious lower-calorie option, great for a weekend brunch with family or friends. It's also a super-flexible recipe for using up what's in your fridge – the only essentials are tomatoes and eggs. Serve with a slice of sourdough bread to dip into the soft egg yolks.

1 Add a teaspoon of olive oil to the pan. Cook the chorizo over medium-low heat for 3 minutes. Remove the chorizo from the pan and set aside, leaving the excess oils on the pan.
2 Add the onion, red pepper, and a pinch of salt and pepper and cook in the oils from the chorizo for 2–3 minutes.
3 Next add in the garlic, cumin, paprika and chilli flakes. Stir through and cook for 2 minutes.
4 Add the chopped tomatoes to the pan and simmer on a medium heat for 15 minutes.
5 Remove from the heat and make 6 indents or wells in the tomato mixture and crack an egg into each one.
6 Using a spoon, gently scoop some of the tomato over the egg whites to help them cook more evenly.
7 Place the pan back on a low heat and cover with a lid for 5 minutes.
8 Remove the lid and sprinkle with feta cheese, chopped parsley, a drizzle of honey and thinly sliced green chilli before serving.

Each portion provides:
- **vitamin B12 128%** RI (3.2mg)
- **vitamin C 95%** RI (76mg)
- **vitamin D 74%** RI (3.7μg)

Vitamin D supports the absorption of calcium and is important for strong bones and muscle function.

BLACK PUDDING AVOCADO TOAST

CALORIES PER SERVING	CARBS (G)	PROTEIN (G)	FAT (G)	FIBRE (G)
432KCAL	25	17	30	8

» EXERCISE DAY

⊕ INJURY RECOVERY

INGREDIENTS

50g black pudding (sliced)

1 tbsp rapeseed oil

1 egg

½ avocado

pinch of salt

pinch of black pepper

¼ tsp chilli flakes

1 slice wholemeal brown bread

SERVES: 1

PREPARATION TIME: 2 MINUTES

COOKING TIME: 10 MINUTES

TOTAL TIME: 12 MINUTES

EQUIPMENT: MEDIUM-SIZED POT, BAKING TRAY, TOASTER, SMALL BOWL

Black pudding and avocado is a dream combination – trust me! Spread on some wholemeal toast and topped with a poached egg, it's a breakfast (or lunch) you'll want to make again and again ... and again. It provides a good hit of protein too.

1 Preheat the oven to 190°C.
2 Put the black pudding slices on a baking tray, drizzle with oil and cook for 3–4 minutes on each side.
3 Meanwhile, poach the egg in a pot of simmering hot water for 3–5 minutes, depending on how well done you like your egg to be.
4 Mash the avocado in a bowl with the back of a fork. Add the salt, pepper and chilli flakes and mix gently.
5 Toast the bread.
6 To serve, spread the avocado onto the toast, followed by the black pudding, and top with the poached egg.

Each portion provides:
- **iron 65%** RI (9.1mg)
- **vitamin D 29%** RI (1.5µg)
- **chloride 147%** RI (1175mg)

This is a great recipe to support blood health, as it's rich in iron – and vitamins D and C and chloride help with iron absorption.

BLACK PUDDING FRITTATA

CALORIES PER SERVING	CARBS (G)	PROTEIN (G)	FAT (G)	FIBRE (G)
727KCAL	31	41	48	6.8

Zz **REST DAY**

(ッ **IMMUNE SUPPORT**

INGREDIENTS

1/2 tbsp olive oil

1 large potato (cooked)

1 onion (chopped)

½ tsp oregano

½ tsp garlic powder

½ tsp smoked paprika

pinch of salt

pinch of pepper

6 mushrooms (sliced)

1 red bell pepper (sliced)

½ head of broccoli (chopped)

6 eggs

150g black pudding (sliced)

60g Cheddar cheese (grated)

Handful fresh coriander
  (chopped), to garnish

SERVES: 2

PREPARATION TIME: 5 MINUTES

COOKING TIME: 15 MINUTES

TOTAL TIME: 25 MINUTES

EQUIPMENT: OVENPROOF SKILLET, SMALL PAN, LARGE MIXING BOWL

Not only does this taste great, but it will also keep you full for hours. It might be one for the weekend or a day when you have a little more time to prepare breakfast, but it's well worth it!

1 Preheat the oven to 190°C.
2 Heat the olive oil in an ovenproof skillet.
3 Chop the potato into small cubes.
4 Add the onion and potato to the skillet with the oregano, garlic powder, paprika and a pinch of salt and pepper. Cook on a medium heat for 2–3 minutes.
5 Add the mushrooms, red pepper and broccoli and cook for a further 5 minutes until soft.
6 Meanwhile, cook the black pudding on a separate pan for 3–4 minutes on each side.
7 Whisk the eggs in a large mixing bowl.
8 Pour the eggs into the skillet over the vegetables, then add the black pudding and grated cheese.
9 Place the skillet in the preheated oven and cook for 5 minutes.
10 Garnish with coriander and serve yourself a hearty slice.

Each portion provides:
- **vitamin C 178%** RI (143mg)
- **vitamin D 120%** RI (6µg)
- **iron 92%** RI (13mg)

The absorption of iron – which is needed for the production of red blood cells – is supported by vitamin C.

BLUESPRESSO

CALORIES PER SERVING	CARBS (G)	PROTEIN (G)	FAT (G)	FIBRE (G)
318KCAL	29	32	8	3

Zz REST DAY

⊕ INJURY RECOVERY

INGREDIENTS

1 espresso shot (cooled)

30g blueberries (frozen)

1 tbsp Greek yoghurt

1 banana

1 scoop vanilla whey protein powder

40ml milk

1 square dark chocolate

SERVES: 1

PREPARATION TIME: 5 MINUTES

TOTAL TIME: 5 MINUTES

EQUIPMENT: BLENDER, ESPRESSO MAKER

This might be a tad controversial, but it has been a big hit with coffee lovers! Enjoy this versatile smoothie for breakfast, lunch, as a snack or as an accompaniment to a main meal for added energy. An added benefit of this smoothie, apart from taste, is the caffeine hit, which makes it a winner as a pre-workout option in the morning.

1 Add the cooled espresso shot to a glass.
2 Blend all the smoothie ingredients and pour in with the espresso shot, then serve and enjoy.

Each portion provides:
- **potassium 41%** RI (821mg)
- **calcium 38%** RI (303mg)
- **magnesium 37%** RI (138mg)

Blueberries contain iron, phosphorus, calcium, magnesium, zinc and vitamin K. Adequate intake of these minerals and vitamins are essential to build and maintain bone structure and strength.

CHIA PROTEIN PUDDING

CALORIES PER SERVING	CARBS (G)	PROTEIN (G)	FAT (G)	FIBRE (G)
572KCAL	44	41	28	11

Zz **REST DAY**

⊕ **INJURY RECOVERY**

INGREDIENTS

2 tbsp Greek yoghurt

100ml milk

2 tsp honey

1 tbsp peanut butter

1 tbsp chia seeds

1 scoop vanilla whey protein
    powder

15g dark chocolate

½ banana (sliced)

½ kiwi (chopped)

SERVES: 1

PREPARATION TIME: 5 MINS

TOTAL TIME: 6+ HOURS

EQUIPMENT: BOWL

I'm often asked, 'How can I incorporate whey protein into my day without having to make a smoothie?' Chia protein pudding is the answer! This easy-to-make snack will be sure to satisfy a sweet tooth and deliver a protein hit. It also makes a great pre-bedtime snack that will support your recovery overnight.

1   Mix the yoghurt, milk, honey, peanut butter, chia seeds and protein powder in a bowl until you have your desired texture – I like mine to be pretty smooth.
2   Place the banana and kiwi on top of the pudding mixture, and grate dark chocolate over the fruit.
3   Leave it in the fridge overnight before eating. Bon appetit!

Each portion provides:
- **calcium 91%** RI (726mg)
- **omega-3 89%** RI (2g)
- **vitamin B12 136%** RI (3.4µg)

One tablespoon of chia seeds contains 79mg calcium, making them a significant non-dairy source of calcium.

CHOCOLATE PUDDLE PANCAKES

CALORIES PER SERVING	CARBS (G)	PROTEIN (G)	FAT (G)	FIBRE (G)
791KCAL	77	24	43	13

>> EXERCISE DAY

⊘ IMMUNE SUPPORT

INGREDIENTS

150g oats

100g Greek yoghurt

1 tbsp cacao powder

1 ripe banana

2 medium eggs

1 tsp honey

50ml milk (more if needed)

60g dark chocolate (85–90%)

50g blueberries

1 tbsp olive oil

1 tsp coconut oil

SERVES: 2

PREPARATION TIME: 5 MINUTES

COOKING TIME: 10 MINUTES

TOTAL TIME: 15 MINUTES

EQUIPMENT: BLENDER, NON-STICK PAN, MICROWAVE, SMALL BOWL

If you fancy something a little sweet but still packed with nutritional value, give these delicious pancakes a try! They're a great way of getting carbohydrates on board in preparation for competition. The high fat content makes them best suited to days when you need to top up your energy – or for a big weekend brunch treat.

1 Place the oats, yoghurt, cacao powder, banana, eggs, honey and milk in the blender, and blend to a smooth batter. (Note: if your batter is too thick, add a little more milk to reach the desired consistency.)

2 Chop up half the chocolate. Add the chopped chocolate and blueberries to the batter. Mix through with a spoon.

3 Heat some of the olive oil in a non-stick pan.

4 Use a ladle to dollop some batter onto the pan. Cook on a medium heat until golden brown on both sides.

5 Repeat until the batter is used up, oiling the pan very lightly for each pancake.

6 Add the remaining chocolate and the coconut oil to a small bowl. Place the bowl in the microwave on the defrost or low setting for 30 seconds. Remove from the microwave and stir. Repeat this process until the chocolate has melted completely and is a smooth, silky consistency.

7 Drizzle the melted chocolate over the pancakes and serve.

Each portion provides:
- **magnesium 67%** RI (250mg)
- **iron 66%** RI (9.3mg)
- **zinc 46%** RI (4.6mg)

Athletes can often be deficient in zinc as it is lost through sweat. It's important to replace these stores to enable greater muscle recovery following exercise and in the lead-up to competition.

CRANBERRY AND PECAN GRANOLA

CALORIES PER SERVING	CARBS (G)	PROTEIN (G)	FAT (G)	FIBRE (G)
203KCAL	13	4	11	3

Zz **REST DAY**

⊕ **INJURY RECOVERY**

INGREDIENTS

240g oats

30g desiccated coconut

30g flaked almonds

40g pecans

40g dried cranberries

3 tbsp honey

2 tbsp coconut oil (melted)

1 tbsp orange zest

2 tbsp orange juice

½ tsp cinnamon

½ tsp ginger

½ tsp nutmeg

½ tsp salt

MAKES: 10 SERVINGS

PREPARATION TIME: 5 MINUTES

COOKING TIME: 35 MINUTES

TOTAL TIME: 40 MINUTES, PLUS COOLING TIME

EQUIPMENT: LARGE BOWL, BAKING PAPER, BAKING TRAY, AIRTIGHT CONTAINER

Enjoy this delicious nutty granola served on top of Greek yoghurt or sprinkled over your porridge in the morning. This really simple recipe is brought to life by the dried cranberries, orange zest and toasted nuts. It's also a great accompaniment to my Yuggy Berry recipe (page 112).

1 Preheat the oven to 180°C.
2 Combine all of the ingredients in a large bowl.
3 Spread the mixture evenly on a baking tray lined with baking paper.
4 Bake in the oven for 15 minutes.
5 Remove from the oven and mix well before placing back in the oven for a further 20 minutes.
6 Allow to cool and then transfer to an airtight container to store.

Each portion provides:
- **manganese 48%** RI (0.97mg)
- **phosphorus 14%** RI (99mg)
- **vitamin E 8%** RI (0.95mg)

Together, manganese and phosphorus support bone health and muscle function.

ESPRESSO OATS

CALORIES PER SERVING	CARBS (G)	PROTEIN (G)	FAT (G)	FIBRE (G)
450KCAL	56	46	5	4

INTENSE EXERCISE DAY

INJURY RECOVERY

INGREDIENTS

50g oats

1 tsp baking soda

1 scoop vanilla whey
   protein powder

1 espresso (made with
   50–80ml water)

1 tbsp honey

150g 0% fat Greek yoghurt

SERVES: 1

PREPARATION TIME: 3 MINUTES

COOKING TIME: 2 MINUTES

TOTAL TIME: 5 MINUTES

EQUIPMENT: SMALL BOWL, MICROWAVE, ESPRESSO MAKER

Try kick-starting your morning with this super-tasty oat breakfast with a caffeine and carb hit in one! It takes only a few minutes to throw together, while delivering over 50g of carbohydrates, making it the perfect breakfast option before training or in preparation for a workout.

1 Mix the oats, baking soda and whey together in a bowl.
2 Add the coffee, half the honey and half the yoghurt, and mix well.
3 Place in the microwave for 1 minute on the standard setting.
4 Remove from the microwave, stir and put back in for another 45–60 seconds (depending on desired consistency).
5 Mix the rest of the yoghurt and honey together and serve over the cooked oats.

Each portion provides:
- **calcium 44%** RI (350mg)
- **manganese 98%** RI (2mg)
- **vitamin B1 48%** RI (0.53mg)

Supplementation with caffeine
has been shown to have
significant benefits for various
aspects of exercise performance
– particularly aerobic endurance.

FRENCH TOAST WITH GREEK YOGHURT

CALORIES PER SERVING	CARBS (G)	PROTEIN (G)	FAT (G)	FIBRE (G)
692KCAL	80	28	22	4

 INTENSE EXERCISE DAY

⊕ INJURY RECOVERY

INGREDIENTS

1 tbsp olive oil

100ml milk

3 eggs

½ tsp cinnamon

4 slices sourdough bread

For the toppings:

2 tbsp Greek yoghurt

1 banana (sliced)

1 tbsp honey

1 handful fresh berries

SERVES: 2

PREPARATION TIME: 2 MINUTES

COOKING TIME: 8 MINUTES

TOTAL TIME: 10 MINUTES

EQUIPMENT: NON-STICK PAN, SMALL BOWL, TRAY OR SHALLOW BOWL

French toast works incredibly well with yoghurt and honey, making a delicious and satisfying breakfast or lunch. This recipe is brilliant to whip up when you're short on time but in need of something tasty and substantial to keep you going for a few hours.

1 Preheat the oil on a non-stick pan.
2 Whisk the milk, eggs and cinnamon together in a small bowl.
3 Pour the egg mix into a flat tray or shallow bowl.
4 Soak the slices of bread in the egg mix, turning them over to absorb all of the liquid.
5 Place the slices of bread on the pan and cook on each side for 3–4 minutes or until lightly browned. You may have to do this in batches, depending on the size of your pan.
6 Remove the French toast from the pan and put onto plates for serving.
7 Serve with a dollop of yoghurt, some sliced banana, honey and fresh berries.

Having adequate carbohydrate stores (glycogen) in the body's muscle tissue and liver supports performance by delaying the onset of fatigue and maintaining energy levels.

MANGOLOCO OATS

CALORIES PER SERVING	CARBS (G)	PROTEIN (G)	FAT (G)	FIBRE (G)
624KCAL	72	30	24	7

 INTENSE EXERCISE DAY

 IMMUNE SUPPORT

INGREDIENTS

Mango base:

1 tsp olive oil

1 thumb-sized piece of ginger
   (peeled and grated)

100g mango (peeled and chopped)

½ tsp cardamom

½ tsp cinnamon

1½ tbsp honey

1 tbsp almond butter

1 tsp lime juice

Creamy oat mix:

40g oats

½ scoop vanilla protein powder

1 tbsp desiccated coconut

1 tsp vanilla extract

100g Greek yoghurt

100ml water

SERVES: 1

PREPARATION TIME: 5 MINUTES

COOKING TIME: 10 MINUTES

TOTAL TIME: 6+ HOURS

EQUIPMENT: SMALL NON-STICK PAN, SMALL BOWL, MASON JAR

Overnight oats save so much time in the morning, and you can easily vary the ingredients and flavours that you use. The desiccated coconut here is a good source of dietary fibre but, as well as that, adds a lovely texture to the pudding-like breakfast.

1 Heat the olive oil on a small non-stick pan. Fry the ginger on a medium heat until golden brown.

2 Add the mango, cardamom, cinnamon, 1 tbsp of honey, almond butter and lime juice.

3 Stirring continuously, cook until soft and aromatic.

4 Place the oats, protein powder, coconut, vanilla extract, yoghurt and water together in a bowl and mix thoroughly.

5 Once the mango mixture has cooled, spoon it into a Mason jar.

6 Next, add the oat mix on top and drizzle over the remaining ½ tbsp of honey.

7 Seal the jar and leave in the fridge to set overnight.

8 Serve – I like to add some fresh berries and extra pieces of mango on the side.

Each portion provides:
- **vitamin C 49%** RI (39mg)
- **phosphorus 59%** RI (410mg)
- **manganese 134%** RI (2.7mg)

Manganese is a trace mineral that plays a role in decreasing inflammation and pain associated with inflammatory disorders and assists in the regulation of blood sugar levels.

MIXED BERRY SMOOTHIE BOWL

CALORIES PER SERVING	CARBS (G)	PROTEIN (G)	FAT (G)	FIBRE (G)
515KCAL	48	30	22	8

>> **EXERCISE DAY**

⊕ **INJURY RECOVERY**

INGREDIENTS

20g mixed nuts

pinch of salt

100g frozen strawberries and
banana

1 tbsp honey

1 scoop whey protein powder
(or 2 tbsp Greek yoghurt)

100ml low-fat milk

For the toppings:

50g fresh berries (strawberries,
raspberries and blueberries)

20g dark chocolate (grated)

SERVES: 1

PREPARATION TIME: 5 MINUTES

COOKING TIME: 15 MINUTES

TOTAL TIME: 20 MINUTES

EQUIPMENT: OVEN, BAKING TRAY, BLENDER

Smoothie bowls are one of my favourite things to have
post-workout – they're quick to make yet deliver a
satisfying and substantial meal. Using frozen fruit rather
than fresh fruit gives an incredible creamy texture, and I
love to top mine with fresh berries and some grated dark
chocolate. This recipe is particularly popular with athletes
aiming to hit their protein targets in a tasty way!

1 Preheat your oven to 170°C. Place the nuts on a tray,
   sprinkle with a little salt and dry roast in the oven for
   1 minute.
2 Blend the frozen fruit, honey, whey/yoghurt and milk on a
   low speed for 2–3 minutes or until fully blended.
3 Pour the blended mix into a bowl.
4 Top with the roasted nuts, fresh berries and grated dark
   chocolate and serve.

Each portion provides:
- **calcium 40%** RI (316mg)
- **magnesium 35%** RI (131mg)
- **potassium 33%** RI (655mg)

Increasing magnesium in the
body is a great way to reduce
muscle tightness.

PEANUT BUTTER YOGHURT TOAST

CALORIES PER SERVING	CARBS (G)	PROTEIN (G)	FAT (G)	FIBRE (G)
344KCAL	48	11	12	5

 INTENSE EXERCISE DAY

⊕ INJURY RECOVERY

INGREDIENTS

1 slice wholegrain brown bread
1 tbsp peanut butter
1 banana
1 tbsp natural yoghurt
½ tbsp honey

SERVES: 1

PREPARATION TIME: 2 MINUTES

COOKING TIME: 2 MINUTES

TOTAL TIME: 4 MINUTES

EQUIPMENT: TOASTER

Taking less than five minutes to make, this recipe makes for a great light breakfast, early afternoon snack, or even a pre-workout or training session option; or if you double the portion size, it's perfect for post-workout too. Together the ingredients provide a great hit of carbs and a decent protein source – and boy, oh boy, it's tasty!

1 Toast the bread.
2 Spread the peanut butter on top of the toasted bread.
3 Mash or slice the banana and spread it over the peanut butter.
4 Top with yoghurt and drizzle over the honey.

Each portion provides:
- **potassium 35%** RI (691mg)
- **magnesium 25%** RI (93mg)
- **chloride 66%** RI (529mg)

Potassium and chloride are two of the main electrolytes needed by the body to maintain healthy function. As electrolytes are lost through bodily fluids, such as sweat, they need to be replaced through nutritional means.

PETER'S QUESADILLA

CALORIES PER SERVING	CARBS (G)	PROTEIN (G)	FAT (G)	FIBRE (G)
605KCAL	40	33	35	5

>> EXERCISE DAY

⟳ IMMUNE SUPPORT

INGREDIENTS

1 ½ tbsp rapeseed oil

1 small red onion (sliced)

1 tsp cumin

½ tbsp paprika

salt and pepper

1 small red bell pepper (sliced)

30g sweetcorn

3 eggs

2 tortilla wraps

150g grated mozzarella

30g cottage cheese

1 tsp garlic powder

juice of ½ lime

1 tbsp fresh coriander

SERVES: 2

PREPARATION TIME: 5 MINUTES

COOKING TIME: 15 MINUTES

TOTAL TIME: 20 MINUTES

EQUIPMENT: NON-STICK PAN, CHOPPING BOARD

Peter Tierney has brought all his creative skills to this delicious dish – a Mexican-inspired recipe combining a toasted tortilla wrap with melted cheese layered over scrambled eggs and vegetables. Quesadillas are a quick and versatile breakfast option that are a big hit with families, and you can vary the vegetables inside.

1 Heat a tablespoon of oil on a large non-stick pan.

2 Add the onion, cumin, paprika and a pinch of salt and pepper to the pan, and fry on a medium heat for 2–3 minutes.

3 Add the red pepper and sweetcorn to the pan and cook for a further 3–4 minutes.

4 Remove the veg from the pan and set aside.

5 Crack the eggs into the pan and lightly scramble.

6 Remove the eggs from the pan and set aside with the veg.

7 Add a half tablespoon of rapeseed oil to the pan. Place 1 wrap on the pan to soak up the oil and flavour. Turn the wrap over and add a layer of grated mozzarella.

8 Spoon the egg and vegetables on top, then add another layer of mozzarella.

9 Place the second wrap on top and cover the pan with a lid for 2 minutes.

10 Remove the lid, place a chopping board on top of the pan and turn quickly so the quesadilla is on the board. Then slide the quesadilla back into the frying pan with a little olive oil to cook the other side. Place the lid on again for 2 minutes.

11 Meanwhile, mix the 3 tablespoons of cottage cheese with the garlic powder, juice of half a lime and pinch of salt and pepper.

12 Garnish with coriander and serve on a chopping board with the cottage cheese.

Each portion provides:
- **vitamin C 113%** RI (91mg)
- **selenium 73%** RI (40μg)
- **calcium 54%** RI (431mg)

Selenium is an essential trace element with antioxidant and immune functions and may potentially improve athletic performance and training recovery for physically active people.

POWER-UP MOCHA SHAKE

CALORIES PER SERVING	CARBS (G)	PROTEIN (G)	FAT (G)	FIBRE (G)
440KCAL	40	26	20	8

» EXERCISE DAY

⊕ INJURY RECOVERY

INGREDIENTS

400ml milk

1 scoop whey protein powder
(vanilla or chocolate)

2 tbsp almond butter

1 banana (frozen)

2 Medjool dates

1 tbsp cacao powder

10 ice cubes

2 shots espresso (optional)

SERVES: 2

PREPARATION TIME: 3 MINUTES

TOTAL TIME: 3 MINUTES

EQUIPMENT: FOOD PROCESSOR OR BLENDER, ESPRESSO MAKER (OPTIONAL)

This creamy chocolate and date smoothie is so nutritious and filling, it's guaranteed to go down a treat. It is also easy to adapt to make it vegan-friendly – simply swap the protein powder and milk for dairy-free alternatives, and there you have it. You can also add a shot of espresso for a caffeine hit on the go!

1   Place all the ingredients in a blender and blitz until they reach a smooth consistency, then serve.

Each portion provides:
- **calcium 51%** RI (411mg)
- **vitamin E 45%** RI (5.4mg)
- **magnesium 41%** RI (154mg)

Magnesium supports calcium's role in bone health by improving bone mineral density and reducing fracture risk.

THE TOFU PORRIDGE QUEEN

CALORIES PER SERVING	CARBS (G)	PROTEIN (G)	FAT (G)	FIBRE (G)
492KCAL	51	18	24	7

≫ EXERCISE DAY

⊕ INJURY RECOVERY

INGREDIENTS

200ml milk (of choice)

100ml water

140g tofu

1 tsp vanilla extract

1 tsp cinnamon

1 tbsp honey (plus extra for drizzling)

1 tbsp almond butter

1 banana

80g porridge oats

6 walnuts

1 tbsp rapeseed oil (for frying)

SERVES: 2

PREPARATION TIME: 5 MINUTES

COOKING TIME: 5 MINUTES

TOTAL TIME: 10 MINUTES

EQUIPMENT: BLENDER, MEDIUM-SIZED SAUCEPAN, SMALL FRYING PAN

If you like to start your morning with a high protein intake for breakfast, you're going to love this spin on the classic porridge! We are doubling down with this porridge recipe, making it with high-protein tofu milk for a creamy consistency. The addition of nuts and fruit works really well with the smooth, silky tofu milk.

1 Place the milk, water, tofu, vanilla extract, cinnamon, honey, almond butter and half the banana in a blender and blitz for 1 minute until smooth. (Leave this to soak overnight if you have time.)

2 Place the tofu milk in a medium-sized pot with the porridge oats.

3 Stirring regularly, cook on a low-medium heat for 5 minutes or until you have reached your desired consistency.

4 Meanwhile, chop the walnuts and slice the rest of the banana.

5 Fry the banana in a little oil on both sides till lightly browned (although if you're pushed for time, you can serve it fresh).

6 Remove the porridge from the heat and serve with the chopped walnuts, banana and a drizzle of honey.

Each portion provides:
- **calcium 55%** RI (441mg)
- **omega-3 45%** RI (1 g)
- **iron 45%** RI (6.3mg)

Iron is an essential nutrient for the production of red blood cells. It also plays a role in energy production, muscle function, DNA synthesis and our immune system.

TUMMY-LOVING CHIA PUDDING

CALORIES PER SERVING	CARBS (G)	PROTEIN (G)	FAT (G)	FIBRE (G)
329KCAL	16	37	13	13

Zz **REST DAY**

⊕ **INJURY RECOVERY**

INGREDIENTS

200g 0% fat Greek yoghurt

½ scoop vanilla protein powder

20g chia seeds

1 tsp vanilla extract

¼ tsp cinnamon

1 tbsp desiccated coconut

Small handful of blueberries

5 strawberries (sliced)

SERVES: 1

PREPARATION TIME: 5 MINUTES

TOTAL TIME: 6+ HOURS

EQUIPMENT: MASON JAR OR LUNCH BOX, BOWL

Make a tasty, low-carb chia-seed pudding in just a few minutes and save yourself some precious time in the morning with this ready-to-go breakfast. The desiccated coconut and chia seeds swell, absorbing the moisture from the yoghurt overnight, leaving you with a thick, creamy pudding waiting for you the next morning.

1 In a bowl, whisk the yoghurt and protein powder together until smooth. Add the chia seeds, vanilla extract, cinnamon and coconut and mix well.

2 Add in the blueberries and gently mix.

3 Layer two-thirds of the sliced strawberries on the bottom of the Mason jar.

4 Pour the yoghurt mix into the jar and top with the rest of the sliced strawberries.

5 Cover and place in the fridge to set for a few hours or overnight.

Each portion provides:
- **omega-3 170%** RI (3.7g)
- **calcium 50%** RI (398mg)
- **vitamin C 50%** RI (40mg)

Omega-3 has shown several health benefits, including improvements in inflammatory conditions and positive neurological effects.

WARMING CARAMELISED BANANA PORRIDGE

CALORIES PER SERVING	CARBS (G)	PROTEIN (G)	FAT (G)	FIBRE (G)
570KCAL	55	31	25	9

>> EXERCISE DAY

⊕ INJURY RECOVERY

INGREDIENTS

40g jumbo oats

250ml milk

1 tsp rapeseed oil

¼ tsp fresh ginger (grated)

½ banana

¼ tsp cinnamon

½ scoop vanilla protein powder

20g milled flaxseed

1 tsp honey

SERVES: 1

PREPARATION TIME: 2 MINUTES

COOKING TIME: 10 MINUTES

TOTAL TIME: 12 MINUTES

EQUIPMENT: MEDIUM-SIZED SAUCEPAN, SMALL PAN

The ginger and cinnamon in this comforting porridge add warmth, light spiciness and a mellow sweetness, making this traditional and nutritious breakfast the perfect go-to for those cold Irish mornings.

1 Add the oats and milk to a saucepan and stir regularly on a medium heat for 5–8 minutes or until it reaches your desired consistency.

2 While the porridge is cooking, heat the oil in a small pan.

3 Fry the ginger on a medium heat for 2 minutes.

4 Slice the banana lengthwise in half, sprinkle with cinnamon and place on the pan with the ginger. Fry the banana until lightly golden on both sides.

5 When the porridge is almost cooked, stir in the protein powder until smooth.

6 Place the milled flaxseed in a bowl and drizzle the honey over it.

7 Pour the porridge into the bowl and place the caramelised banana and ginger on top.

Each portion provides:
- **vitamin B12 93%** RI (2.3µg)
- **calcium 56%** of RI (450mg)
- **magnesium 44%** (167mg)

Calcium has many roles,
including bone formation and
density, muscle contraction,
protein synthesis and
maintaining heart health.

YUGGY BERRY

CALORIES PER SERVING	CARBS (G)	PROTEIN (G)	FAT (G)	FIBRE (G)
532KCAL	21	29	37	15

Zz REST DAY

⊕ INJURY RECOVERY

INGREDIENTS

200g plain yoghurt

100g raspberries

30g granola

1 tbsp flaxseed

1 tbsp desiccated coconut

½ tbsp chia seeds

SERVES: 1

PREPARATION TIME: 5 MINUTES

TOTAL TIME: 5 MINUTES

EQUIPMENT: MASON JAR, BOWL

A super-tasty and creamy breakfast or a quick and easy snack, Yuggy Berry tastes great and is visually appealing. The expression 'eat with your eyes' is certainly true because when a dish looks good it gives us even more reasons to enjoy and celebrate the food we eat! And why not make up a batch of my Cranberry and Pecan Granola (page 90) to use in this recipe?

1   Spoon half the yoghurt into the jar.
2   Add a layer of raspberries on top.
3   In a separate bowl, combine the granola, flaxseed, coconut and chia seeds. Spoon half of the granola mix evenly on top of the raspberries.
4   Repeat steps 1–3 using the rest of the ingredients.

Each portion provides:
- **omega-3 156%** RI (3.4mg)
- **vitamin B12 60%** RI (1.5µg)
- **selenium 47%** RI (26µg)

Vitamin B12 and omega-3 support and protect healthy blood and nerve cells in the body. Omega-3 is also a natural anti-inflammatory.

YUMMY OVERNIGHT VEGAN OATS

CALORIES PER SERVING	CARBS (G)	PROTEIN (G)	FAT (G)	FIBRE (G)
422KCAL	52	30	10	14

Zz REST DAY

⊙ IMMUNE SUPPORT

INGREDIENTS

40g oats

1 tbsp chia seeds

250ml unsweetened oat milk

1 scoop plant-based protein
   powder

30g raspberries

15g blueberries

30g strawberries

SERVES: 1

PREPARATION TIME: 5 MINUTES

TOTAL TIME: 6+ HOURS

EQUIPMENT: MASON JAR

Preparing your oat-based breakfast the night before is a great idea when looking to save time the next morning. Yummy Overnight Vegan Oats is truly an all-rounder, as it's suitable for vegan and dairy-free diets while providing carbs, protein and plenty of important nutrients.

1 Place the oats, chia seeds, oat milk and vegan protein powder in a Mason jar and mix well.
2 Chop the berries to desired size and add to the jar with the oats and mix well.
3 Seal the jar and place in the fridge overnight.

Each portion provides:
- **omega-3 88%** RI (1.9mg)
- **vitamin C 131%** RI (105mg)
- **magnesium 29%** RI (110mg)

Many of the minerals found in chia seeds are known to be beneficial to bone health, including calcium, magnesium, and phosphorus.

LUNCH

BACON, EGG AND AVOCADO BAGEL

CALORIES PER SERVING	CARBS (G)	PROTEIN (G)	FAT (G)	FIBRE (G)
560KCAL	50	37	24	11

» **EXERCISE DAY**

⟳ **IMMUNE SUPPORT**

INGREDIENTS

4 bacon medallions

2 eggs

2 bagels

1 avocado

1 tbsp lemon juice

½ tsp cayenne pepper

½ tsp salt

½ tsp black pepper

2 tbsp cream cheese

4 cherry tomatoes (halved)

SERVES: 2

PREPARATION TIME: 5 MINUTES

COOKING TIME: 10 MINUTES

TOTAL TIME: 15 MINUTES

EQUIPMENT: TOASTER, NON-STICK PAN, SMALL BOWL

A seriously tasty and satisfying bagel sandwich, filled with guacamole, cream cheese, crispy bacon and an egg cooked just how you like it! Top it off with fresh tomatoes and a sprinkle of salt and black pepper, and I guarantee you this one will keep you going well into the afternoon!

1. Cook the medallions under the grill for 5 minutes until lightly browned on either side.
2. Meanwhile, cook the egg how you like it – poached, fried or scrambled!
3. Separate and toast the bagels.
4. Mash the avocado in a small bowl using a fork. Mix in the lemon juice, cayenne pepper, salt and black pepper.
5. To assemble the bagel, spread some cream cheese on one half of each bagel, followed by the mashed avocado.
6. Add the medallions, egg and cherry tomatoes, and close the sandwich with the other half of the bagel before serving.

Each portion provides:
- **vitamin B12 92%** RI (2.3µg)
- **vitamin D 45%** RI (2.2µg)
- **zinc 38%** RI (3.8mg)

Vitamin B12 can only be found naturally in animal foods such as red meat, milk, fish and eggs. However, it can be consumed through foods that have been fortified; common examples include nutritional yeast, breakfast cereals and plant milks.

BULGUR BROCCOLI SALAD WITH TOASTED PUMPKIN SEEDS

CALORIES PER SERVING	CARBS (G)	PROTEIN (G)	FAT (G)	FIBRE (G)
648KCAL	68	23	26	10

>> EXERCISE DAY

 IMMUNE SUPPORT

INGREDIENTS

1 vegetable stock cube

280ml hot water

150g bulgur wheat

100ml red wine

1 tbsp olive oil

1 onion (chopped)

2 cloves garlic (crushed)

50g chorizo (chopped)

1 red chilli (finely chopped)

6 mushrooms (chopped)

1 head broccoli (chopped)

3 tbsp pumpkin seeds

SERVES: 2

PREPARATION TIME: 5 MINUTES

COOKING TIME: 40 MINUTES

TOTAL TIME: 45 MINUTES

EQUIPMENT: JUG, POT, NON-STICK PAN, CASSEROLE DISH

This broccoli salad is so easy, yet it's one of the most satisfying salads I make. I often serve it by itself for lunch or add some fish or meat for a larger meal. It works particularly well with barbecued chicken or the Lemon Curry Trout on page 234.

1. Add the vegetable stock cube to a jug and pour in the hot water to make your liquid stock.
2. Pour the stock into a pot and add the bulgur wheat and half the wine, then bring the liquid to the boil. Reduce heat and leave to simmer for 20–30 minutes or as per packet instructions.
3. Meanwhile, heat the olive oil on a large pan, then add the onions, garlic, chorizo and chilli. Cook on a medium heat for 5 minutes.
4. Preheat the oven to 180°C.
5. Add the rest of the red wine, the mushrooms and the broccoli to your pan and mix well. Leave to cook on a medium heat for a further 5 minutes.
6. Spoon the bulgur wheat evenly into a casserole dish.
7. Pour the contents of the pan over the bulgur wheat and spread out.
8. Sprinkle the pumpkin seeds on top.
9. Place the casserole dish in the oven for 7–10 minutes until the seeds and broccoli are slightly browned.

Each portion provides:
- **vitamin K 345%** RI (259mg)
- **vitamin C 58%** (48mg)
- **potassium 73%** RI (1458mg)

Vitamin K increases bone density, specifically assisting with the formation of blood clots; regulates calcium levels, bone production and metabolism; and manages blood sugar levels and supports heart health.

CAJUN SALMON BURRITO BOWL

CALORIES PER SERVING	CARBS (G)	PROTEIN (G)	FAT (G)	FIBRE (G)
639KCAL	30	39	40	8

Zz REST DAY

⊕ INJURY RECOVERY

INGREDIENTS

200g salmon fillet

1 tbsp rapeseed oil

1 tsp Cajun spice

1 onion (chopped)

2 cloves of garlic (minced)

50g mushrooms (sliced)

handful of spinach

50g green beans

4 cherry tomatoes (halved)

70g long grain white rice

For the sauce:

½ tsp dill

1 tbsp cucumber (grated)

1 tbsp fresh lemon juice

½ tsp garlic (minced)

2 tbsp rapeseed oil

200g Greek yoghurt

For the guacamole:

1 avocado (peeled and
   stone removed)

1 tbsp rapeseed oil

1 tbsp fresh lemon juice

SERVES: 2

PREPARATION TIME: 5 MINUTES

COOKING TIME: 20 MINUTES

TOTAL TIME: 25 MINUTES

EQUIPMENT: NON-STICK PAN, SMALL POT, MEDIUM-SIZED MIXING BOWL, BAKING TRAY, 2 SMALL BOWLS, TIN FOIL

This is a nutritional powerhouse of a meal – a great option for anyone looking to gain the nutritional benefits of fish without having to spend hours in the kitchen. The use of fresh ingredients combined with fresh fish delivers an abundance of flavours and textures you're sure to love!

1 Preheat your oven to 180°C.
2 In a medium-sized bowl, add the salmon, a tablespoon of oil and the Cajun spice and mix well.
3 Place the salmon fillet on a tin-foil-lined tray, and cook in the oven for about 15 minutes.
4 Meanwhile, in a pan, add a little rapeseed oil, onion, garlic, mushrooms, spinach, green beans and cherry tomatoes and cook until soft.
5 Bring a pot of water – approximately 150ml, or double the volume of rice – to the boil. Add the rice and cook for 12 minutes or until water evaporates.
6 To make the sauce, place the dill, cucumber, lemon juice, garlic and rapeseed oil in a bowl with the yoghurt and stir to combine.
7 For the guacamole, place the avocado, olive oil and lemon juice in a small bowl, and mash with a fork.
8 Serve the salmon and vegetables on a bed of rice, topped with the yoghurt dressing and guacamole.

Each portion provides:
- **vitamin B12 198%** RI (5µg)
- **vitamin D 185%** RI (9µg)
- **omega-3 143%** RI (3g)

Oily fish, such as salmon, are brilliant sources of omega-3 fatty acids, which have been shown to have anti-inflammatory effects in the body.

CHORIZO TUNA STEAKS

CALORIES PER SERVING	CARBS (G)	PROTEIN (G)	FAT (G)	FIBRE (G)
349KCAL	7	43	16	3

⊘ IMMUNE SUPPORT

⊕ INJURY RECOVERY

INGREDIENTS

2 tuna steaks

1 tbsp rapeseed oil, plus extra
    for frying

1 clove garlic (crushed)

100g mushrooms (chopped)

50g chorizo (sliced)

1 red bell pepper (sliced)

1 tsp cumin seeds

1 tsp rosemary leaves

salt

1 lemon

8 cherry tomatoes (chopped)

SERVES: 2

PREPARATION TIME: 1 HOUR

COOKING TIME: 15 MINUTES

TOTAL TIME: 1 HOUR 15 MINUTES

EQUIPMENT: NON-STICK PAN, GRIDDLE OR BARBECUE

Tuna steak is a meaty fish that is great for barbecuing or pan-frying. It works really well with a fresh mango avocado salsa or garden salad. For days that you want a higher carbohydrate meal, serve with baby potatoes or rice for a real crowd-pleaser!

1 Marinate the tuna in rapeseed oil and garlic for at least an hour.

2 When your tuna steaks have been marinating for 45 minutes, preheat the oven to 180℃.

3 Heat some oil on a pan. Add the mushrooms, chorizo, red pepper, cumin seeds, rosemary and some salt and cook on a medium heat for 10 minutes.

4 Meanwhile, heat up a griddle or barbecue. Place the tuna on the griddle or barbecue, squeeze the juice of a lemon on top and cook on each side for 1–2 minutes.

5 Add the chopped tomatoes into your vegetable pan with another pinch of salt.

6 Place the pan in the oven for 5 minutes.

7 Remove from the oven and serve.

Each portion provides:
- **selenium 252%** RI (139μg)
- **vitamin B12 141%** RI (3.5μg)
- **vitamin C 138%** RI (110mg)

Evidence shows a strong correlation between low levels of selenium and muscle fatigue in athletes.

CITRUS QUINOA AVOCADO SALAD

CALORIES PER SERVING	CARBS (G)	PROTEIN (G)	FAT (G)	FIBRE (G)
556KCAL	44	16	48	13

» **EXERCISE DAY**

⊕ **INJURY RECOVERY**

INGREDIENTS

4 tbsp pomegranate seeds

4 scallions (chopped)

1 handful fresh parsley (chopped)

4 tbsp flaked almonds (toasted)

300g quinoa (cooked and cooled)

3 tbsp extra virgin olive oil

zest and juice of ½ lime

zest and juice of ½ orange

pinch of salt

pinch of black pepper

1 avocado

SERVES: 2

PREPARATION TIME: 5 MINUTES

TOTAL TIME: 5 MINUTES

EQUIPMENT: LARGE BOWL

This refreshing and nourishing salad packs a punch when it comes to flavour and texture! It's quick to toss together and works well on a rest day or to bring with you to work for lunch. For added protein, throw in some diced tofu or chicken.

1   Place the pomegranate seeds, scallions, parsley and almonds in a medium bowl.
2   Mix in your cooked and cooled quinoa.
3   Toss with olive oil, orange and lime zest, orange and lime juice, salt and pepper.
4   Chop your avocado just before serving to make sure it's as fresh as possible, and fold it gently in.

Each portion provides:
- **vitamin K 115%** RI (86µg)
- **vitamin C 63%** RI (50mg)
- **iron 47%** RI (6.6mg)

Iron is an important component of haemoglobin, the substance in red blood cells that carries oxygen from your lungs to the rest of your body.

CLAUDIA'S POTATO SALAD WITH BOILED EGGS

CALORIES PER SERVING	CARBS (G)	PROTEIN (G)	FAT (G)	FIBRE (G)
236KCAL	27	14	9	3

>> **EXERCISE DAY**

✓ **IMMUNE SUPPORT**

INGREDIENTS

4 eggs

2 large potatoes (approx. 400g, boiled)

4 pickles (chopped)

4 tbsp pickle juice

1 onion (chopped)

1 tsp wholegrain mustard

1 tsp white wine vinegar

4 tbsp Greek yoghurt

¼ tsp salt

¼ tsp pepper

½ tsp fresh dill (chopped)

SERVES: 4

PREPARATION TIME: 10 MINUTES

COOKING TIME: 10 MINUTES

TOTAL TIME: 20 MINUTES

EQUIPMENT: POT, 2 BOWLS

The best potato salad on the planet – simple yet delicious and works with so many dishes. This recipe came from Claudia, a wonderful family friend who lost her battle with cancer a number of years ago. She was gifted in the kitchen and created so many wonderful recipes. Thank you, Claudia, for influencing us Daveys with your amazing smiles and wonderful meals.

Enjoy with a barbecue, a steak dinner or even alongside a sandwich for lunch – you really can't go wrong with this recipe.

1. Place the eggs in a pot of cold water. Bring the water to the boil.
2. Once boiling, start your timer. Cook the eggs for 8–10 minutes.
3. Remove from the water and place in a bowl of cold water.
4. Leave them to cool before peeling off the shells.
5. In a large bowl, roughly chop the boiled potatoes and eggs.
6. Add the remaining ingredients and mix until fully combined, then serve.

Each portion provides:
- **chloride 79%** RI (635mg)
- **vitamin D 33%** RI (1.6µg)
- **selenium 33%** RI (18µg)

This recipe can be used to support bone health and the maintenance of healthy hair, skin and nails.

CREAMY CHORIZO PASTA

CALORIES PER SERVING	CARBS (G)	PROTEIN (G)	FAT (G)	FIBRE (G)
552KCAL	55	28	26	11

>> EXERCISE DAY

⟳ IMMUNE SUPPORT

INGREDIENTS

SERVES: 4

PREPARATION TIME: 5 MINUTES

COOKING TIME: 20 MINUTES

TOTAL TIME: 25 MINUTES

EQUIPMENT: FOOD PROCESSOR, NON-STICK PAN, MEDIUM-SIZED POT

For the sauce:

1 avocado

100g 0% fat Greek yoghurt

1 tbsp rapeseed oil

1 tbsp lemon juice

1 clove garlic (crushed)

50–100ml water

3 tbsp lemon juice

For the pasta:

6 bacon medallions (chopped)

60g chorizo (chopped)

1 onion (chopped)

4 sun-dried tomatoes (chopped)

300g wholewheat spaghetti

chilli flakes (to taste)

salt and pepper

handful fresh coriander
   (chopped), to garnish

This phenomenal pasta dish is full of flavour and sure to hit the spot when you're in need of something packed with energy and taste! The creamy avocado sauce complements the saltiness of the bacon and chorizo, while the sun-dried tomatoes add a lovely sweetness to the dish.

1 Place all the ingredients for the sauce in a food processor with 50ml water (add more if you want the sauce a little thinner).
2 Blitz until smooth. Add salt and pepper to taste.
3 Heat some oil on a medium-sized pan.
4 Add the medallions, chorizo, onion and sun-dried tomatoes to the pan and fry until lightly browned.
5 Bring a pot of water to the boil and cook the spaghetti for 12–15 minutes.
6 Drain the spaghetti. Pour the spaghetti onto the pan with the chorizo, bacon, onion and tomatoes, pour over the creamy avocado sauce and mix.
7 Season with chilli flakes, salt and pepper and garnish with fresh coriander.

Each portion provides:
- **manganese 109%** RI (2.2mg)
- **zinc 35%** RI (3.5mg)
- **selenium 30%** RI (16.3μg)

Manganese is a trace mineral, which your body needs in small amounts for the normal functioning of your brain and your nervous and enzyme systems.

CREAMY GARDEN-PEA CHICKEN PASTA

CALORIES PER SERVING	CARBS (G)	PROTEIN (G)	FAT (G)	FIBRE (G)
682KCAL	58	47	29	12

>>> INTENSE EXERCISE DAY

 IMMUNE SUPPORT

INGREDIENTS

120g linguine

1 tbsp rapeseed oil

1 onion (chopped)

2 cloves of garlic (crushed)

200g chicken breast (chopped)

1 tsp oregano

1 red bell pepper (sliced)

100g chestnut mushrooms
   (chopped)

6 asparagus spears (chopped)

6 sun-dried tomatoes (chopped)

100g garden peas

1 tbsp tomato purée

100g Greek yoghurt

50g parmesan

salt and black pepper

SERVES: 2

PREPARATION TIME: 5 MINUTES

COOKING TIME: 30 MINUTES

TOTAL TIME: 35 MINUTES

EQUIPMENT: NON-STICK PAN, MEDIUM-SIZED POT

This pasta is a huge winner on all fronts! The ingredients are straightforward and easy to source, but let me assure you, it will go down a treat. Garden peas are a great addition to almost any pasta dish – their fresh flavour bursts with each bite.

1 Bring a pot of water to the boil. Add the linguine and cook for 10–12 minutes or as per packet instructions.
2 Meanwhile, heat the rapeseed oil in a non-stick pan and fry the onion for 3–4 minutes.
3 Add the garlic, chicken, oregano and a pinch of salt. Cook on a medium heat for 5 minutes.
4 When the pasta is cooked, strain it and leave it to the side.
5 Next, add the red pepper, mushrooms and asparagus to your pan. Cook for 5 minutes, until soft.
6 Mix in the sun-dried tomatoes and garden peas and leave to cook for 10 minutes.
7 Add the pasta, tomato purée and Greek yoghurt to the pan and mix well.
8 Season with a little salt and pepper, grate the parmesan over the pasta and serve.

Each portion provides:
- **selenium 75%** RI (41 ug)
- **vitamin E 56%** RI (6.7mg)
- **folate 49%** RI (98µg)

Folate is needed in the body to form healthy red blood cells. A lack of folate in the diet can lead to folate deficiency anaemia.

CREAMY SALMON MEGA MIX

CALORIES PER SERVING	CARBS (G)	PROTEIN (G)	FAT (G)	FIBRE (G)
618KCAL	69	35	23	8

>>> INTENSE EXERCISE DAY

⌄ IMMUNE SUPPORT

INGREDIENTS

400g salmon fillets

1 tbsp rapeseed oil

1 tbsp lemon juice

1 tsp dill (dried)

1 onion (chopped)

2 cloves garlic (crushed)

1 red bell pepper (chopped)

10 mushrooms (chopped)

1 courgette (chopped)

½ tsp fresh basil (chopped)

½ tsp oregano

½ tsp chilli powder

400g tin chopped tomatoes

100g Greek yoghurt

280g pasta (uncooked weight)

salt and pepper

fresh dill, to garnish

parmesan flakes, to garnish

SERVES: 4

PREPARATION TIME: 5 MINUTES

COOKING TIME: 25 MINUTES

TOTAL TIME: 30 MINUTES

EQUIPMENT: NON-STICK PAN, MEDIUM-SIZED POT, BAKING TRAY

I call this recipe a mega mix because not only is it mega on flavour, but it's also a mega source of each macronutrient and numerous micronutrients! This creamy salmon pasta hits the spot when it comes to flavour and filling you up – the fresh taste of dill and lemon works particularly well with the delicate flavours from the salmon.

1 Preheat the oven to 180°C.
2 Coat the salmon with a tablespoon of oil, lemon juice and dill.
3 Place the salmon on a tray and bake in the oven for 10–12 minutes.
4 While the salmon is baking, heat some oil in a large pan.
5 Add the onion and garlic with a pinch of salt and sauté for 5 minutes.
6 Add the vegetables (not including the tomatoes) and the remaining herbs and spices. Mix through and leave to cook for 10 minutes.
7 Meanwhile, bring a pot of water to the boil and cook the pasta as per packet instructions. Once cooked, drain.
8 Add the pasta, tomatoes and yoghurt into the pan with the vegetables, season to taste and mix.
9 When the salmon is cooked, add it to the pan and mix through before serving with a garnish of dill and parmesan.

Each portion provides:
- **omega-3 151%** RI (3.3mg)
- **vitamin D 95%** RI (4.7µg)
- **selenium 77%** RI (43µg)

Vitamin D is critical to many biological processes, with research showing a strong correlation between sufficient levels of vitamin D and optimal muscle function.

ENERGISE PRAWN QUINOA SALAD

CALORIES PER SERVING	CARBS (G)	PROTEIN (G)	FAT (G)	FIBRE (G)
650KCAL	60	32	29	7

>>> INTENSE EXERCISE DAY

⊘ IMMUNE SUPPORT

INGREDIENTS

150g quinoa

10 cashew nuts

1 pinch of salt

200g king prawns

1 tbsp sesame seed oil

2 scallions (chopped)

1 red chilli pepper (diced)

1 tbsp fresh lemon juice

1 bag wild salad leaves

8 cherry tomatoes (chopped)

For the salad dressing:

3 tbsp olive oil

3 tbsp balsamic vinegar

1 tbsp honey

1 tsp wholegrain mustard

5 basil leaves (roughly chopped)

5 mint leaves (roughly chopped)

SERVES: 2

PREPARATION TIME: 10 MINUTES

COOKING TIME: 25 MINUTES

TOTAL TIME: 35 MINUTES

EQUIPMENT: MEDIUM-SIZED POT, NON-STICK PAN, SMALL BOWL, LARGE BOWL

This prawn quinoa salad is packed full of nutrients and flavour. Fresh mint and basil leaves mixed through a salad are a game changer – no salad should be bland, and this one certainly isn't! It's also a great source of carbohydrates, mostly from the quinoa.

1 Pour the quinoa into a medium-sized saucepan with 400ml water. Bring to a boil, cover with a lid and reduce the heat. Simmer for 15 minutes.
2 Toast the cashew nuts in a non-stick pan with a pinch of salt over a medium heat for 3–4 minutes. Remove from the pan and set aside.
3 Add the prawns, sesame oil, scallions and chilli pepper to the pan and cook for 5 minutes, until the prawns are almost fully cooked.
4 Pour the cooked quinoa and lemon juice on top of the prawns and mix well.
5 For the dressing, mix all the ingredients together in a small bowl. Taste to test for sweetness – you may need more honey or balsamic depending on your personal taste.
6 Wash and dry the salad leaves and place in a large bowl.
7 Drizzle half of the dressing over the leaves, add your tomatoes and mix through.
8 Serve the quinoa and prawn mixture on a bed of the salad leaves, topped off with the cashew nuts and the rest of the salad dressing drizzled on top.

Each portion provides:
- **vitamin C 47%** RI (38mg)
- **selenium 67%** RI (37μg)
- **vitamin B12 52%** RI (1.3g)

Vitamin B12 plays an important role in the maintenance of healthy blood and nerve cells in the body.

GO FISH YUMMY SPAGHETTI

CALORIES PER SERVING	CARBS (G)	PROTEIN (G)	FAT (G)	FIBRE (G)
551KCAL	53	42	20	6

>> EXERCISE DAY

⊘ IMMUNE SUPPORT

INGREDIENTS

240g spaghetti

1 tbsp olive oil

1 onion (chopped)

30g chorizo (chopped)

2 cloves of garlic (minced)

1 red bell pepper (sliced)

100g mushrooms (chopped)

150g salmon fillet (chopped)

150g tuna steak (chopped)

150g prawns

400g passata

5 leaves basil (finely chopped)

½ tsp oregano

1 tsp paprika

80g parmesan cheese (grated)

salt and black pepper

SERVES: 4

PREPARATION TIME: 5 MINUTES

COOKING TIME: 25 MINUTES

TOTAL TIME: 30 MINUTES

EQUIPMENT: LARGE NON-STICK PAN, MEDIUM-SIZED POT

This easy fish spaghetti in a ridiculously simple tomato sauce is guaranteed to be a winner if you're a lover of fish! I got used to eating this type of dish on holiday in Spain and Portugal and now love making my own version. It doesn't just deliver big on flavour: it also serves over 50% of your recommended daily intake of omega-3 fatty acids per portion.

1 Bring a pot of water to the boil.
2 Add the spaghetti and cook as per packet instructions.
3 Meanwhile, heat the oil on a large pan.
4 Fry the onion and chorizo on a medium heat for 5 minutes.
5 Add the garlic, red pepper and mushrooms and cook for a further 5 minutes.
6 Add the salmon and tuna steak to the pan. Mix in the prawns and cook on a medium heat for 5 minutes.
7 Next mix in the passata, basil, oregano, paprika and salt. Leave to simmer for 10 minutes.
8 Drain the spaghetti and add it to the pan, mixing well to fully coat in the sauce.
9 Sprinkle the parmesan cheese over the pasta and serve with some black pepper.

Each portion provides:
- **vitamin B12 171%** RI (4.3µg)
- **vitamin C 95%** (76mg)
- **omega-3 63%** (1.4mg)

Vitamin B12 helps to keep your body's blood and nerve cells healthy, and repairs cell damage following activities, such as high-intensity exercise.

JERK CHICKEN BURGER

CALORIES PER SERVING	CARBS (G)	PROTEIN (G)	FAT (G)	FIBRE (G)
496KCAL	43	54	12	5

» EXERCISE DAY

⊘ IMMUNE SUPPORT

INGREDIENTS

300g chicken breast

2 tbsp rapeseed oil

½ tsp dried thyme

2 tsp jerk seasoning

2 tbsp lime juice

2 large burger buns

½ beef tomato (chopped)

¼ pineapple (chopped)

¼ red onion (chopped)

½ head lettuce leaves

2 tbsp ketchup

Each portion provides:
- **vitamin K 80%** RI (60 ug)
- **selenium 51%** RI (28.2mg)
- **vitamin C 45%** RI (36mg)

Vitamin C is an important antioxidant that boosts our immune system and is particularly needed for the formation of blood vessels, cartilage, muscle and collagen in bones.

SERVES: 2

PREPARATION TIME: 25 MINUTES

COOKING TIME: 15 MINUTES

TOTAL TIME: 40 MINUTES

EQUIPMENT: BARBECUE OR GRIDDLE PAN, ROLLING PIN, SHALLOW BOWL, CLING FILM

The first time I had jerk chicken was a few years ago in Jamaica, where you can get it on most street corners and at local food markets. It was so good that when I got home from that trip, making my own version was one of the first things I did! This is my simple jerk chicken burger, topped with fresh pineapple and red onion.

1 Wrap the chicken breasts loosely in cling film and whack them with a rolling pin to flatten them out.
2 In a shallow bowl, combine the oil, thyme, jerk seasoning and 1 tbsp of lime juice. Add the chicken breasts, coating them fully in the dressing.
3 Cover the chicken and leave in the fridge to marinate for 20 minutes.
4 Preheat the barbecue or griddle pan.
5 Remove the chicken from the fridge and place on the hot pan. Cook the chicken for 5–7 minutes on each side, and remove from the heat when cooked through.
6 Toast the burger buns on the barbecue or griddle pan for 1–2 minutes.
7 To assemble, layer the chicken breast between the burger buns, topped with tomato, sliced pineapple, red onion, lettuce, a dollop of ketchup and a drizzle of lime juice.
8 Serve with a side of sweet potato and parsnip chips spiced with salt and paprika!

PRAWN AND SWEET POTATO SALAD

CALORIES PER SERVING	CARBS (G)	PROTEIN (G)	FAT (G)	FIBRE (G)
408KCAL	36	19	21	7

Zz REST DAY

IMMUNE SUPPORT

INGREDIENTS

For the salad:

1 red pepper (chopped)

1 sweet potato (chopped)

2 tbsp rapeseed oil

200g prawns

½ tsp smoked paprika

½ tsp garlic granules

salt

½ red onion (chopped)

100g sweetcorn

2 large handfuls of spinach

For the dressing:

1 clove garlic (minced)

2 tbsp olive oil

1 tbsp lemon juice

Each portion provides:
- **vitamin C 176%** RI (141mg)
- **vitamin A 117%** RI (939µg)
- **vitamin K 95%** RI (71µg)

Vitamins A and C are water-soluble vitamins and antioxidants. Antioxidants help protect our cells from damage caused by free radicals.

SERVES: 2

PREPARATION TIME: 5 MINUTES

COOKING TIME: 40 MINUTES

TOTAL TIME: 45 MINUTES

EQUIPMENT: BAKING TRAY, NON-STICK PAN, LARGE BOWL, SMALL BOWL

Sometimes salads are thought of as 'boring' or 'not satisfying'. If that's what you think then you've been eating the wrong salads! This salad is delicious, full of different flavours and textures. The tangy, garlicky dressing brings out the taste of the vegetables and pairs perfectly with the prawns and sweet potato. I promise you it will not disappoint!

1 Preheat the oven to 180°C.
2 Add the red pepper and sweet potato to a baking tray and lightly coat them in rapeseed oil and a little sea salt.
3 Place them in the oven to roast for 35–40 minutes, until cooked through.
4 Heat some more oil on a pan. Coat the prawns in the smoked paprika and garlic granules. Add them to the pan and fry on a medium heat until cooked, about 3–4 minutes on each side.
5 Place the red onion, sweetcorn and spinach in a large bowl.
6 For the dressing, mix the crushed garlic, olive oil, lemon juice and a good pinch of salt in a small bowl.
7 Pour the dressing over the salad.
8 Add the sweet potato, pepper and prawns and mix well, fully coating the salad in the dressing, before serving.

KIMCHI TOASTIE

CALORIES PER SERVING	CARBS (G)	PROTEIN (G)	FAT (G)	FIBRE (G)
659KCAL	55	42	30	3

>> EXERCISE DAY

 IMMUNE SUPPORT

INGREDIENTS

1 tsp rapeseed oil

100g chicken (cooked)

4 slices sourdough bread (approx. 200 g)

2 tbsp butter

2 tbsp grated parmesan cheese

60g Cheddar cheese

60g kimchi

2 handfuls wild salad leaves

SERVES: 2

PREPARATION TIME: 5 MINUTES

COOKING TIME: 10 MINUTES

TOTAL TIME: 15 MINUTES

EQUIPMENT: FRYING PAN

If you want a mouth-wateringly delicious sandwich to look forward to on your lunch break, this is for you! Kimchi is spicy fermented cabbage, a Korean dish that is made similarly to sauerkraut. It goes surprisingly well with parmesan cheese – you've got to give this one a go! It's great served with sweet potato chips and chunky tomato relish.

1 Heat a drop of oil on a non-stick pan.
2 Roughly shred the cooked chicken.
3 Spread butter on one side of each slice of bread.
4 Take two of the slices, and sprinkle a quarter of the parmesan cheese on each buttered side.
5 On the non-buttered side of those slices, layer the Cheddar cheese, kimchi, chicken and salad leaves.
6 Place the other slices of bread on top, with the buttered sides facing up.
7 Sprinkle the rest of the parmesan cheese on top.
8 Gently place the sandwiches onto the pan and fry on a medium heat until the Cheddar cheese has melted and the bread is lightly browned on each side (approx. 3–5 minutes each side).

Each portion provides:
- **selenium 71%** RI (39μg)
- **calcium 56%** RI (446mg)
- **vitamin K 53%** RI (40μg)

Fermented foods, such as kimchi, have been shown to support gut health, which is linked to overall health and immunity and decreasing markers of inflammation in the body.

LENTIL CURRY WITH ROASTED BALSAMIC POTATOES

CALORIES PER SERVING	CARBS (G)	PROTEIN (G)	FAT (G)	FIBRE (G)
534KCAL	69	21	19	12

 INTENSE EXERCISE DAY

 IMMUNE SUPPORT

INGREDIENTS

300g sweet potato (chopped)

2 carrots (chopped)

1 courgette (chopped)

2 tbsp rapeseed oil

pinch of salt

2 tbsp balsamic vinegar

1 onion (chopped)

2 cloves garlic (minced)

½ tbsp turmeric

½ tbsp curry powder

5 leaves basil (chopped)

1 tbsp tikka masala paste

200g coconut milk

400g tin chopped tomatoes

1 tbsp honey

100g peas

200g chickpeas

200g red lentils

150ml water

Handful fresh coriander,
   to garnish

SERVES: 4

PREPARATION TIME: 5 MINUTES

COOKING TIME: 40 MINUTES

TOTAL TIME: 45 MINUTES

EQUIPMENT: BAKING TRAY, LARGE NON-STICK SAUCEPAN

This delicious meat-free curry is packed with incredible Indian flavours. The balsamic vinegar in this recipe really brings the dish to another level! And, as it takes less than an hour to prepare, it is perfect for batch cooking to enjoy for lunch the next day. For a higher-carb meal, serve with quinoa or rice.

1. Preheat the oven to 200°C.
2. Toss the sweet potatoes, carrots and courgette in 1 tbsp rapeseed oil, salt and balsamic vinegar.
3. Place the potato, carrot and courgette mix onto a baking tray and into the preheated oven for 15 minutes.
4. When the vegetables are almost ready to come out, heat ½ tbsp oil in a non-stick saucepan.
5. Add the onion and garlic, and sauté on a medium heat for 5 minutes.
6. Remove the potatoes, carrots and courgette from the oven. Add them to the saucepan with the onions and garlic and mix well.
7. Next, add the turmeric, curry powder, basil, tikka masala paste, coconut milk, chopped tomatoes, honey, peas, chickpeas, lentils and 150ml of water to the saucepan and mix well.
8. Leave to simmer for 15–20 minutes, then garnish with coriander and serve.

Each portion provides:
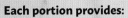
- **fibre 48%** RI (12g)
- **iron 53%** RI (7.4mg)
- **vitamin A 146%** RI (1.17mg)

Indigestible fibre (prebiotics) play an important role in enhancing gut health and immunity. It can also improve symptoms of IBS and leave you feeling satisfied after a meal.

MD'S BULGUR WHEAT SALMON

CALORIES PER SERVING	CARBS (G)	PROTEIN (G)	FAT (G)	FIBRE (G)
580KCAL	42	35	30	6

>> EXERCISE DAY

⊘ IMMUNE SUPPORT

INGREDIENTS

2 red bell peppers (chopped)

8 cherry tomatoes (chopped)

3 cloves of garlic (finely chopped)

2 tbsp rapeseed oil

salt and pepper

200g bulgur wheat

1 vegetable stock cube

juice of ½ a lemon

400g salmon fillets

100g feta cheese (cubed)

20g hazelnuts

SERVES: 4

PREPARATION TIME: 5 MINUTES

COOKING TIME: 40 MINUTES

TOTAL TIME: 45 MINUTES

EQUIPMENT: BAKING DISH

This has become a huge hit in the Davey household for lots of reasons. First, because it's outrageously tasty and satisfying – but also because it works brilliantly as a sharing dish with minimal fuss involved. Just place it in the middle of the table and allow everyone to dig in!

1   Preheat the oven to 180°C.
2   To a baking dish, add the peppers, tomatoes and garlic with olive oil and some salt and pepper, then place in the oven. Roast for 15 minutes.
3   Mix the stock cube with 400ml of boiling water.
4   Remove the dish from the oven and pour the bulgur wheat over the vegetables. Pour the stock and lemon juice into the dish and mix well.
5   Place the dish in the oven to roast for 5–7 minutes, then remove, stirring to ensure even absorption of the stock.
6   Make some space in the dish for the fish and place the salmon into it. Sprinkle the feta on top and place the dish back in the oven for a further 5 minutes.
7   Remove the dish from the oven, sprinkle over the hazelnuts, then put the dish back in the oven and cook for another 5–10 minutes, until the salmon is cooked through.

Each portion provides:
- **vitamin D 186%** RI (9.3μg)
- **vitamin B12 180%** RI (4.5μg)
- **omega-3 142%** RI (3.1g)

This recipe supports your bones and muscle function because it is a great source of vitamin D and vitamin B12.

PAUL MANNION'S SMOKED TOFU SATAY

CALORIES PER SERVING	CARBS (G)	PROTEIN (G)	FAT (G)	FIBRE (G)
695KCAL	58	30	38	14

» EXERCISE DAY

⊘ IMMUNE SUPPORT

INGREDIENTS

1 tbsp extra virgin olive oil

1 red onion (chopped)

400g smoked tofu (chopped)

1 tbsp soy sauce

3 cloves garlic (crushed)

salt and pepper

1 tsp smoked paprika

200g chestnut mushrooms

1 head broccoli (chopped)

½ courgette (chopped)

1 tbsp sweet chilli sauce

1½ tbsp curry powder

400ml coconut milk

4 nests egg noodles

40g cashew nuts

fresh coriander, to garnish

For the satay:

3 tbsp peanut butter

1 tbsp soy sauce

1 tbsp sweet chilli sauce

1 tbsp lemon juice

½ tsp chilli powder

100ml water

SERVES: 4   **PREPARATION TIME:** 5 MINUTES

COOKING TIME: 35 MINUTES   **TOTAL TIME:** 40 MINUTES

EQUIPMENT: NON-STICK PAN, MEDIUM SAUCEPAN, SMALL SAUCEPAN, SMALL BOWL

Paul Mannion created this recipe and it has all the hallmarks of an athlete's top-quality meal. It strikes a good balance between protein and carbohydrates and works as an everyday recipe or a post-exercise meal.

1 Heat the olive oil on a non-stick pan.
2 Add the onion and sauté on a medium heat for 5 minutes, until translucent.
3 Add the tofu and soy sauce and cook for 4–5 minutes, stirring often.
4 Add the garlic, a pinch of salt and pepper and smoked paprika and mix gently.
5 Add the mushrooms, broccoli and courgette to the pan and cook for 5–10 minutes, until soft.
6 Add the sweet chilli sauce, curry powder and half of the coconut milk. Mix well and simmer for 5–10 minutes.
7 Meanwhile, add the noodles to a pot of boiling water and cook for 8–12 minutes (or as per packet instructions). Once cooked, drain and set aside.
8 For the satay sauce, mix all of the ingredients together in a small bowl.
9 Pour the sauce into a small pan and add the other half of the coconut milk. Heat gently on a low heat for 5 minutes, stirring regularly.
10 Once the sauce is a nice smooth consistency, remove it from the heat.
11 Combine the noodles with the vegetables. Mix the satay sauce through to fully coat the noodles.
12 Sprinkle with cashew nuts and fresh coriander and serve.

Each portion provides:
- **vitamin C 75%** RI (60mg)
- **potassium 55%** RI (1101mg)
- **fibre 54%** RI (14g)

Potassium is one of two main electrolytes needed by the body. Electrolytes help regulate nerve and muscle function, and maintain hydration.

ROAST VEGETABLE AND BBQ CHICKEN SALAD WITH PERI-PERI DRESSING

CALORIES PER SERVING	CARBS (G)	PROTEIN (G)	FAT (G)	FIBRE (G)
754KCAL	68	57	28	12

⋙ INTENSE EXERCISE DAY

⊕ INJURY RECOVERY

INGREDIENTS

For the salad:

2 chicken breasts (approx. 300g)

2 sweet potatoes (approx. 400g, chopped)

2 carrots (chopped)

1 tbsp olive oil

½ tsp paprika

½ tsp dried oregano

pinch of salt

3 handfuls spinach

½ red onion (diced)

8 cherry tomatoes (chopped)

1 roasted red bell pepper (chopped)

4 gherkins (chopped)

50g feta cheese (chopped)

For the dressing:

1 tbsp olive oil

4 tbsp Greek yoghurt

1 tbsp peri-peri seasoning

2 tsp honey

2 tbsp balsamic vinegar

½ tsp garlic powder

few sprigs of fresh dill

SERVES: 2

PREPARATION TIME: 10 MINUTES

COOKING TIME: 45 MINUTES

TOTAL TIME: 55 MINUTES

EQUIPMENT: BARBECUE, BAKING TRAY, LARGE SALAD BOWL, SMALL BOWL

This salad makes a really balanced meal that will leave you feeling very satisfied – not to mention it's super tasty and full of flavour. I love to use barbecue chicken, but it works well with all kinds of barbecue meats.

1 Cook the chicken breasts on the barbecue, for 7–10 minutes each side.
2 Preheat the oven to 200°C.
3 Toss the sweet potatoes and carrots in a tablespoon of olive oil along with the paprika, dried oregano and a pinch of salt. Place on a tray and roast in the oven for 25 minutes, then set aside to cool.
4 Add the spinach, onion, tomatoes, pepper, gherkins and feta cheese to a large bowl and mix well to fully combine.
5 For the dressing, add the olive oil, Greek yoghurt, peri-peri seasoning, honey, balsamic vinegar, garlic powder and fresh dill to a small bowl and mix well.
6 Add the cooled vegetables to the salad mix.
7 Pour the dressing over the salad and toss to cover in the peri-peri dressing.
8 Chop the chicken, scatter over the salad and serve.

Each portion provides:
- **vitamin C 261%** RI (209mg)
- **selenium 66%** RI (36μg)
- **calcium 59%** RI (474mg)

Calcium is essential to maintaining bone formation and density, muscle contraction, protein synthesis and heart health.

SMOKY CHICKEN PASTA SALAD

CALORIES PER SERVING	CARBS (G)	PROTEIN (G)	FAT (G)	FIBRE (G)
622KCAL	78	40	17	11

>>> INTENSE EXERCISE DAY

⟳ IMMUNE SUPPORT

INGREDIENTS

140g pasta

3 tbsp olive oil

2 tbsp lemon juice

2 tbsp balsamic vinegar

½ tsp salt

6 cherry tomatoes (chopped)

½ red onion (sliced)

200g chicken breast (diced)

2 tsp smoked paprika

½ tsp garlic powder

½ tsp chilli powder

1 red bell pepper (chopped)

100g beetroot (cooked and
    chopped)

150g mixed salad leaves

SERVES: 2

PREPARATION TIME: 5 MINUTES

COOKING TIME: 20 MINUTES

TOTAL TIME: 25 MINUTES

EQUIPMENT: NON-STICK PAN, MEDIUM-SIZED POT, LARGE BOWL, SMALL BOWL

This quick and simple dish is packed with flavour and nutrition. The crunch from the fresh vegetables goes perfectly with the smoky-flavoured chicken, and it's all tossed in a tangy sweet dressing. So simple, yet so delicious.

1 Bring a pot of water to the boil. Cook the pasta for 10–12 minutes or as per packet instructions. Once cooked, drain and set aside to cool.

2 Meanwhile, for the dressing, mix two tablespoons of olive oil, lemon juice, balsamic vinegar and salt together in a small bowl.

3 Place the tomatoes and onion in a large bowl and pour over the dressing.

4 Coat the chicken in the smoked paprika, garlic powder and chilli powder.

5 Heat some oil on a non-stick pan, add the chicken and fry on a medium heat for 5–7 minutes on either side until cooked through and slightly browned.

6 Add the red pepper and beetroot to the bowl with the tomatoes and onions.

7 When the chicken has cooked, add to the bowl of vegetables with the pasta and mixed leaves, and toss to fully coat in the dressing before serving.

Each portion provides:
- **vitamin C 164%** RI (132mg)
- **selenium 59%** RI (32mg)
- **vitamin K 54%** RI (41mg)

There is evidence that vitamin K can increase the cardiac output of athletes, essentially improving aerobic endurance capacity.

SPANISH-STYLE FISH

CALORIES PER SERVING	CARBS (G)	PROTEIN (G)	FAT (G)	FIBRE (G)
508KCAL	47	41	17	11

>> **EXERCISE DAY**

⊘ **IMMUNE SUPPORT**

INGREDIENTS

2 medium potatoes (cubed)

100g chorizo (chopped)

1 large red onion (chopped)

2 cloves of garlic (crushed)

4 scallions (chopped)

1 red bell pepper (chopped)

1 yellow bell pepper (chopped)

½ courgette (chopped)

½ aubergine (chopped)

½ tsp smoked paprika

½ tsp oregano

2 tbsp lemon juice

500g fish mix (salmon, smoked haddock and cod)

400g tinned chopped tomatoes

200g tinned chickpeas

200g tinned cannellini beans

handful fresh coriander (chopped)

SERVES: 4

PREPARATION TIME: 5 MINUTES

COOKING TIME: 25 MINUTES

TOTAL TIME: 30 MINUTES

EQUIPMENT: MEDIUM-SIZED POT, LARGE NON-STICK PAN

I like to use salmon, smoked haddock and cod in this dish but feel free to incorporate the fish of your choice. This combination of fresh fish and vegetables along with the smoky flavours from the chorizo and paprika really makes for a big bowl of happiness and satisfaction!

1 Bring a pot of water to the boil and add the potatoes. Cook for 10 minutes.

2 Add the chorizo and onion to a large non-stick pan and cook on a medium heat for 3–4 minutes.

3 Drain the potatoes, then add to the pan. Mix them around to coat them in the red oil from the chorizo, then cook on a high heat for 2–3 minutes.

4 Turn the heat down to medium before adding the garlic, scallions, peppers, courgette, aubergine, smoked paprika and oregano to the pan. Cook for 5–7 minutes, stirring often.

5 Add the lemon juice and fish mix and stir them through the vegetables.

6 Cover the pan and leave to cook for 5 minutes.

7 Next add the chopped tomatoes, chickpeas, cannellini beans and coriander.

8 Leave to cook on a medium heat for 5 minutes, allowing the flavours to further develop, before serving.

Each portion provides:
- **vitamin C 149%** RI (119mg)
- **potassium 65%** RI (1296mg)
- **vitamin K 56%** RI (42μg)

Potassium is involved in muscle and nerve contraction. The frequency and degree to which your muscles contract is heavily dependent on the amount of potassium in the body, so athletes need to ensure adequate potassium intake.

SPICY ALMOND HEMP FRIED CHICKEN

CALORIES PER SERVING	CARBS (G)	PROTEIN (G)	FAT (G)	FIBRE (G)
453KCAL	6	48	26	4

⋙ INTENSE EXERCISE DAY

⊕ INJURY RECOVERY

INGREDIENTS

300g chicken fillet

1 egg

1 tsp honey

30g ground almonds

30g shelled hemp

1 tsp chipotle pepper sauce

½ tsp oregano

1 tsp smoked paprika

1 tbsp olive oil, plus extra
  to grease the tray

SERVES: 2

PREPARATION TIME: 5 MINUTES

COOKING TIME: 15 MINUTES

TOTAL TIME: 20 MINUTES

EQUIPMENT: TWO SHALLOW BOWLS, NON-STICK PAN, BAKING TRAY

This simple, nutritious and slightly nutty take on chicken tenders is fun to make and guaranteed to be loved by all! Enjoy served with homemade chips, a fresh garden salad or for lunch in a wrap to help you meet your protein targets throughout the day.

1 Preheat the oven to 190°C.
2 Slice the chicken fillets lengthways into strips.
3 In a shallow bowl, whisk the egg and honey together.
4 Combine the ground almonds, hemp, chipotle sauce, oregano and smoked paprika in another shallow bowl.
5 Dip a chicken strip into the egg mixture, then into the ground almond mix, making sure to coat generously. Set aside and repeat for the remaining chicken strips.
6 Heat the olive oil on a high heat on a non-stick pan. Fry the chicken strips for 2–3 minutes each side.
7 Place the chicken strips on a baking tray lightly coated in olive oil and cook in the oven for a further 10 minutes, until the chicken is cooked through and golden brown on the outside. Serve up with a dip of your choice.

Each portion provides:

- **omega-3 62%** RI (1.4 g)
- **magnesium 43%** RI (161mg)
- **vitamin E 35%** RI (4.2mg)

Vitamin E helps to promote
a healthy immune system,
potentially helping to prevent
the dip in immune function
following strenuous exercise.

SALMON HASH

CALORIES PER SERVING	CARBS (G)	PROTEIN (G)	FAT (G)	FIBRE (G)
722KCAL	48	50	37	8

» EXERCISE DAY

⊘ IMMUNE SUPPORT

INGREDIENTS

3 potatoes (approx. 400g, cubed)

1 large salmon fillet

olive oil

salt and pepper

1 onion (chopped)

1 clove garlic (crushed)

6 mushrooms (chopped)

1 red bell pepper (chopped)

5 eggs

½ tsp chilli powder

50g Cheddar cheese (grated)

Each portion provides:
- **vitamin D 187%** RI (9.3µg)
- **vitamin C 165%** RI (132mg)
- **omega-3 148%** RI (3.3mg)

Vitamin C has the potential to reduce the length of a cold or flu. The recommended intake of vitamin C when sick is 1g per day.

SERVES: 2

PREPARATION TIME: 5 MINUTES

COOKING TIME: 30 MINUTES

TOTAL TIME: 35 MINUTES

EQUIPMENT: NON-STICK STAINLESS STEEL PAN (SUITABLE FOR OVEN), MEDIUM-SIZED POT, MEDIUM-SIZED BOWL

This flavour-packed meal is great for any day of the week when you want something hearty. Salmon works really well with egg and cheese, both of which are good sources of fat and will be sure to keep you full for hours!

1   Preheat the oven to 180°C.
2   Bring a pot of water to the boil. Add the potatoes and parboil for 10 minutes, then drain.
3   Season your salmon with oil, salt and pepper, then bake for 8–10 minutes, chop and set aside.
4   Meanwhile, heat some oil on a pan. Add the onion, garlic, mushrooms and red pepper and sauté for 5–10 minutes, until soft.
5   Add the potatoes to the pan with the vegetables and fry for 5 minutes.
6   Crack all 5 eggs into a bowl and whisk together with your chilli powder. Pour the egg mix into the pan over the potatoes and vegetables.
7   Add the chopped salmon to the pan on top of the mixture and stir through.
8   Sprinkle the cheese over the mixture and bake in the oven at 180°C for 10 minutes.

SNACKS

AFFOGATO

CALORIES PER SERVING	CARBS (G)	PROTEIN (G)	FAT (G)	FIBRE (G)
441KCAL	33	22	25	3

⋙ **INTENSE EXERCISE DAY**

⊕ **INJURY RECOVERY**

INGREDIENTS

200g frozen Greek yoghurt
25g 80% dark chocolate
1 tbsp honey
1 espresso

SERVES: 1

PREPARATION TIME: 2 MINUTES

COOKING TIME: 5 MINUTES

TOTAL TIME: 7 MINUTES

EQUIPMENT: GLASS BOWL, SAUCEPAN, ESPRESSO MAKER

This recipe is my take on the classic affogato, meaning 'drowned' in Italian. It uses just four simple ingredients and takes less than 10 minutes to make! Drown the ice-cold frozen yoghurt in warm honey coffee and melted dark chocolate to give yourself a heavenly energy-boosting treat! I love to make this when friends come for dinner – they love digging at the dark chocolate that gathers at the bottom of the dish.

1. Melt the dark chocolate in a glass bowl over a saucepan of simmering water.
2. Place the frozen yoghurt in a glass.
3. Mix the honey, espresso and melted dark chocolate until smooth.
4. Pour the espresso mix over the frozen yoghurt and serve.

Each portion provides:
- **vitamin B12 62%** RI (2μg)
- **selenium 39%** RI (22μg)
- **calcium 38%** RI (303mg)

Coffee is a source of caffeine, bioactive compounds and antioxidants (polyphenols, catechins and flavonoids). The benefits of caffeine consumption include stimulation of brain function and improvement in mood and physical performance.

ALMOND BUTTER TOAST

CALORIES PER SERVING	CARBS (G)	PROTEIN (G)	FAT (G)	FIBRE (G)
335KCAL	38	12	15	6

 **INTENSE EXERCISE DAY**

INGREDIENTS

1 tsp rapeseed oil

1 apple (cut into slices)

pinch of cinnamon

2 slices porridge bread (or wholemeal brown bread)

1 tbsp almond butter

2 tsp honey

2 tbsp Greek yoghurt

SERVES: 2

PREPARATION TIME: 2 MINUTES

COOKING TIME: 10 MINUTES

TOTAL TIME: 12 MINUTES

EQUIPMENT: TOASTER, PAN

What makes this recipe work so well is the addition of slow-digesting ingredients like almond butter and fruit. It's perfect if you need a quick snack as you rush out the door to training.

1 Heat the oil on a pan.
2 Add the apple and cinnamon to the pan.
3 Cook on a medium heat for 8–10 minutes, until soft.
4 Toast the bread.
5 Spread the almond butter on the toasted bread.
6 Place the apple slices on the toast, drizzle over the honey and top with Greek yoghurt.

Each portion provides:
- **vitamin E 23%** RI (2.8mg)
- **calcium 22%** RI (172mg)
- **manganese 49%** RI (0.99mg)

This recipe can be used in preparation for or to recover from strenuous training or a competition.

BANANA BLUEBERRY PECAN BREAD

CALORIES PER SERVING	CARBS (G)	PROTEIN (G)	FAT (G)	FIBRE (G)
213KCAL	14	6	15	4.5

Zz REST DAY

✓ IMMUNE SUPPORT

INGREDIENTS

3 free-range eggs

1 tbsp coconut oil

2 bananas

20g blueberries

1 tsp vanilla extract

120g porridge oats

3 tbsp chopped pecans

2 tbsp ground almonds

2 tbsp milled flaxseed

4 tbsp desiccated coconut

2 tsp baking powder

1 tsp cinnamon

SERVES: 10

PREP TIME: 15 MINUTES

COOK TIME: 45 MINUTES

TOTAL TIME: 1 HOUR

EQUIPMENT: BLENDER, 2LB LOAF TIN, BAKING PAPER, WIRE COOLING RACK

This healthy alternative to regular bread uses oats to provide the bulk of the carbohydrate, while the banana, cinnamon and vanilla provide a sweet taste to complement the roasted nuts. Enjoy on its own or spread some fresh jam and peanut butter to fuel your workout.

1 Preheat the oven to 180°C.
2 In a blender, blitz the eggs, coconut oil, bananas, blueberries and vanilla extract until smooth.
3 Mix the rest of the ingredients in a large bowl.
4 Add the wet mix to the dry ingredients and mix well to form a wet dough.
5 Pour into a 2lb loaf tin lined with baking paper.
6 Bake for 45 minutes, or until a toothpick inserted into the centre of the loaf comes out clean.
7 Allow to cool on a wire rack for 15 minutes before slicing and serving.

Each portion provides:
- **manganese 55%** RI (1.1mg)
- **phosphorus 31%** RI (220mg)
- **omega-3 25%** RI (0.54g)

Nuts are a great source of omega-3 fatty acid, a natural anti-inflammatory that may help improve joint pain caused by inflammation.

BERRY BARS

CALORIES PER SERVING	CARBS (G)	PROTEIN (G)	FAT (G)	FIBRE (G)
222KCAL	26	8	10	3

>> EXERCISE DAY

INGREDIENTS

250g oats

125g mixed nuts and seeds

pinch of salt

3 medium eggs

2 bananas

2 tbsp honey

50g blueberries

75g raspberries

SERVES: 10

PREPARATION TIME: 5 MINUTES

COOKING TIME: 25 MINUTES

TOTAL TIME: 30 MINUTES, PLUS COOLING TIME

EQUIPMENT: BLENDER, MIXING BOWL, BAKING TIN, BAKING PAPER

These oaty berry bars are the perfect lunchbox filler. They make for a delicious midday snack with a cup of tea or coffee and will provide you with plenty of slow-releasing energy. The bitter-sweet berries add a lovely punch of flavour to these bars, and they're also a source of antioxidants.

1 Preheat the oven to 180°C.
2 Line a baking tin with baking paper.
3 Combine the oats, nuts, seeds and salt in a bowl.
4 Blitz the bananas, eggs and honey in a blender for 2 minutes, until smooth.
5 Pour the banana and egg mixture into the bowl with the oats and mix well to fully combine.
6 Fold in the blueberries and raspberries with a spoon.
7 Pour the batter into the prepared tin.
8 Bake in the preheated oven for 20–25 minutes, until cooked through.
9 Place on a wire rack and allow to cool completely before slicing into bars.

Each portion provides:
- **manganese 67%** RI (1.3mg)
- **copper 28%** RI (0.28mg)
- **phosphorus 25%** RI (172mg)

Copper is an essential trace mineral and plays an important role in iron metabolism and formation of haemoglobin.

CHOCOLATE MOUSSE

CALORIES PER SERVING	CARBS (G)	PROTEIN (G)	FAT (G)	FIBRE (G)
222KCAL	20	12	10	3

» EXERCISE DAY

⊕ INJURY RECOVERY

INGREDIENTS

125ml almond milk
   (or milk of choice)
80g dark chocolate
2 tbsp maple syrup
   (or honey)
1 tsp vanilla extract
¼ tsp sea salt
3 tbsp fresh orange juice
   (optional)
280g low-fat Greek yoghurt

SERVES: 3

PREPARATION TIME: 10 MINUTES

COOKING TIME: 5 MINUTES, PLUS 15 MINUTES COOLING TIME

REFRIGERATE TIME: 5 HOURS

TOTAL TIME: 5 HOURS 30 MINUTES

EQUIPMENT: MICROWAVE

This protein-rich chocolate mousse is ridiculously creamy and velvety, not to mention easy to make. Anyone who follows me knows that I am a big fan of dark chocolate, so, for me, this recipe is a winner for taste – and sometimes I spice things up even more by stirring some orange zest into the mixture. It's also a pretty healthy treat.

1 Heat the milk in the microwave for 80 seconds
2 Add the chocolate and mix until fully melted.
3 Stir in the maple syrup, vanilla extract, orange juice (if using) and salt and mix well.
4 Allow it to cool for about 15 minutes.
5 Add the yoghurt and whisk until smooth and creamy.
6 Divide the mixture equally between 3 bowls or glasses.
7 Place in the fridge for at least 5 hours to set.

Each portion provides:
- **calcium 18%** RI (146mg)
- **copper 40%** RI (0.4mg)
- **manganese 45%** RI (0.9mg)

Calcium, copper and manganese contribute to the development and protection of bone mass.

CRISPY HOMEMADE CHIPS

CALORIES PER SERVING	CARBS (G)	PROTEIN (G)	FAT (G)	FIBRE (G)
220KCAL	36	4	7	4

>>> INTENSE EXERCISE DAY

INGREDIENTS

400g potatoes (cut into wedges)

1 tbsp rapeseed oil

½ tsp sea salt

½ tsp paprika

½ tsp black pepper

SERVES: 2

PREPARATION TIME: 5 MINUTES

COOKING TIME: 25 MINUTES

TOTAL TIME: 30 MINUTES

EQUIPMENT: LARGE POT, KITCHEN ROLL, BAKING TRAY, BAKING PAPER

Chunky homemade potato chips are a great accompaniment to any number of dishes. Enjoy alongside a meaty burger, with a cheesy lasagne or dipped in hummus as a snack. There is no limit to what you can serve these hearty chips with!

1. Preheat the oven to 250°C.
2. Bring a pot of water to the boil and add the potato wedges. Parboil the potatoes for 5 minutes.
3. Drain and dry off the potatoes with kitchen roll.
4. Line a baking tray with a sheet of baking paper.
5. Place the potatoes on the lined tray and coat in the rapeseed oil and seasoning.
6. Bake for 15–20 minutes, turning the potatoes halfway through.
7. Remove from the oven when golden brown and crisp.

Each portion provides:
- **chloride 112%** RI (898mg)
- **potassium 45%** RI (909mg)
- **vitamin C 35%** RI (28mg)

Muscles and neurons are often
referred to as the 'electrical
tissues' of the body, and rely on
the movement of electrolytes,
such as potatssium and chloride,
through the fluid inside,
between and outside the cells.

EILEEN'S BUNS

CALORIES PER SERVING	CARBS (G)	PROTEIN (G)	FAT (G)	FIBRE (G)
263KCAL	46	6	6	3

⋙ INTENSE EXERCISE DAY

INGREDIENTS

160g raisins

1 teabag

1 tsp mixed spice

1 tsp cinnamon

50g cold butter, diced

500g self-raising flour

1 tsp baking powder

pinch of salt

1 egg

300ml milk

1 tbsp honey

SERVES: 12

PREPARATION TIME: 5 MINUTES

COOKING TIME: 20 MINUTES

TOTAL TIME: 25 MINUTES

EQUIPMENT: 2 SMALL BOWLS, LARGE BOWL, CUPCAKE TIN OR BAKING TRAY, WIRE RACK

It's hard to beat your mother's baking, and I had to include this recipe for the joy they bring with a little butter and jam. These are the buns my mother will make when she knows I am coming home from Dublin. They are just such a treat when I have spent some time out on the farm and I come in hungry.

1   Preheat the oven to 180°C.
2   Soak the raisins in a bowl of hot water with the tea bag, ½ tsp cinnamon and ½ tsp of mixed spice.
3   In a large bowl, combine the butter, flour, baking powder, ½ tsp cinnamon, ½ tsp mixed spice and pinch of salt. Mix together, using your hands to break up the butter, to form a crumbly mixture.
4   Beat the egg in a small bowl and mix in the milk and honey.
5   Slowly pour the egg mix into the flour mix, stirring well as you do so.
6   Drain the raisins and fold them into the batter.
7   Knead the ingredients together.
8   Spoon into a lightly greased cupcake tin or onto a flat baking tray that has been lined with baking paper.
9   Bake for 18–20 minutes, then tip onto a wire rack to cool.

Each portion provides:
- **phosphorus 32%** RI (222mg)
- **manganese 19%** RI (0.36mg)
- **chloride 15%** RI (122mg)

Maintaining a sufficient dietary intake of phosphorus is thought to increase your peak power output.

BANANA CHIA OAT BREAD

CALORIES PER SERVING	CARBS (G)	PROTEIN (G)	FAT (G)	FIBRE (G)
263KCAL	46	6	6	3

EXERCISE DAY

INGREDIENTS

130g oats

3 tbsp mixed dried fruit

1 scoop vanilla protein powder

2 tbsp chia seeds

1 tsp baking soda

2 tsp cinnamon

½ tsp nutmeg

3 free-range eggs

1 tbsp almond butter

1 tbsp coconut oil

2 bananas

150g low-fat Greek yoghurt

For the glaze:

1 medium egg

1 tsp honey

½ tsp cinnamon

½ tsp sea salt

SERVES: 12 **PREPARATION TIME:** 5 MINUTES

COOKING TIME: 50 MINUTES **TOTAL TIME:** 55 MINUTES

EQUIPMENT: LARGE BOWL, SMALL BOWL, BLENDER, LOAF TIN, WIRE RACK, BAKING PAPER, PASTRY BRUSH

During lockdown, it seemed banana-bread making became contagious! I decided to reinvent mine by adding some different flavours and textures, and I think this tastes even better than the original! This loaf is like a fruit brack but high in protein and nutrients – perfect for lunchboxes or an evening snack.

1 Preheat the oven to 180°C.
2 Line a loaf tin with baking paper.
3 Mix the oats, mixed fruit, protein powder, chia seeds, baking soda, cinnamon and nutmeg together in a large bowl.
4 In a blender, blitz the eggs, almond butter, coconut oil, bananas and Greek yoghurt for 2 minutes, until smooth.
5 Pour the wet mix into the large bowl with the dry ingredients and mix well until fully combined.
6 Pour the batter into the lined loaf tin and place in the oven for 45 minutes.
7 While the loaf is baking, make the glaze by whisking the egg in a small bowl with the honey and cinnamon.
8 After 45 minutes, take the fruit loaf out of the oven and brush the glaze over the top and sprinkle the sea salt on top.
9 Place the bread back into the oven for 5 minutes or until a toothpick inserted into the centre of the loaf comes out clean.
10 Allow to cool on a wire rack before slicing and serving.

Each portion contains:
- **omega-3 16%** RI (0.36g)
- **phosphorus 23%** RI (163mg)
- **manganese 31%** RI (0.62mg)

Phosphorus is an electrolyte required for developing bones and teeth, maintaining pH balance, synthesizing proteins, metabolising carbohydrates and fats, and generating energy.

LEAN QUEEN YOGHURT AND BERRIES

CALORIES PER SERVING	CARBS (G)	PROTEIN (G)	FAT (G)	FIBRE (G)
262KCAL	12	28	11	5

Zz **REST DAY**

☑ **IMMUNE SUPPORT**

INGREDIENTS

150g Greek yoghurt
½ scoop whey protein powder
50g strawberries
50g raspberries

SERVES: 1

PREPARATION TIME: 3 MINUTES

TOTAL TIME: 3 MINUTES

EQUIPMENT: SMALL BOWL

This refreshing snack is so simple and convenient! It's light, yet high in protein, and works well between meals, on a rest day or even as a pre-bedtime snack.

1 In a bowl, combine the Greek yoghurt and whey protein by mixing with a fork until well combined.
2 Top with the berries and enjoy.

Each portion provides:
- **vitamin C 56%** RI (45mg)
- **calcium 40%** RI (324mg)
- **vitamin B12 45%** RI (1.1µg)

Vitamin C is an important antioxidant that boosts our immune system and is needed in particular for the formation of blood vessels.

MUNCHY MUESLI BARS

CALORIES PER SERVING	CARBS (G)	PROTEIN (G)	FAT (G)	FIBRE (G)
202KCAL	29	6	7	5

>> **EXERCISE DAY**

INGREDIENTS

400g muesli (no added sugar,
    oats, nuts and dried fruit mix)

3 tbsp chia seeds

2 tbsp desiccated coconut

1 tsp salt

1 banana

3 tbsp honey

2 tbsp almond butter

2 free-range eggs

SERVES: 12

PREPARATION TIME: 10 MINUTES

COOKING TIME: 20 MINUTES, PLUS COOLING TIME

TOTAL TIME: 2 HOURS 30 MINUTES

EQUIPMENT: LARGE BOWL, FOOD PROCESSOR, BAKING TIN, BAKING PAPER

These Munchy Muesli Bars are so versatile: have them with breakfast, on the go or with a cup of joe. They are packed full of energy and nutrients, and are sure to keep you going until your next meal. So simple to make, using basic ingredients and sweetened with only banana and honey, this is a recipe you'll come back to again and again!

1 Preheat the oven to 175°C.
2 Line a baking tin with baking paper.
3 Place the dry ingredients in a bowl and mix.
4 In a food processor, blend the banana, honey, almond butter and eggs until smooth.
5 Mix the wet ingredients with the dry ingredients to form a dough.
6 Pour the mix into the lined baking tin and spread evenly.
7 Bake for 20 minutes, or until golden brown.
8 Remove from the oven, allow to cool for 2 hours, then chop into bars.

Each portion provides:
- **chloride 48%** RI (382mg)
- **manganese 46%** RI (0.93mg)
- **phosphorus 22%** RI (151mg)

This recipe can be used to support electrolyte balance in the body.

NO-BAKE CHOCOLATE PROTEIN BALLS

CALORIES PER SERVING	CARBS (G)	PROTEIN (G)	FAT (G)	FIBRE (G)
221KCAL	21	11	10	5

» EXERCISE DAY

INGREDIENTS

200g oats

3 scoops whey protein powder

50g mixed nuts

50g mixed dried fruit

3 tbsp chia seeds

2 tbsp honey

50–70ml milk

100g dark chocolate

1 tbsp coconut oil

SERVES: 10

PREPARATION TIME: 15 MINUTES

TOTAL TIME: 1 HOUR 15 MINUTES

EQUIPMENT: MEDIUM-SIZED BOWL, MICROWAVE, BAKING PAPER, PLATE

This no-bake recipe requires minimal fuss and will kit your fridge out with a handy go-to pre- or post-exercise snack. Covering the balls in melted chocolate and leaving them in the fridge to set gives a lovely chocolate crunch when you bite into them.

1 Add the dry ingredients to a medium-sized bowl and mix well.
2 Add honey and mix well again.
3 Add the milk bit by bit, slowly, and mix well until the mixture becomes clumpy. Don't allow it to get too wet – if it does, add some more whey and oats to make it less sticky!
4 Using a tablespoon and your hands, form the mixture into medium-sized balls.
5 Melt the dark chocolate with the coconut oil in the microwave (see page 88), then roll each protein ball in the chocolate and place on a lined plate. (If you don't fancy the chocolate coating, skip this step.)
6 When you have formed all the balls, put the plate in the fridge and allow them to set for about an hour.

Each portion provides:
- **manganese 58%** RI (1.2mg)
- **copper 35%** RI (0.35mg)
- **phosphorus 27%** RI (187mg)

Manganese is a trace mineral that plays a role in maintaining homeostasis in the body.

ORANGE SPLIT JELLIES

CALORIES PER SERVING	CARBS (G)	PROTEIN (G)	FAT (G)	FIBRE (G)
177KCAL	27	15	0	0

>> EXERCISE DAY

⊕ INJURY RECOVERY

INGREDIENTS

4 gelatine sheets

100ml cold water

1 packet orange jelly cubes

100ml hot water

1 tsp honey

100ml orange juice

50ml MiWadi orange sugar-free
   (undiluted)

100g 0% fat Greek yoghurt

MAKES: 16

PREPARATION TIME: 10 MINUTES

COOKING TIME: 5 MINUTES

TOTAL TIME: 4 HOURS 15 MINUTES

EQUIPMENT: 2 SAUCEPANS,
2 JUGS, ICE-CUBE TRAY, KITCHEN
PAPER, SMALL BOWL

Keep these tangy, chewy jellies in the fridge for a great treat to enjoy between meals or around your training sessions. They're also a great way of increasing your protein and collagen intake.

1 Place the gelatine sheets in a bowl and cover with the cold water. Leave to soak for 5 minutes.
2 Meanwhile, break up the cubes of jelly and place them in a pot.
3 Pour the hot water over the cubes of jelly. Add in the honey and mix well until the cubes are almost fully dissolved.
4 Remove the gelatine sheets from the water and pat dry using kitchen paper.
5 Pour the cold water into the pot and place the gelatine sheets in too.
6 Put the pot on a low–medium heat on the hob, add the orange juice and stir well until the sheets are fully dissolved.
7 Remove from the heat, and separate the liquid into 2 jugs. Put ⅓ of the mix in one jug and ⅔ of the mix in another.
8 Pour the MiWadi into the jug with ⅔ of the mix and stir well.
9 Pour this liquid into the ice-cube tray, filling each cup only ⅔ of the way.
10 Leave to set for 30 minutes in the fridge.
11 In the meantime, mix the yoghurt into the jug with ⅓ of the gelatine liquid.
12 Stir well until fully combined and there are no lumps.
13 When 30 minutes have passed, remove the tray from the fridge and fill up each cup with the yoghurt mixture.
14 Leave to set for at least 3 hours in the fridge or, for best results, overnight.
15 Remove the jellies carefully from the tray and enjoy!

Each portion provides:
- **chloride 16%** RI (132mg)
- **vitamin C 9%** RI (8mg)
- **calcium 8%** RI (63mg)

Collagen has been shown to support the repair of bones, tendons, connective tissues and muscles.

PEANUT BUTTER AND BERRY FLAPJACKS

CALORIES PER SERVING	CARBS (G)	PROTEIN (G)	FAT (G)	FIBRE (G)
270KCAL	34	8	12	4

» EXERCISE DAY

⊕ INJURY RECOVERY

INGREDIENTS

2 ripe bananas

2 tbsp honey

4 tbsp crunchy peanut butter

½ tsp cinnamon

50g blueberries

½ apple (grated)

200g porridge oats

40g mixed nuts

40g mixed dried fruit

40g mixed seeds

pinch of salt

SERVES: 8

PREPARATION TIME: 5 MINUTES

COOKING TIME: 30 MINUTES

TOTAL TIME: 35 MINUTES, PLUS COOLING TIME

EQUIPMENT: LARGE BOWL, BAKING TIN, BAKING PAPER

These oat-based bars are a great high-carb, on-the-go snack, a winning combination of slow- and fast-digesting carbohydrates. They provide healthy fats from the nuts and seeds and antioxidants from the fresh and dried berries.

1 Preheat the oven to 180°C.
2 Line a baking tin with baking paper.
3 In a large bowl, mash the bananas and mix in the honey, peanut butter and cinnamon.
4 Next, fold in the blueberries and grated apple.
5 Add the oats, nuts, fruit, seeds and salt and mix well until fully combined.
6 Spread the mixture evenly in the lined baking tin.
7 Place the tin in the oven for 30 minutes.
8 Remove and allow to cool before chopping into bars.

Each portion provides:
- **manganese 75%** RI (1.5mg)
- **chloride 38%** RI (307mg)
- **omega-6 26%** RI (3.6mg)

These flapjacks work well as a carb-loading treat or as a high-GI snack (combined with a protein shake) as part of a recovery strategy.

PEANUT BUTTER AND BANANA COOKIES

CALORIES PER SERVING	CARBS (G)	PROTEIN (G)	FAT (G)	FIBRE (G)
169KCAL	18	4	9	3

» **EXERCISE DAY**

⊕ **INJURY RECOVERY**

INGREDIENTS

150g oats

2 tbsp milled flaxseed

2 tbsp desiccated coconut

1 tsp baking soda

1 tsp salt

2 bananas

3 tbsp honey

5 tbsp peanut butter

2 tbsp coconut oil

SERVES: 10

PREPARATION TIME: 5 MINUTES

COOKING TIME: 12 MINUTES

TOTAL TIME: 17 MINUTES

EQUIPMENT: FOOD PROCESSOR, MIXING BOWL, BAKING PAPER, BAKING TRAY

These simple peanut butter cookies are so wholesome and delicious, you won't believe it!

Sweetened with nothing other than banana and honey, they make for a tasty snack that will be sure to satisfy your sweet tooth between meals and are a great accompaniment to your evening cup of tea.

1 Preheat the oven to 190°C.
2 Line a baking tray with baking paper.
3 Blitz the oats in a food processor until they reach a flour-like consistency.
4 Place all the dry ingredients in a bowl and mix well.
5 Blitz the bananas, honey, peanut butter and coconut oil in the food processor until smooth.
6 Pour the bananas mixture into the bowl with the dry ingredients and mix well.
7 Using your hands, roll the dough into small balls and flatten into the shape of a cookie on the lined tray.
8 Bake for 10–12 minutes, until golden brown.

Each portion provides:
- **manganese 42%** RI (0.84mg)
- **omega-3 21%** RI (0.47g)
- **potassium 10%** RI (196mg)

Nuts and seeds are brilliant
sources of omega-3, a type of
polyunsaturated fatty acid.

PORRIDGE BREAD WITH MIXED SEEDS

CALORIES PER SERVING	CARBS (G)	PROTEIN (G)	FAT (G)	FIBRE (G)
245KCAL	30	10	10	5

>> **EXERCISE DAY**

⊕ **INJURY RECOVERY**

INGREDIENTS

350g oats

2 tsp baking soda

½ tsp salt

30g chia seeds

30g sunflower seeds

30g pumpkin seeds

2 medium free-range eggs

500g Greek yoghurt

1 tbsp honey

SERVES: 10

PREPARATION TIME: 10 MINUTES

COOKING TIME: 1 HOUR 5 MINUTES

TOTAL TIME: 1 HOUR 15 MINUTES

EQUIPMENT: LARGE BOWL, SMALL BOWL, 9X5-INCH LOAF TIN, BAKING PAPER

An extremely simple and versatile oat-based bread, this can be used as an accompaniment to breakfast or lunch or as a snack around training.

1 Preheat the oven to 180°C.
2 Line a 9×5-inch loaf pan with baking paper.
3 In a large bowl, mix the oats, baking soda, salt and seeds together.
4 Whisk the eggs together in a small bowl.
5 Add the eggs, yoghurt and honey to the oat mixture and stir until well combined.
6 Pour the mix into the loaf tin.
7 Place in the oven for 65 minutes.
8 Carefully remove the bread from the tin, set aside and allow to cool.

Each portion provides:
- **omega-3 29%** RI (0.63g)
- **phosphorus 45%** RI (317mg)
- **manganese 73%** RI (1.5mg)

Oats are a slow-releasing energy source, which makes this bread an ideal snack, particularly when combined with a protein source such as eggs or meat.

PROTEIN BOMBS AWAY

CALORIES PER SERVING	CARBS (G)	PROTEIN (G)	FAT (G)	FIBRE (G)
279KCAL	22	12	16	4

» EXERCISE DAY

⊕ INJURY RECOVERY

INGREDIENTS

70g mixed nuts

1 tbsp coconut oil

pinch of salt

2 tbsp peanut butter

2 tbsp honey

200g oats

2 scoops whey protein powder

1 tbsp shelled hemp

150g dark chocolate (roughly chopped)

50ml milk

SERVES: 10

PREPARATION TIME: 15 MINUTES

REFRIGERATOR TIME: 2 HOURS

TOTAL TIME: 2 HOURS 15 MINUTES

EQUIPMENT: LARGE BOWL, SMALL BOWL, MICROWAVE, BAKING TRAY, BAKING PAPER

These chocolate protein bombs are a tasty snack to add to your meal plan. Prepare them at the weekend or early in the week, and they are sure to save you time and stop you from reaching for other, less nutritious snacks throughout the week.

1 Preheat the oven to 180°C.
2 Put the nuts on a baking tray and drizzle over ½ tbsp coconut oil and a pinch of salt. Roast in the oven for 6–7 minutes. Take the tray out and shake the nuts to turn halfway through.
3 Spoon the peanut butter and honey into a small bowl and mix to create a paste.
4 In a large bowl, combine the nuts, oats, whey protein, hemp and 50g of the dark chocolate.
5 Add the peanut butter and honey paste and rub into the mixture using the tips of your fingers.
6 Slowly pour in the milk, mixing well as you do. (Add more milk if needed, or if the mixture becomes too wet, add some more oats or protein powder).
7 Melt the remaining 100g of dark chocolate in a small bowl with ½ tbsp of coconut oil (see page 88).
8 Using your hands, shape the mixture into balls and then roll them in the melted dark chocolate.
9 Place the balls on a plate or a tray lined with baking paper, and leave in the fridge for at least 2 hours to set.

Each portion provides:
- **manganese 48%** RI (0.97mg)
- **phosphorus 18%** RI (125mg)
- **magnesium 15%** RI (57mg)

Manganese plays a role in the formation of cartilage and bones, so this recipe can be used to support bone health.

PROTEIN BOOSTED BATTLE BARS

CALORIES PER SERVING	CARBS (G)	PROTEIN (G)	FAT (G)	FIBRE (G)
331KCAL	16	12	24	4

Zz **REST DAY**

⊕ **INJURY RECOVERY**

INGREDIENTS

250g mixed nuts

70g oats

2 scoops whey protein powder

50g shelled hemp

½ tsp salt

250g 80% dark chocolate (melted, see page 88)

2 tbsp honey

SERVES: 12

PREPARATION TIME: 5 MINUTES

REFRIGERATOR TIME: 2 HOURS

TOTAL TIME: 2 HOURS 5 MINUTES

EQUIPMENT: LARGE BOWL, MICROWAVE, BAKING TIN, BAKING PAPER

These chocolate nut bars are always a hit – the battle is not eating them all in one go! The high fat content in these bars is sure to keep you satisfied between meals, making them great for rest days when you still need to boost your energy requirements without all the carbs.

1 Line a baking tin with baking paper.
2 Mix all the dry ingredients together in a bowl.
3 Pour the melted chocolate and honey over the dry ingredients and mix until fully combined.
4 Spoon the mixture into the baking tin.
5 Place in the fridge to set for 2 hours.
6 Remove from the fridge and chop into 12 bars.

Each portion provides:
- **magnesium 31%** RI (117mg)
- **vitamin E 24%** RI (2.8mg)
- **iron 23%** RI (3.2mg)

These bars deliver a delicious hit of chocolate while containing less than 10g sugar per serving.

PUDDLE BARS

CALORIES PER SERVING	CARBS (G)	PROTEIN (G)	FAT (G)	FIBRE (G)
217KCAL	20	9	11	4

» EXERCISE DAY

⟳ IMMUNE SUPPORT

INGREDIENTS

1 sweet potato (approx. 300g)

3 eggs

3 tbsp peanut butter

2 tbsp honey

100g oats

2 scoops whey protein powder
(vanilla or chocolate)

3 tbsp desiccated coconut

150g dark chocolate

SERVES: 12

PREPARATION TIME: 5 MINUTES

COOKING TIME: 50 MINUTES

TOTAL TIME: 55 MINUTES, PLUS COOLING TIME

EQUIPMENT: BAKING TRAY, BAKING PAPER, SMALL BOWL, MEDIUM BOWL, LARGE BOWL, BAKING TIN

This naturally sweetened fudgy brownie recipe uses just 8 simple ingredients to give 12 indulgent chocolate bars. Adding chunks of chocolate to the mix makes for an even gooier treat, with puddles of melted chocolate in the middle... mind the splash when you take a bite!

1 Preheat the oven to 200°C. Line a baking tray and a baking tin with baking paper.

2 Poke holes in the sweet potato using a fork. Place it on the tray and bake it for 30 minutes until soft. (You could also steam it, but be careful it doesn't become too mushy.)

3 Remove the skin and mash the sweet potato in a medium bowl using the back of a fork.

4 Whisk the eggs and mix in with the sweet potato.

5 Mix in the peanut butter and honey.

6 Combine the oats, whey and coconut in a large bowl.

7 Add the egg mixture and stir well.

8 Melt 100g of the chocolate in a small bowl in the microwave (see page 88), and add to the mix.

9 Chop the remaining chocolate and mix it through the batter.

10 Pour the batter into the lined tin. Bake in the preheated oven for 12–15 minutes until cooked through.

11 Allow to cool before cutting into 12 bars.

Each portion provides:
- **manganese 38%** RI (0.77mg)
- **copper 31%** RI (0.31mg)
- **vitamin E 16%** RI (1.9mg)

Vitamin E is an antioxidant that plays a role in protecting our cells from damage caused by free radicals. The presence of free radicals in the body is increased following periods of strenuous activity or injury to the body.

RASPBERRY JELLY DELIGHT

CALORIES PER SERVING	CARBS (G)	PROTEIN (G)	FAT (G)	FIBRE (G)
403KCAL	63	17	9	3

 INTENSE EXERCISE DAY

⊕ INJURY RECOVERY

INGREDIENTS

1 packet raspberry jelly
  (approx. 135g)
4 tbsp 0% fat Greek yoghurt
1 tsp honey
50g mixed berries
40g dark chocolate
½ tsp coconut oil

SERVES: 1

PREPARATION TIME: 5 MINUTES

COOKING TIME: 5 MINUTES

TOTAL TIME: 6+ HOURS

EQUIPMENT: MASON JAR, 2 SMALL BOWLS, MICROWAVE

This delicious jelly recipe is topped with a layer of thick creamy yoghurt, sweet berries and rich dark chocolate, making it the perfect healthy treat that you can enjoy between meals, alongside your lunch or for dessert!

1 Make the jelly as per the packet instructions.
2 Pour the jelly mixture into a Mason jar or bowl and refrigerate overnight.
3 Mix the yoghurt and honey together in a small bowl.
4 Dollop the yoghurt onto the jelly.
5 Top with mixed berries.
6 Melt the dark chocolate with the coconut oil in a small bowl in the microwave (see page 88), and drizzle over the top.
7 Place back in the fridge for 5 minutes to allow the chocolate to set, or serve immediately.

Each portion provides:
- **vitamin C 20%** RI (16mg)
- **calcium 19%** RI (150mg)
- **potassium 15%** RI (305mg)

Gelatin has been shown to support recovery from tendon injuries.

RASPBERRY-ROONS

CALORIES PER SERVING	CARBS (G)	PROTEIN (G)	FAT (G)	FIBRE (G)
212KCAL	8	7	17	4

ᶻᶻ REST DAY

◔ IMMUNE SUPPORT

INGREDIENTS

50g oats

100g desiccated coconut

2 scoops whey protein powder
   (vanilla flavour)

2 tbsp coconut oil (melted)

1 tbsp honey

50–70ml milk (plus more if
   needed)

For the toppings:

1 tbsp rapeseed oil

100g raspberries

½ tbsp honey

40g 85% dark chocolate

¼ tsp coconut oil

sea salt

20g desiccated coconut

SERVES: 9

PREPARATION TIME: 5 MINUTES

COOKING TIME: 15 MINUTES

TOTAL TIME: 6+ HOURS

EQUIPMENT: LARGE BOWL,
SMALL POT, BAKING PAPER,
BAKING TIN, SMALL BOWL,
MICROWAVE

These Raspberry-Roons are a real treat! The contrast between the tanginess of the raspberries and bitterness of the dark chocolate on top of the crumbly oat base is nothing short of delicious.

1 Preheat the oven to 200°C.
2 Mix the oats, coconut and protein powder together in a large bowl.
3 Add the coconut oil and honey and mix well.
4 Add the milk bit by bit, slowly, and mix until the mixture becomes clumpy and starts to stick together without becoming too wet.
5 Spoon the mix into a baking tin lined with baking paper and press down well. It should be about 1cm thick.
6 Place in the oven and bake for 8–10 minutes, or until lightly golden, then leave to cool.
7 Meanwhile, heat some oil in a small pot.
8 Mash the raspberries in a small bowl using the back of a fork.
9 Add the raspberries to the pot and mix half a tablespoon of honey through them. Leave to simmer for 3 minutes before removing from the heat.
10 Leave the raspberries to cool.
11 When cooled, spread the raspberry mix over the coconut base.
12 Melt the dark chocolate in a small bowl in the microwave with a quarter of a teaspoon of coconut oil for approximately 60 seconds.
13 Pour the melted chocolate evenly over the layer of raspberries and spread using a blunt knife.
14 Sprinkle some sea salt and coconut on top and leave to set in the fridge overnight, before cutting into 9 squares.

Each portion provides:
- **manganese 27%** RI (0.54mg)
- **copper 17%** RI (0.17mg)
- **magnesium 8%** RI (29mg)

These are a good source of fat and protein, the most satisfying macronutrients, so will be sure to keep you going between meals or on the go.

SUPERCHARGER RICE CAKES

CALORIES PER SERVING	CARBS (G)	PROTEIN (G)	FAT (G)	FIBRE (G)
302KCAL	41	7	12	3

» **EXERCISE DAY**

INGREDIENTS

2 tbsp cashew butter
2 plain rice cakes
1 banana

SERVES: 1
PREPARATION TIME: 2 MINUTES
TOTAL TIME: 2 MINUTES

Supercharger Rice Cakes are a great snack option if you are feeling hungry between main meals and want an energy boost. The combination of carbohydrate from the rice cakes and banana also provides a fast-acting energy source, which makes this an ideal pre-exercise snack.

1 Thinly spread a tablespoon of cashew butter over each rice cake.
2 Chop the banana and place it on top.

Each portion provides:
- **potassium 31%** RI (615mg)
- **phosphorus 31%** RI (217mg)
- **chloride 29%** RI (232mg)

Chloride helps promote iron absorption, so when combined with foods rich in iron, the absorption of the iron significantly increases.

DINNER

CHEAT'S RISOTTO

CALORIES PER SERVING	CARBS (G)	PROTEIN (G)	FAT (G)	FIBRE (G)
415KCAL	59	19	11	4

» **EXERCISE DAY**

INGREDIENTS

2 tbsp olive oil

1 onion (chopped)

1 clove garlic (crushed)

salt and pepper

200g cooked ham (roughly
    chopped)

300g arborio rice

1 vegetable stock cube

1 litre boiling water

200g peas (frozen)

30g parmesan cheese

SERVES: 4

PREPARATION TIME: 5 MINUTES

COOKING TIME: 25 MINUTES

TOTAL TIME: 30 MINUTES

EQUIPMENT: LARGE PAN WITH LID

If you want to shake up your pre-performance meal with something that is quick and easy but doesn't compromise on flavour, then look no further! Risotto rice is high in carbohydrates and low in fibre, which is an all-round winner when you want to top up your fuel in preparation for competition.

1 Heat the olive oil in a large pan, add the onion, garlic and a pinch of salt and pepper and fry for 5 minutes on a low-medium heat, until the onion is soft and translucent.
2 Add the ham to the pan.
3 Place the vegetable stock cube in 1 litre of water and stir until dissolved.
4 Add the rice and vegetable stock to the pan, stir well and cover with a lid.
5 Bring to the boil before reducing the heat and simmering for 15 minutes, until the rice is tender and it has absorbed all the liquid.
6 Stir in the peas and cook for an additional 3 minutes.
7 Sprinkle the parmesan cheese on top and serve.

Each portion provides:
- **chloride 134%** RI (1074mg)
- **omega-3 31%** RI (0.69 g)
- **zinc 27%** RI (2.7mg)

Chloride is involved in many bodily functions, such as the regulation of fluids and blood pressure.

CHIA BASE PIZZA

CALORIES PER SERVING	CARBS (G)	PROTEIN (G)	FAT (G)	FIBRE (G)
625KCAL	70	35	24	8

>>> INTENSE EXERCISE DAY

INGREDIENTS

350g plain white flour

3 tbsp chia seeds

½ tsp dried yeast

½ tsp chilli flakes

½ tsp garlic powder

2 tbsp honey

salt and pepper

300ml warm water

2 tbsp olive oil

For the toppings

200g passata

100g cheese (grated)

5 sun-dried tomatoes

200g cooked chicken breast

½ red onion (chopped)

6 mushrooms (chopped)

6 cherry tomatoes (quartered)

basil leaves (to garnish)

SERVES: 4

PREPARATION TIME: 5-12 HOURS

COOKING TIME: 15 MINUTES

TOTAL TIME: 5-12 HOURS 15 MINUTES

EQUIPMENT: LARGE BOWL, ROLLING PIN, BAKING TRAYS

Pizzas are delicious, provide lots of energy and can be fun for the whole family to make together. It's a meal that athletes can use to fuel up before competition (go easy on the cheese) and also for a tasty recovery meal afterwards! This recipe is easy, tasty and has a bit of a kick if you include the chilli.

1 Add the flour, chia seeds, yeast, chilli flakes, garlic powder, honey and a pinch of salt and pepper to a large bowl. Stir in the warm water and the oil. Using your hands, mix well to form a dough.

2 Leave the dough to rise overnight or for at least 5 hours at room temperature. (Alternatively, if you want a flat base, leave the dough for a shorter period, between 30 and 60 minutes.)

3 When ready to cook, heat the oven to 220°C.

4 Using your knuckles, knead the dough on a floured surface, trying to avoid it getting sticky. Add a little more flour if the mixture is too wet.

5 Divide the dough into 4 equal pieces.

6 Use a rolling pin, roll the pieces into round pizza shapes, and place each on a lightly floured baking tray.

7 Add your toppings however you like them and bake for 10–15 minutes, depending on the thickness of the pizzas, or until the crust is brown.

Chia seeds are loaded with antioxidants, vitamins, minerals and fibre, making them a great addition to this recipe.

BOLD CHORIZO AND BLACK PUDDING CHICKEN WITH SPICED WEDGES

CALORIES PER SERVING	CARBS (G)	PROTEIN (G)	FAT (G)	FIBRE (G)
791KCAL	76	53	30	8

 INTENSE EXERCISE DAY

IMMUNE SUPPORT

INGREDIENTS

For the wedges:

2 potatoes (cut into wedges)

1 sweet potato (cut into wedges)

1 tbsp extra virgin olive oil

1 tsp cumin

1 tsp smoked paprika

1 tsp ground pepper

1 tsp salt

1 tbsp coconut oil

For the chorizo chicken:

90g chorizo (chopped)

1 onion (chopped)

2 cloves garlic (minced)

50g black pudding (chopped)

350g chicken breast (chopped)

½ tsp dried oregano

½ courgette (chopped)

8 chestnut mushrooms (chopped)

4 tbsp fresh cream

2 handfuls spinach

90g apple sauce (to serve)

Each portion provides:

- **vitamin C 80%** RI (64mg)
- **selenium 59%** RI (33µg)
- **iron 43%** RI (6.1mg)

SERVES: 3

PREPARATION TIME: 5 MINUTES

COOKING TIME: 35 MINUTES

TOTAL TIME: 40 MINUTES

EQUIPMENT: BAKING TRAY, MEDIUM-SIZED BOWL, NON-STICK PAN

This dish is outrageously tasty! And it's made using such simple ingredients – nothing fancy, just good food packed full of flavour. Serve it with these spiced potato wedges and a dollop of apple sauce and you have yourself a recipe that is guaranteed to be a major crowd-pleaser.

For the wedges:

1 Preheat the oven to 200°C.
2 Toss the potato and sweet potato wedges with the olive oil, cumin, paprika, pepper and salt in a medium bowl.
3 Spread the wedges out evenly over a baking tray greased with coconut oil.
4 Bake for 15 minutes, then flip them over and bake for an additional 10 minutes, or until golden brown and cooked through.

For the chicken:

1 Meanwhile, fry the chorizo and onion on a non-stick pan over a medium heat until the onion is translucent.
2 Add the garlic and black pudding to the pan and cook for 5 minutes. Turn the black pudding halfway through.
3 Add the chicken and oregano to the pan and cook for a further 5 minutes.
4 Next add the courgette, mushrooms and cream. Mix well.
5 Cover and simmer on a low-medium heat for 15–20 minutes.
6 Serve with the spiced potato wedges and apple sauce.

CHICKEN AND BACON TAGLIATELLE IN TOMATO SAUCE

CALORIES PER SERVING	CARBS (G)	PROTEIN (G)	FAT (G)	FIBRE (G)
555KCAL	65	52	10	6

>>> INTENSE EXERCISE DAY

INGREDIENTS

1 tbsp olive oil

1 onion (chopped)

2 cloves of garlic (crushed)

½ tsp chilli flakes

2 tsp smoked paprika

300g chicken breast (chopped)

4 bacon medallions (diced)

280g tagliatelle (uncooked)

1 tbsp tomato purée

400g tinned tomatoes

200g low-fat cottage cheese

1 tbsp honey

1 handful basil leaves (chopped)

salt and black pepper

Each portion provides:
- **chloride 126%** RI (1010mg)
- **selenium 70%** RI (38.5µg)
- **vitamin B1 65%** RI (0.71mg)

Carbohydrate loading increases muscular glycogen stores far beyond resting levels and ensures that muscle glycogen stores are replenished and maximised.

SERVES: 4

PREPARATION TIME: 5 MINUTES

COOKING TIME: 45 MINUTES

TOTAL TIME: 50 MINUTES

EQUIPMENT: NON-STICK PAN, LARGE POT

Although this pasta dish is made using the simplest of ingredients, I assure you it is packed full of flavour! This homemade creamy tomato sauce is so simple that even someone with the most basic cooking skills will be able to perfect it. To increase the nutritional content, just add in any of your favourite vegetables.

1. Heat the olive oil in a non-stick pan.
2. Add the onion and sauté on a medium heat until translucent.
3. Add the garlic, chilli and smoked paprika and cook for 3 minutes, stirring continuously.
4. Add the chicken and bacon to the pan and cook for 10–15 minutes or until they're cooked through, stirring continuously.
5. While the chicken and bacon are cooking, bring a pot of water to the boil. Once the water has been brought to the boil, cook the tagliatelle for 10–12 minutes or as per packet instructions.
6. Add the tomato purée, tin of tomatoes, cottage cheese, honey and basil to the pan, and leave to simmer on a medium to low heat for 10–15 minutes.
7. Drain the tagliatelle and add to the pan. Sprinkle over some salt and black pepper.
8. Mix well to fully coat the tagliatelle in the sauce before serving.

CHICKEN KORMA

CALORIES PER SERVING	CARBS (G)	PROTEIN (G)	FAT (G)	FIBRE (G)
590KCAL	24	44	35	10

Zz REST DAY

⊕ INJURY RECOVERY

INGREDIENTS

For the chicken:

3 chicken breasts (chopped)

2 tbsp rapeseed oil

2 cloves garlic (crushed)

2 tsp curry powder

½ tsp salt

½ tsp black pepper

1 onion (peeled and chopped)

1 red chilli (diced)

1 yellow bell pepper (chopped)

1 aubergine (chopped)

6 sun-dried tomatoes (chopped)

For the sauce:

2 onions (peeled and chopped)

3 cloves garlic (crushed)

½ red chilli

½ green chilli

2 tbsp coconut oil

2 thumb-sized pieces of ginger (grated)

250ml reduced-fat coconut cream

2 tbsp Greek yoghurt

2 tsp curry powder

1 tsp turmeric

1 tsp cinnamon

salt and pepper

½ tsp cumin

zest of 1 lemon

1 tbsp honey

1 tbsp fresh coriander (finely chopped)

SERVES: 3 **PREPARATION TIME:** 1 HOUR

COOKING TIME: 1 HOUR **TOTAL TIME:** 2 HOURS

EQUIPMENT: MEDIUM-SIZED BOWL, LARGE NON-STICK PAN, BLENDER, LARGE SAUCEPAN

This easy chicken korma recipe is a delicious take on the classic Indian dish. It is mild and creamy, sure to be a real crowd-pleaser for any occasion. It can be served with traditional rice or an alternative such as cauliflower rice – a great option to reduce the calories and carbohydrate level of a meal without compromising on enjoyment.

1 Marinate the chicken with half the rapeseed oil, some garlic, curry powder, salt and black pepper in a medium bowl and set aside in the fridge for at least an hour.

2 When the chicken is marinated, place the rest of the garlic, chilli, onion and 1 tbsp oil in a pan and cook for 2–3 minutes, until the onions begin to brown.

3 Add the chicken and cook thoroughly, roughly 5 minutes.

4 Next, add the yellow pepper, aubergine and sun-dried tomatoes and cook for another 3–5 minutes.

5 To make the korma sauce, place the onions, garlic, chillies and a little water in a blender and blitz until creamy.

6 In a large saucepan, heat the coconut oil over medium heat. Add the mixture from the blender and cook for 2–3 minutes, stirring continuously.

7 Add the ginger, coconut cream, yoghurt, spices, lemon zest and honey and mix together.

8 Turn the heat down to low and simmer for 30–40 minutes until the sauce has reduced, making sure to stir continuously.

9 Garnish with fresh coriander and serve with cauliflower, brown or white rice.

Each portion provides:
- **vitamin C 128%** RI (103mg)
- **vitamin E 59%** RI (7mg)
- **selenium 35%** RI (19μg)

Vitamins C and E are essential vitamins and potent antioxidants with anti-inflammatory properties, playing a significant role in improving immunity and reducing inflammation.

CHICKEN PIE WITH GARLIC POTATOES

CALORIES PER SERVING	CARBS (G)	PROTEIN (G)	FAT (G)	FIBRE (G)
652KCAL	54	48	27	8

>> **EXERCISE DAY**

⊕ **INJURY RECOVERY**

INGREDIENTS

5 medium potatoes (approx. 1kg)

2 cloves garlic (chopped)

2 tbsp butter

2 tbsp rapeseed oil

1 onion (chopped)

3 chicken breasts (chopped)

10 button mushrooms (chopped)

2 handfuls baby spinach

½ tbsp fresh oregano

100ml cream

120g Cheddar cheese (grated)

salt and ground pepper

SERVES: 4

PREPARATION TIME: 5 MINUTES

COOKING TIME: 45 MINUTES

TOTAL TIME: 50 MINUTES

EQUIPMENT: MEDIUM-SIZED POT, NON-STICK PAN, CASSEROLE DISH

Creamy chicken and mushrooms topped with a layer of garlic potatoes and melted Cheddar cheese – a proper tasty and wholesome recipe, to say the least!

1 Preheat the oven to 190°C.
2 Cut potatoes into thick slices (roughly 5mm) and parboil for 5 minutes, then drain.
3 Add the chopped garlic, some pepper, butter and 1 tbsp of oil into the pot with the drained potatoes and mix well. Cook over a medium heat for 2–3 minutes.
4 Heat 1 tbsp of oil on a non-stick pan.
5 Sauté the onion with a pinch of salt for 2–3 minutes.
6 Add the chicken pieces to the pan and cook for 10–15 minutes, or until they are almost done.
7 Add the mushrooms, baby spinach, fresh oregano and cream and mix well.
8 Spoon the chicken and vegetables into the casserole dish.
9 Next, layer the garlic potatoes on top, then place the dish in the oven at 190°C for about 25 minutes, or until the potatoes are just cooked through.
10 Remove from the oven and sprinkle the grated cheese on top. Place the dish back in the oven for 2–3 minutes to melt the cheese, then serve.

Each portion provides:
- **potassium 101%** RI (2010mg)
- **vitamin C 57%** RI (45mg)
- **zinc 35%** RI (3.5mg)

Vitamin C, also known as ascorbic acid, may reduce the length of a cold or flu. The recommended intake of vitamin C when sick is 1g per day.

COCONUT DAHL AND EASY NAAN

CALORIES PER SERVING	CARBS (G)	PROTEIN (G)	FAT (G)	FIBRE (G)
463KCAL	70	21	11	12

INGREDIENTS

1 tbsp rapeseed oil

2 onions (diced)

3 cloves garlic (minced)

1 thumb-sized piece of ginger (peeled and grated)

½ tbsp ground turmeric

1 tsp ground cumin

½ tbsp paprika

½ tbsp garam masala

400g lentils

1 vegetable stock cube

450ml hot water

400ml coconut milk

200g tinned chopped tomatoes

1 tbsp tomato purée

1 tsp chilli purée

1 tbsp honey

2 tbsp lime juice

For the naan:

190g flour (plus extra for rolling)

1 tsp baking soda

1 tsp garlic powder

1 tbsp fresh coriander (finely chopped)

½ tsp salt

250g 0% fat Greek yoghurt

1 tbsp rapeseed oil

SERVES: 4 **PREPARATION TIME:** 5 MINUTES

COOKING TIME: 30 MINS **TOTAL TIME:** 35 MINUTES

EQUIPMENT: LARGE SKILLET, LARGE BOWL, SMALL PAN

This healthy take on a traditional Indian dish really hits the spot! The easy-to-make naan bread is super tasty and a good source of protein.

1 Heat a tablespoon of rapeseed oil on a medium heat on a large skillet. Add the onion and sauté until translucent.

2 Add the garlic and ginger and fry for 3 minutes. Next, add the spices, fully coating the onion.

3 Rinse the lentils and drain before adding them to the skillet with the onion.

4 Dissolve the vegetable stock cube in 450ml of hot water, then add to the skillet. Mix well and simmer for 10 minutes, until most of the liquid has been absorbed.

5 Next add the coconut milk, tomatoes, tomato purée, chilli purée and honey. Mix well and leave to simmer for a further 10 minutes.

6 While the dahl is simmering, prepare your naan bread by mixing the flour, baking soda, garlic powder, coriander and salt together in a bowl. Then add the yoghurt and use your hands to form into a ball of dough.

7 Flour a clean, flat surface and transfer the dough onto it. Divide the dough into 8 pieces and shape into small flat circles.

8 Heat a little oil on a medium heat on a small pan. Fry each piece for 3–4 minutes on each side, putting some oil on the pan before each one.

9 Remove the dahl from the heat, squeeze over the lime juice, mix well and serve with naan bread and warm rice!

Each portion provides:
- **chloride 54%** RI (433mg)
- **fibre 47%** RI (12 g)
- **vitamin B1 32%** RI (0.35mg)

Salt consists of sodium and chloride and is important for normal physiologic function. High sweat rates in athletes result in loss of both fluids and sodium, and athletes therefore need to replace these through their diet.

CODDIN' ME CURRY

CALORIES PER SERVING	CARBS (G)	PROTEIN (G)	FAT (G)	FIBRE (G)
451KCAL	60	24	13	9

>> **EXERCISE DAY**

 IMMUNE SUPPORT

INGREDIENTS

400g cod fillets

2 large sweet potatoes (peeled
   and chopped)

1 tbsp rapeseed oil

1 onion (chopped)

2 cloves of garlic (crushed)

1 thumb-sized piece ginger
   (grated)

½ chilli pepper (finely sliced)

1 courgette (sliced)

2 red bell peppers (chopped)

1 tsp smoked paprika

1 tsp garam masala

1 tsp cumin seeds

1 tsp turmeric

400ml reduced-fat coconut milk

1 tbsp honey

1 tbsp lemon juice

2 handfuls spinach

SERVES: 4

PREPARATION TIME: 5 MINUTES

COOKING TIME: 40 MINUTES

TOTAL TIME: 45 MINUTES

EQUIPMENT: LARGE NON-STICK PAN, MEDIUM-SIZED POT, STEAMER

Who doesn't love a good curry? This recipe is a delicious way to incorporate more fish into your diet. The reduced-fat coconut milk used here makes it suitable for an exercise day; use regular coconut milk if you want to increase the fat content. And for something a little extra, why not try making my Easy Naan on page 216?

1 Steam or bake the cod fillets and leave to one side while preparing the curry.

2 Bring a pot of water to the boil, add the sweet potatoes and cook for 5–8 minutes, until tender. Drain and set aside.

3 Meanwhile, heat the oil in a large non-stick pan. Add the onion, garlic, ginger and chilli and fry for 5 minutes on medium heat.

4 Add the courgette and bell peppers and cook for another 5 minutes, until soft.

5 Next, add the spices and drained sweet potato and mix well. Leave to cook for a further 5 minutes.

6 Add the coconut milk, honey and lemon juice and simmer for 10 minutes.

7 Add the cod fillets and spinach. Stir to break the cod fillets up through the curry and leave to simmer for a further 5 minutes, then serve.

Each portion provides:
- **vitamin A 228%** RI (1823µg)
- **vitamin C 218%** RI (175mg)
- **selenium 49%** RI (27µg)

Ginger and turmeric contain antioxidant as well as anti-inflammatory properties, making this an excellent recipe for aiding recovery from muscle-related injuries involving stress and inflammation.

CRISPY BALSAMIC TOFU AND ROAST VEG WITH CHICKPEA PASTA

CALORIES PER SERVING	CARBS (G)	PROTEIN (G)	FAT (G)	FIBRE (G)
479KCAL	47	30	19	12

>> EXERCISE DAY

+ INJURY RECOVERY

SERVES: 3 **PREPARATION TIME:** 1 HOUR

COOKING TIME: 45 MINUTES **TOTAL TIME:** 1 HOUR 45 MINUTES

EQUIPMENT: BAKING TRAY, SMALL BOWL, SMALL PAN, MEDIUM POT

INGREDIENTS

For the tofu:

2 tbsp balsamic vinegar

½ tbsp soy sauce (or tamari if gluten-free)

1 tbsp honey

1 tbsp garlic powder

300g firm tofu (pressed to remove water and cubed)

For the pasta:

5 cherry tomatoes (roughly chopped)

1 bell pepper (roughly chopped)

1 courgette (roughly chopped)

1 aubergine (roughly chopped)

250g mushrooms (roughly chopped)

1 red onion (roughly chopped)

2 cloves of garlic (peeled but left whole)

1 tbsp rapeseed oil, plus extra for frying

4 tbsp balsamic vinegar

1 tsp salt

1 tsp black pepper

1 tsp chilli flakes

150g chickpea pasta (or regular pasta if not gluten-free)

grated parmesan or nutritional yeast (to serve)

This recipe is a great all-rounder! It's suitable for vegetarians while being gluten- and dairy-free – not to mention it's uber-wholesome and comforting: ideal to pop into the oven after a long day at work.

1 In a small bowl, mix the balsamic vinegar, soy sauce/tamari, honey and garlic powder. Add the cubes of tofu and coat in the sauce. Place into the fridge to marinate for an hour.

2 Preheat the oven to 180°C.

3 Place the vegetables and garlic on a baking tray and drizzle with 1 tablespoon of oil and 3 tablespoons of balsamic vinegar. Season with salt, black pepper and chilli flakes and mix well.

4 Make some space on one side of the tray, lay out the tofu pieces and drizzle with any excess sauce.

5 Place in the preheated oven for 20 minutes.

6 Remove from the oven, turn the vegetables and tofu and add another tablespoon of balsamic vinegar. Cook for a further 20 minutes.

7 Meanwhile, cook the pasta in a pot of boiling water as per packet instructions.

8 Heat some oil on a small pan. Remove the tofu from the tray and fry on the pan until slightly crispy.

9 Remove the vegetables from the oven and pick out the garlic cloves.

10 Use the back of a fork to mash the garlic and mix it through the vegetables.

11 Drain the pasta and combine with the vegetables and tofu.

12 Mix well and enjoy served with some grated parmesan – or nutritional yeast to keep it dairy-free.

Each portion provides:
- **calcium 91%** RI (731mg)
- **copper 70%** RI (0.7mg)
- **potassium 61%** RI (1218mg)

Sufficient levels of dietary copper are linked with a reduced risk of osteoporosis.

CHORIZO BEEF BURGERS

CALORIES PER SERVING	CARBS (G)	PROTEIN (G)	FAT (G)	FIBRE (G)
243KCAL	8	25	12	0.8

Zz REST DAY

⊕ INJURY RECOVERY

INGREDIENTS

100g chorizo (diced)

1 clove garlic (crushed)

1 spring onion (finely chopped)

2 tbsp maple syrup

500g lean beef mince

½ tsp chilli powder

½ tsp paprika

pinch of salt

pinch of black pepper

1 tbsp barbecue sauce

1 tbsp tomato purée

1 tbsp rapeseed oil

Each portion provides:
- **vitamin B12 75%** RI (1.9μg)
- **zinc 45%** RI 4.5mg)
- **iron 13%** RI (1.8mg)

Iron and vitamin B12 are needed for the production of red blood cells, which carry oxygen around the body. This recipe can be used to support recovery, particularly in instances of blood loss.

SERVES: 5

PREPARATION TIME: 5 MINUTES

COOKING TIME: 15 MINUTES

TOTAL TIME: 20 MINUTES

EQUIPMENT: NON-STICK PAN, LARGE BOWL

Nothing beats making your own beef burgers, and these are so simple to make and are a great protein source. By making your own burgers, you know exactly what's in there and can make them to suit your taste preferences. Be sure not to overcook the meat so that it is nice and juicy. During the summer you can pop them on the barbecue for an extra smoky flavour.

1 Place a non-stick pan on a medium heat and add chorizo, garlic and chopped spring onion. Fry for 3–4 minutes.

2 Add the maple syrup and fry for another 1–2 minutes. Once the spring onion is lightly browned, remove the mix from the pan and allow to cool for a few minutes.

3 Add the beef mince, chilli powder, paprika, salt and pepper, barbecue sauce and tomato purée to a large bowl and, using your hands, mix well.

4 Add the fried chorizo mix to the beef mince and mix well.

5 Form into 5 burger patties.

6 Heat the oil on the non-stick pan over a medium heat.

7 Place the burgers on the pan and cook for 5 minutes on each side before serving as desired.

ENCHILADAS WITH GUACAMOLE

CALORIES PER SERVING	CARBS (G)	PROTEIN (G)	FAT (G)	FIBRE (G)
389KCAL	46	23	12	6

>> EXERCISE DAY

⟳ IMMUNE SUPPORT

MAKES: 10 ENCHILADAS **PREPARATION TIME:** 5 MINUTES

COOKING TIME: 35 MINUTES **TOTAL TIME:** 40 MINUTES

EQUIPMENT: NON-STICK PAN, SMALL POT, SMALL BOWL, BAKING DISH, MICROWAVE

INGREDIENTS

2 tbsp rapeseed oil

1 onion (diced)

500g chicken fillets (chopped)

2 red bell peppers (sliced lengthways)

½ tsp cumin

½ tsp dried oregano

2 tbsp sweet chilli sauce

2 tbsp soy sauce

¼ tsp salt

¼ tsp pepper

250g rice (cooked)

240g tinned black beans

10 tortillas

100g grated Cheddar cheese

1 avocado

juice of ½ lime

For the sauce:

2 cloves garlic (crushed)

1 red onion (diced)

2 tbsp balsamic vinegar

1 tbsp honey

2 tsp oregano

¼ tsp salt

¼ tsp pepper

500g tomato passata

1 tbsp plain white flour

Enchiladas are a traditional Mexican food – this version features tender chicken, black beans and a mouth-watering tomato sauce.

1 Heat a tablespoon of oil in a large non-stick pan.
2 Add the onion and fry on a medium heat for 5 minutes.
3 Add the chicken and cook for 4–5 minutes on either side.
4 Next add the red peppers, cumin, oregano, sweet chilli, soy sauce, salt and pepper to the pan. Cook for a further 8–10 minutes, until the peppers are soft.
5 Heat the rice in the microwave for 2 minutes then add to the pan with the beans. Mix well.
6 Next, make the sauce by heating a tablespoon of rapeseed oil in a small pot over a medium heat. Once hot, add the garlic and onion and fry for 5 minutes, stirring continuously to avoid burning.
7 Add the vinegar, honey, seasonings, passata and flour and mix well. Leave to simmer for 5–7 minutes, stirring often.
8 Preheat the oven to 180°C.
9 To assemble, divide the chicken and vegetables between the 10 tortillas and fold to create parcels.
10 Place the filled tortilla parcels in a baking dish. Pour over the tomato sauce and place the enchiladas in the preheated oven for 5 minutes.
11 Remove the dish from the oven, sprinkle with cheese and place back in the oven for 2–3 minutes.
12 Meanwhile, in a small bowl, mash the avocado using the back of a fork. Add the lime juice and season with a pinch of salt and pepper.
13 Serve the enchiladas with a dollop of the mashed avocado.

Vitamin C is necessary for tissue repair; it speeds up the healing processes of those tiny tears in your muscles following periods of strenuous activity or injury to the body.

Each portion provides:
- **vitamin C 70%** RI (56mg)
- **potassium 36%** RI (725mg)
- **vitamin E 30%** RI (2.3mg)

GET SHAKY SALMON PASTA BAKE

CALORIES PER SERVING	CARBS (G)	PROTEIN (G)	FAT (G)	FIBRE (G)
657KCAL	45	45	33	6

» EXERCISE DAY

⟳ IMMUNE SUPPORT

INGREDIENTS

240g fusilli

400g salmon fillets

juice of ½ lemon

5 sprigs fresh dill

1 tbsp rapeseed oil

1 onion (chopped)

1 red pepper (chopped)

1 courgette (chopped)

10 mushrooms (chopped)

2 cloves garlic (chopped)

½ tsp oregano

½ tsp cumin

½ tsp paprika

1 pinch salt

1 pinch black pepper

100g Greek yoghurt

160g Cheddar cheese (grated)

SERVES: 4   **PREPARATION TIME:** 5 MINUTES

COOKING TIME: 30 MINUTES   **TOTAL TIME:** 35 MINUTES

EQUIPMENT: POT, BAKING TRAY, BAKING PAPER, NON-STICK PAN, CASSEROLE DISH

Looking for a wholesome midweek dinner to satisfy the whole family? Look no further! This delicious salmon pasta bake with sautéed vegetables and creamy Greek yoghurt is sure to go down a treat!

1 Preheat the oven to 200°C.
2 Bring a pot of water to the boil. Add the pasta and cook for 10–12 minutes or as per packet instructions. Drain and set aside.
3 Place the salmon fillets on a baking tray lined with baking paper. Drizzle over the lemon juice and place the fresh dill on top. Bake for 10–12 minutes.
4 Meanwhile, heat the oil on a non-stick pan.
5 Sauté the onion on a medium-high heat for 2–3 minutes.
6 Add the red pepper, courgette, mushrooms, garlic, oregano, spices, salt and black pepper. Mix well and sauté for 7–8 minutes on a medium heat, stirring often.
7 Remove the salmon from the oven and take the skin off.
8 Add the salmon to the pan with the veggies and mix through to break the fillets up.
9 Add the pasta and yoghurt to the pan and mix well to fully combine.
10 Pour the contents of the pan into a casserole dish and bake in the oven at 200°C for 5 minutes.
11 Remove from the oven, top with the cheese and replace in the oven for a further 5 minutes until the cheese has melted.

Each portion provides:
- **omega-3 139%** RI (3.1 g)
- **vitamin B12 214%** (5.4μg)
- **vitamin D 186%** (9.3μg)

Vitamin D is an essential nutrient that has been shown to support optimum muscle function, bone health and the avoidance of respiratory infections.

HALF 'N' HALF AUBERGINE LASAGNE

CALORIES PER SERVING	CARBS (G)	PROTEIN (G)	FAT (G)	FIBRE (G)
494KCAL	47	28	22	5

» EXERCISE DAY

⊕ INJURY RECOVERY

INGREDIENTS

1 head broccoli (chopped)

1 aubergine (chopped)

8 mushrooms (sliced)

2 peppers (chopped)

2 tbsp rapeseed oil

½ tsp salt

250g pasta sheets

1 onion (diced)

3 cloves of garlic (chopped)

1 tbsp dried oregano

½ tbsp ground coriander

1 tsp cumin

400g chopped tomatoes

400g passata

100g fresh mozzarella (sliced)

50g red Cheddar cheese (grated)

For the cheese sauce:

500g cottage cheese

1 free-range egg

400g Greek yoghurt

1 tbsp rapeseed oil

SERVES: 6   **PREPARATION TIME:** 5 MINUTES

COOKING TIME: 30 MINUTES   **TOTAL TIME:** 35 MINUTES

EQUIPMENT: BAKING TRAY, CASSEROLE DISH, LARGE NON-STICK PAN, MEDIUM-SIZED POT, 2 MEDIUM-SIZED BOWLS, TIN FOIL

This hearty vegetarian recipe is sure to leave you feeling satisfied, with its creamy cheese sauce, topped with a layer of melted mozzarella and Cheddar cheese.

1   Preheat the oven to 180°C.
2   Place the broccoli, aubergine, mushrooms and peppers on a baking tray with 1 tablespoon of oil and the salt and roast for 15 minutes.
3   Meanwhile, pre-cook the pasta sheets as per packet instructions.
4   To make the sauce, mix the cottage cheese, egg, yoghurt, olive oil and parsley in a bowl and set aside.
5   Heat a tablespoon of oil on a large non-stick pan.
6   Add the onion, garlic, dried oregano, coriander and cumin and fry on a medium heat for 5 minutes.
7   Remove the vegetables from the oven. Add to a bowl and mix in the onion mixture, chopped tomatoes and passata.
8   In a large casserole dish, place a layer of pasta sheets, overlapping to avoid spaces.
9   Pour half the vegetables and tomato sauce over the sheets and spread evenly.
10 Next, pour on half of the cheese sauce and spread evenly.
11 Repeat steps 8–10 to add another layer.
12 Top it with the sliced mozzarella and grated Cheddar.
13 Cover with tin foil and place in the oven for 15 minutes.
14 Remove the tin foil and bake for a further 5 minutes to brown the cheese before serving.

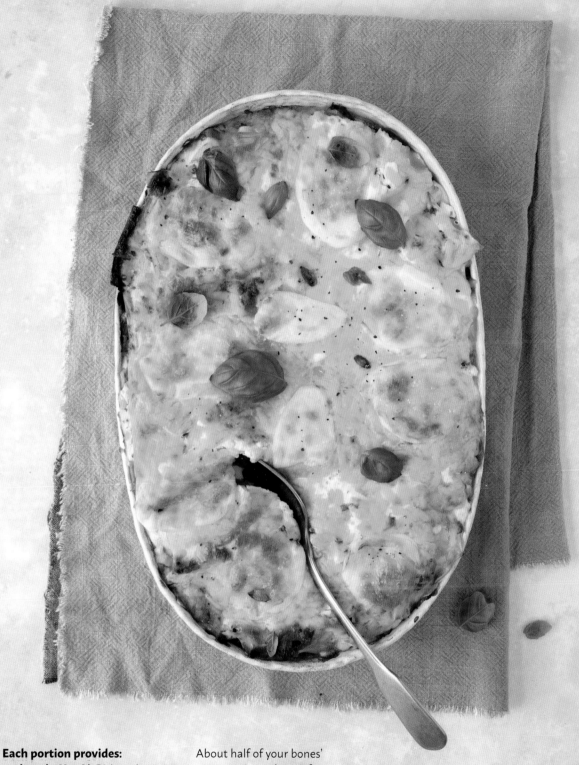

Each portion provides:
- **vitamin K 75%** RI (56µg)
- **phosphorus 68%** RI (475mg)
- **calcium 49%** RI (392mg)

About half of your bones' structure is made up of protein, so sufficient intake of protein following a bone fracture speeds up the healing process and improves bone formation.

HARISSA CHICKEN BURGER

CALORIES PER SERVING	CARBS (G)	PROTEIN (G)	FAT (G)	FIBRE (G)
560KCAL	27	52	27	4

Zz **REST DAY**

⊕ **INJURY RECOVERY**

INGREDIENTS

2 chicken breasts

2 cloves garlic (minced)

½ tsp dried thyme

2 tbsp rapeseed oil

2 tsp harissa

juice of 1 lime

2 burger buns

To garnish:

½ beef tomato (sliced)

½ red onion (sliced)

2 handfuls lettuce leaves

50g Cheddar cheese (sliced or grated)

¼ cucumber (sliced)

SERVES: 2

PREPARATION TIME: 25 MINUTES

COOKING TIME: 10 MINUTES

TOTAL TIME: 35 MINUTES

EQUIPMENT: CLING FILM, ROLLING PIN, MEDIUM-SIZED BOWL, BARBECUE OR GRIDDLE PAN

This delicious, quick and satisfying feel-good recipe delivers a massive 52g of protein! Harissa is a Tunisian hot chilli pepper paste made with roasted red peppers that works incredibly well with chicken... and this burger is no exception! Serve with some roasted sweet potato wedges for a wholesome evening meal.

1 Place the chicken breasts between 2 pieces of cling film and, using the rolling pin, gently pound until flattened.

2 Mix the minced garlic, thyme, oil, harissa and half the lime juice in a bowl.

3 Add the chicken to the bowl and gently rub the marinade into the chicken. Leave to marinate for 20 minutes in the fridge.

4 Heat up the barbecue or griddle pan.

5 Cook the chicken for 5 minutes on each side or until cooked through. Remove from the heat.

6 Toast the burger buns for 1–2 minutes.

7 Place a chicken breast on the bottom of each bun and top with tomato, red onion, some cheese, a handful of lettuce and some cucumber.

8 Squeeze over the rest of the lime juice, add the top buns and serve.

Each portion provides:
- **calcium 76%** RI (608mg)
- **vitamin K 100%** RI (75μg)
- **phosphorus 45%** RI (615mg)

Specific amino acids – the
building blocks of proteins –
such as lysine can increase the
amount of calcium absorbed
into the bone matrix, aiding the
regeneration of bone tissue.

LAMB CHILLI CON CARNE

CALORIES PER SERVING	CARBS (G)	PROTEIN (G)	FAT (G)	FIBRE (G)
560KCAL	27	52	27	4

Zz REST DAY

ⓒ IMMUNE SUPPORT

INGREDIENTS

1 tbsp rapeseed oil

1 onion (chopped)

3 red chilli peppers (finely
    chopped)

2 cloves garlic (minced)

2 bell peppers (chopped)

600g lamb mince

5 tsp cumin

2 tsp cinnamon

1 tbsp paprika

400g tinned chopped tomatoes

juice of 1 lime

400g tinned kidney beans

2 tbsp tomato purée

1 handful fresh coriander
    (chopped)

1 tbsp honey

SERVES: 4

PREPARATION TIME: 5 MINUTES

COOK TIME: 35 MINUTES

TOTAL TIME: 40 MINUTES

EQUIPMENT: LARGE COOKING POT

Lamb chilli is a great alternative to beef. Fresh lamb combines wonderfully with spices and fresh herbs to provide a really tasty and nutritious meal. Cumin is the main flavoring ingredient in this chilli, adding delicious nutty, peppery and warm notes.

1 Heat the oil in a pot and sauté the onion on medium heat for 5 minutes before adding the chillies, garlic and bell peppers.
2 Add the minced lamb, cumin, cinnamon and paprika to the pan, making sure to continually mix.
3 Cook until the meat turns brown, then add the chopped tomatoes and simmer for 20 minutes.
4 Add the lime juice, kidney beans and tomato purée and stir well.
5 Leave to simmer for another 5 minutes.
6 Add the chopped fresh coriander and honey to taste, and then serve with rice. This also works well with sour cream, guacamole, Cheddar cheese and lettuce.

Each portion provides:
- **iron 66%** RI (9.3mg)
- **vitamin B12 120%** RI (3µg)
- **vitamin C 232%** RI (186mg)

Cumin seeds don't just add
flavour – they've been used
in traditional medicine for
centuries for their antioxidant
properties.

LEMON CURRY TROUT

CALORIES PER SERVING	CARBS (G)	PROTEIN (G)	FAT (G)	FIBRE (G)
447KCAL	39	34	18	4

» EXERCISE DAY

⊘ IMMUNE SUPPORT

INGREDIENTS

500g trout fillet
6 cherry tomatoes
1 tbsp rapeseed oil
pinch of salt
6 potatoes (medium sized)

Lemon curry sauce:
1 clove garlic (minced)
2 tbsp rapeseed oil
2 tbsp lemon juice
1 tbsp honey
1 tsp curry powder
1 tbsp balsamic vinegar
1 tbsp mustard
1 tsp garam masala
pinch of salt

SERVES: 4

PREPARATION TIME: 10 MINUTES

COOKING TIME: 20 MINUTES

TOTAL TIME: 30 MINUTES

EQUIPMENT: SMALL BOWL, STEAMER, BAKING PAPER, BAKING TRAY

This simple dish brings you an explosion of flavours – sweetness from the honey, tanginess from the balsamic vinegar and tartness from the lemon. But the fresh, delicate flavour of the fresh trout bursts through the sauce to make this a delicious fish curry with a twist. Serve alongside steamed potatoes for a source of carbohydrates.

1 Preheat the oven to 180°C.
2 To prepare the sauce, mix all the ingredients together in a bowl to form a paste.
3 Place the whole piece of trout on a lined baking tray and pour the sauce over to fully coat it.
4 Sprinkle the tomatoes with a pinch of salt and drizzle with rapeseed oil, and then place beside the trout.
5 Place the tray in the oven and cook for 20 minutes.
6 Meanwhile, steam the potatoes for 10–15 minutes (depending on size) until tender.
7 Remove the trout from the oven and serve with the potatoes.

Each portion provides:
- **vitamin D 205%** RI (10.2μg)
- **vitamin B12 155%** RI (3.9μg)
- **omega 3 101%** RI (2.2 g)

Oily fish are brilliant sources of omega-3, a type of polyunsaturated fatty acid and natural anti-inflammatory.

MEATBALLS AND CHIPS

CALORIES PER SERVING	CARBS (G)	PROTEIN (G)	FAT (G)	FIBRE (G)
528KCAL	44	40	22	6

» EXERCISE DAY

⊘ IMMUNE SUPPORT

INGREDIENTS

For the chips

4 potatoes (approx. 550g,
   cut into even chip slices)

1 tbsp rapeseed oil

sea salt

For the meatballs

30g chorizo (diced)

1 onion (chopped)

1 clove garlic (crushed)

2 tbsp rapeseed oil

8 mushrooms (chopped)

1 bell pepper (chopped)

500g lean beef mince

1 tbsp barbecue sauce

2 tbsp tomato purée

½ tsp chilli powder

½ tbsp paprika

salt

black pepper

1 tin of chopped tomatoes

2 tbsp honey

1 tsp mixed herbs

80g Cheddar cheese (grated)

SERVES: 4 **PREPARATION TIME:** 5 MINUTES

COOKING TIME: 50 MINUTES **TOTAL TIME:** 55 MINUTES

EQUIPMENT: BAKING TRAY, BAKING PAPER, MEDIUM-SIZED POT, NON-STICK PAN, CASSEROLE DISH, LARGE BOWL

Who doesn't love a good wholesome dinner of meatballs and chips? This recipe delivers big on flavour: the tomato sauce has a hint of sweetness from the honey, a smoky flavour from the paprika and tanginess from the barbecue sauce. It's one for all the family to gather around and enjoy!

1 Preheat the oven to 180°C and bring a pot of water to the boil.

2 Add the potatoes to the pot of boiling water and parboil for 8–10 minutes until slightly soft.

3 Line a baking tray with baking paper, drain the potatoes and spread them out on the paper.

4 Sprinkle over some sea salt and drizzle with the oil, and set aside until step 13.

5 Fry the chorizo, onion and garlic on a medium heat for 5 minutes, then remove to a large bowl and set aside.

6 Put some oil on the pan and fry the mushrooms and bell pepper for 10 minutes.

7 While the vegetables are cooking, add the minced beef, barbecue sauce, tomato purée, chilli powder, paprika and some salt and pepper into the bowl with the fried chorizo mix. Mix well using your hands, then form the mixture into 8 meatballs.

8 Next, spoon the vegetables into a casserole dish and cook in the preheated oven for 10 minutes.

9 Meanwhile, fry the meatballs on the pan on medium heat until browned all over.

10 Place the meatballs in the dish along with the vegetables.

11 Mix the tinned tomatoes, honey, mixed herbs and a pinch of salt together in a small bowl.

12 Pour the tomato sauce over the meatballs and vegetables and place both them and your tray of chips in the oven for 20 minutes. (The chips may be ready a little more quickly, so check them after 15 minutes.)

13 Remove both the dish and the tray from the oven. Sprinkle your meatballs with the cheese and return to the oven for 5 more minutes, until the cheese is golden brown and bubbling.

Each portion provides:
- **vitamin B12 119%** RI (3μg)
- **zinc 70%** RI (7mg)
- **iron 24%** RI (3.4mg)

Vitamin B12 is involved in the formation of red blood cells, which carry oxygen through your body and regulate DNA.

NANNY D'S FRIED POTATO WITH BACON AND VEGGIES

CALORIES PER SERVING	CARBS (G)	PROTEIN (G)	FAT (G)	FIBRE (G)
738KCAL	47	56	37	9

》 EXERCISE DAY

✓ IMMUNE SUPPORT

INGREDIENTS

400g potatoes (chopped)

2 tbsp olive oil

1 onion (chopped)

2 cloves garlic (chopped)

150g chicken breast (diced)

200g bacon (diced)

6 chestnut mushrooms (chopped)

½ courgette (sliced)

1 red bell pepper (sliced)

½ tsp salt

½ tsp black pepper

6 cherry tomatoes (chopped)

60g Cheddar cheese (grated)

Each portion provides:
- **vitamin C 174%** RI (139mg)
- **selenium 57%** RI (32μg)
- **zinc 51%** RI (5mg)

Vitamin C has an important role in immune function, collagen synthesis and cortisol synthesis.

SERVES: 2

PREPARATION TIME: 5 MINUTES

COOKING TIME: 30 MINUTES

TOTAL TIME: 35 MINUTES

EQUIPMENT: NON-STICK PAN, MEDIUM-SIZED POT

As a teenager, this was one of my favourite things to come home to after school! You could smell the fried bacon and onions as you walked down the lane to my grandmother's house. My sister and I would sit in Nanny's kitchen enjoying the grub while watching *The Den*. Sharing this recipe with your family will be sure to create great memories, as it has for me!

1. Bring a pot of water to the boil.
2. Add the potatoes to the water and parboil for 8 minutes, then drain.
3. Meanwhile, heat the oil in a pan and fry the onion on a medium heat for 5 minutes, until soft.
4. Add the garlic and chicken and cook for 6–8 minutes until the chicken is almost cooked through.
5. Preheat the oven to 180°C.
6. Next, add the bacon, mushrooms, courgette, bell pepper, salt and black pepper to the pan and fry for 5 minutes.
7. Add the potatoes to the pan with a tablespoon of olive oil. Leave to brown slightly for 5 minutes.
8. Next sprinkle the chopped cherry tomatoes and grated cheese over the top and put in the preheated oven for 5 minutes until the cheese is nicely melted.

POTATO STEAK BOWL

CALORIES PER SERVING	CARBS (G)	PROTEIN (G)	FAT (G)	FIBRE (G)
667KCAL	55	39	33	10

>> EXERCISE DAY

⟳ IMMUNE SUPPORT

SERVES: 2 **PREPARATION TIME:** 5 MINUTES

COOKING TIME: 25 MINUTES **TOTAL TIME:** 30 MINUTES

EQUIPMENT: NON-STICK PAN, BAKING TRAY, 3 BOWLS

INGREDIENTS

2 medium potatoes (sliced)

3 tbsp rapeseed oil

½ tsp garlic powder

½ tsp cumin seeds

½ tsp salt

2 tbsp lime juice

2 tbsp soy sauce

1 thumb-sized piece ginger
(grated)

½ tsp chilli powder

1 tbsp honey

200g lean beef steak (sliced into
even strips, less than 2cm thick)

1 onion (sliced)

2 cloves garlic (crushed)

1 red bell pepper (sliced)

1 yellow bell pepper (sliced)

30g French beans

½ tsp smoked paprika

For the tzatziki:

¼ cucumber (grated)

2 tbsp Greek yoghurt

1 tsp dill (fresh or dried)

1 tbsp lime juice

Not only is this recipe easy to make and super tasty, but it is also packed with fresh seasonal ingredients that pack a big nutritional punch. Potatoes and steak will provide the carbohydrate and protein, while the mix of vegetables offers vitamins, minerals and an abundance of fibre.

1 Preheat the oven to 200°C.
2 Toss the sliced potatoes with 1 tablespoon of rapeseed oil, the garlic powder, cumin seeds and salt, place on a baking tray and roast in the oven for 20–25 minutes. Turn the potatoes halfway through cooking.
3 Meanwhile, in a bowl, mix the lime juice, soy sauce, ginger, chilli powder and honey.
4 Add the steak strips to the bowl, mixing well to coat the meat.
5 Heat 1 tablespoon of rapeseed oil in a non-stick pan over medium–high heat.
6 Add the onion and garlic and sauté for 4–5 minutes.
7 Add the chopped bell peppers, French beans and smoked paprika and cook for 5 minutes. Remove the vegetables from the pan into a bowl and set aside.
8 Add 1 tablespoon of oil to the pan and sear the steak. Allow to cook for 3 to 4 minutes (medium) on each side.
9 Mix the ingredients for the tzatziki together in a small bowl.
10 To assemble, divide the potato slices between two bowls, then top with the steak, onion, peppers and French beans, and a dollop of tzatziki.

Each portion provides:
- **vitamin C 295%** RI (236mg)
- **vitamin B12 84%** RI (2.1 ug)
- **iron 34%** RI (4.8mg)

Iron has many benefits, helping with cognitive function, immune function, gastrointestinal function and regulation of body temperature as well as blood health.

SALMON SPAGHETTI

CALORIES PER SERVING	CARBS (G)	PROTEIN (G)	FAT (G)	FIBRE (G)
519KCAL	46	33	23	8

» EXERCISE DAY

⟳ IMMUNE SUPPORT

INGREDIENTS

200g spaghetti

2 salmon fillets

2 tbsp rapeseed oil (plus extra
 for drizzling)

1 tbsp lemon juice

1 onion (chopped)

2 cloves garlic (crushed)

salt and black pepper

1 tsp dried oregano

6 mushrooms (chopped)

100g garden peas

6 sun-dried tomatoes (chopped)

1 red pepper (roasted or fresh,
 sliced)

2 tbsp tomato purée

100g Greek yoghurt

50g parmesan cheese (shavings)

SERVES: 4

PREPARATION TIME: 5 MINUTES

COOKING TIME: 25 MINUTES

TOTAL TIME: 30 MINUTES

EQUIPMENT: BAKING TRAY, MEDIUM-SIZED PAN

This quick and easy nutritious dish provides a great source of all three macronutrients, making it a great option for training days.

1 Place a pot of water on a medium heat and bring to the boil. Preheat the oven to 180°C.
2 Cook the pasta as per packet instructions.
3 Meanwhile, place the salmon fillets in an ovenproof dish, drizzle with a tablespoon of rapeseed oil and the lemon juice and cook in the oven for 10 minutes.
4 Heat 1 tablespoon of oil in a medium-sized pan and sauté the onion and garlic with some salt and pepper and the oregano for 5 minutes.
5 Next add the mushrooms, garden peas, sun-dried tomatoes and red pepper and cook until soft.
6 Add the tomato purée and yoghurt and mix well.
7 When the pasta is cooked, strain it and pour it into the pan with the vegetables.
8 Remove the salmon from the oven and mix it through the pasta to break it up.
9 Stir the parmesan cheese through the pasta before serving.

Each portion provides:
- **vitamin B12 103%** RI (2.6μg)
- **omega-3 99%** RI (5.9mg)
- **vitamin C 81%** RI (65mg)

Vitamin B12 and omega-3 play an important role in the support and protection of healthy blood and nerve cells in the body.

TANGY TASTY PRAWN CURRY

CALORIES PER SERVING	CARBS (G)	PROTEIN (G)	FAT (G)	FIBRE (G)
582KCAL	65	23	26	5

≫ **INTENSE EXERCISE DAY**

⟳ **IMMUNE SUPPORT**

INGREDIENTS

1 tbsp rapeseed oil

1 onion (chopped)

2 cloves garlic (crushed)

1 thumb-sized piece ginger
   (grated)

1 pinch salt

100g chestnut mushrooms
   (chopped)

1 red bell pepper (chopped)

1 yellow bell pepper (chopped)

400g prawns

3 tbsp balsamic vinegar

2 tbsp mango chutney

400ml coconut milk

1 tbsp curry powder

1 tbsp dried basil

1 tbsp fresh oregano

240g rice

2 handfuls baby spinach

SERVES: 4

PREPARATION TIME: 5 MINUTES

COOKING TIME: 30 MINUTES

TOTAL TIME: 35 MINUTES

EQUIPMENT: LARGE NON-STICK PAN, MEDIUM-SIZED POT

Curries are a great way of packing in flavour and nutrients. This curry combines both savoury and sweet flavours from the curry powder, ginger and mango chutney, while the coconut milk offers a lovely creaminess. For a lower-calorie recipe, swap to reduced-fat coconut milk.

1 Bring a pot of water to the boil, allowing for two parts water to one part rice.
2 Add the rice to the boiling water and leave to simmer until cooked or the water has been absorbed (approx. 20 minutes).
3 Meanwhile, heat the oil in a non-stick pan.
4 Once hot, fry the onion, garlic, ginger and salt on a medium heat for 5–6 minutes.
5 Add the mushrooms and peppers to the pan and cook for 10 minutes until soft.
6 Add in the prawns, balsamic vinegar, mango chutney, coconut milk, curry powder, basil and oregano. Mix through and leave to simmer on a medium heat for 10 minutes or until prawns are cooked through.
7 Finally, add the spinach leaves to the curry and stir through until wilted – then serve up.

Each portion provides:
- **vitamin C 134%** RI (108mg)
- **copper 53%** RI (0.53mg)
- **manganese 65%** RI (1.3mg)

There is some evidence that copper can delay exhaustion time and enhance endurance by increasing oxygenation. Foods that are good sources of copper include shellfish, nuts, legumes, buckwheat and organ meats.

DRINKS AND SMOOTHIES

BERRY HAPPY KEFIR SMOOTHIE

CALORIES PER SERVING	CARBS (G)	PROTEIN (G)	FAT (G)	FIBRE (G)
488KCAL	45	37	18	9

>> EXERCISE DAY

⟲ IMMUNE SUPPORT

INGREDIENTS

150ml unflavoured kefir

1 tbsp almond butter

1 scoop protein powder

100g frozen berries

½ banana

1 tsp honey

2 tbsp oats

½ thumb-sized piece of ginger
(optional)

100ml water

5 ice cubes

SERVES: 1

PREPARATION TIME: 5 MINUTES

TOTAL TIME: 5 MINUTES

EQUIPMENT: BLENDER

Keep your gut happy with this creamy kefir smoothie! As well as being nutritious, it is also a quick high-energy option, perfect to whip up when you're in need of something substantial to keep you going. It packs a punch of high-quality protein, fats, carbohydrates and fibre.

1. Place all the ingredients in a blender and blitz. For a thicker or thinner smoothie, adjust the amount of water and ice cubes.
2. Serve up in your favourite glass, and enjoy!

Each portion provides:
- **vitamin E 52%** RI (6.2mg)
- **calcium 34%** RI (272mg)
- **vitamin C 38%** RI (30.2mg)

Kefir is a fermented milk drink. Fermented foods have been shown to support gut health, which is linked to overall health and immunity.

BOOSTER C JUICE

CALORIES PER SERVING	CARBS (G)	PROTEIN (G)	FAT (G)	FIBRE (G)
169KCAL	39	3	0	1

» EXERCISE DAY

⊘ IMMUNE SUPPORT

INGREDIENTS

300ml orange juice

2 tbsp fresh lemon juice

2 tbsp fresh lime juice

juice of ½ grapefruit

3 ice cubes

SERVES: 1

PREPARATION TIME: 5 MINUTES

TOTAL TIME: 5 MINUTES

EQUIPMENT: BLENDER

The mixture of fruits in this recipe combine really well to deliver a refreshing flavour that packs a whopping 141mg of vitamin C – enough to cover your daily recommended intake. Vitamin C is recognised in the history books for being the antidote for the disease scurvy.

1 Place all of the ingredients together in a blender and blitz.
2 Add more ice cubes if you'd like the juice a bit thicker.

Each portion provides:
- **vitamin C 176%** RI (141mg)
- **potassium 34%** RI (682mg)
- **vitamin B1 27%** RI (0.3mg)

This recipe can be used to support the immune system in recovery from illness such as the common cold, thanks to its high levels of vitamin C.

DROP A BEET 'SHOT'

CALORIES PER SERVING	CARBS (G)	PROTEIN (G)	FAT (G)	FIBRE (G)
85KCAL	19	2	0	2

» **EXERCISE DAY**

INGREDIENTS

2 medium fresh beetroots

200ml coconut water

1 tbsp lemon juice

2 tsp honey

2 fresh mint leaves

SERVES: 2

PREPARATION TIME: 2 MINUTES

TOTAL TIME: 2 MINUTES

EQUIPMENT: FOOD PROCESSOR

This zesty beetroot drink is packed full of goodness – a great way of consuming a high amount of nutrients in a small portion, and the refreshing taste makes it all the better! Make sure not to 'drop a beet' on your good clothes!

1   Blitz all of the ingredients together in a food processor for 2 minutes until completely smooth.

Each portion provides:
- **vitamin C 14%** RI (11mg)
- **potassium 17%** RI (339mg)
- **folates 62%** RI (124µg)

Beetroots are high in nitrates, which get converted into nitric oxide in the body. Nitric oxide causes blood vessels to widen, causing blood flow to increase and allowing more oxygen and nutrients to be delivered to the muscles as they work.

FRESH MINT BANANA SMOOTHIE

CALORIES PER SERVING	CARBS (G)	PROTEIN (G)	FAT (G)	FIBRE (G)
450KCAL	44	36	15	5

>>> INTENSE EXERCISE DAY

(+) INJURY RECOVERY

INGREDIENTS

200ml milk

1 scoop vanilla whey protein
  powder

10g oats

1 handful mint leaves

1 tbsp Greek yoghurt

1 banana

5 ice cubes

SERVES: 1

PREPARATION TIME: 5 MINS

TOTAL TIME: 5 MIN

EQUIPMENT: BLENDER

Fresh mint brings a delicious, lively flavour to this protein smoothie! It's ideal for recovery after training or competition or even a delicious snack.

1   Place all ingredients in a blender and blitz. For a thinner or thicker smoothie, add more milk or adjust the number of ice cubes.

Each portion provides:
- **calcium 63%** RI (504mg)
- **potassium 56%** RI (1121mg)
- **vitamin B12 78%** RI (1.9µg)

This recipe replenishes energy stores and electrolytes, so it's a good bet for post-performance recovery.

G&T RECOVERY TEA

CALORIES PER SERVING	CARBS (G)	PROTEIN (G)	FAT (G)	FIBRE (G)
106KCAL	25	2	0	1

» EXERCISE DAY

⊘ IMMUNE SUPPORT

INGREDIENTS

600ml water (boiling)

1 thumb-sized piece of fresh ginger (grated)

1 tbsp ground turmeric

juice of 1 lemon

2 tsp honey

SERVES: 2

PREPARATION TIME: 2 MINUTES

TOTAL TIME: 5 MINUTES

EQUIPMENT: POT, TEA STRAINER

Ginger and turmeric are combined here for a refreshing tea with an appealing hue. Turmeric is the spice that gives curry its yellow colour and has been used for thousands of years in India as a medical herb. Ginger is a flowering plant that originated in China and is closely related to turmeric.

1 Pour the boiling water into a pot over medium heat.
2 Add the ginger, turmeric, lemon juice and honey.
3 Simmer for 3 minutes.
4 Pour the tea evenly into two mugs through a strainer.

Each portion provides:
- **vitamin C 65%** RI (52mg)

Ginger is high in anti-inflammatory and antioxidant properties.

HOT CHOCOLATE

CALORIES PER SERVING	CARBS (G)	PROTEIN (G)	FAT (G)	FIBRE (G)
266KCAL	19	11	16	5

>> **EXERCISE DAY**

⊕ **INJURY RECOVERY**

INGREDIENTS

500ml milk

4 tsp cacao powder

1 tsp honey

2 squares dark chocolate

SERVES: 2

COOKING TIME: 10 MINUTES

TOTAL TIME: 10 MINUTES

EQUIPMENT: SMALL POT

This chocolatey treat makes for a delicious and comforting hot drink – ideal for those colder evenings when you need something to warm you from within! You can experiement with adding cinnamon and ginger powder for extra warmth and nutrients too.

1 Add the milk to a small pot and place over a medium heat. Heat for 3–4 minutes until quite warm.
2 Mix the cacao powder into a paste with a drop of hot water and add to the pot with the milk.
3 Add the honey and chocolate and mix until the chocolate is fully melted through before serving.

Each portion provides:
- **vitamin B12 94%** RI (2.3μg)
- **phosphorus 49%** RI (345mg)
- **calcium 41%** RI (328mg)

Aside from calcium, milk also offers electrolytes such as phosphorus, sodium and potassium, making it more hydrating than water alone.

MANGO SPLIT SMOOTHIE

CALORIES PER SERVING	CARBS (G)	PROTEIN (G)	FAT (G)	FIBRE (G)
427KCAL	52	34	10	1.4

>>> INTENSE EXERCISE DAY

⊘ IMMUNE SUPPORT

INGREDIENTS

2 scoops vanilla protein powder

200g natural yoghurt

300g mango (fresh or frozen)

1 banana

100g spinach

1 tsp fresh ginger

½ tsp ground turmeric

¼ tsp black pepper

2 tsp honey

200ml milk

8–10 ice cubes

SERVES: 2

PREPARATION TIME: 3 MINUTES

TOTAL TIME: 5 MINUTES

EQUIPMENT: BLENDER

This creamy mango smoothie is chock-full of many different vitamins and minerals, as well as being a great source of carbohydrates and protein. It's also filled with nutrients with anti-inflammatory properties that will support your recovery from a training session, common cold or injury.

1   Place all of the ingredients in a blender and blitz until completely smooth. For a thicker or thinner smoothie, adjust the amount of milk and ice cubes.

Each portion provides:
- **vitamin C 86%** RI (69mg)
- **calcium 47%** RI (372mg)
- **vitamin A 37%** RI (299mg)

Given its high levels of vitamin C, this is an excellent recipe to support the immune system.

SPEEDY RECOVERY SMOOTHIE

CALORIES PER SERVING	CARBS (G)	PROTEIN (G)	FAT (G)	FIBRE (G)
344KCAL	56	21	4	7

>>> INTENSE EXERCISE DAY

 IMMUNE SUPPORT

INGREDIENTS

30g grapes

100g strawberries

1 banana

5 cherries, pitted

1 handful of spinach

1 tbsp honey

1 tsp ginger

1 scoop of whey powder

200ml unsweetened almond milk

6 ice cubes

SERVES: 1

PREPARATION TIME: 3 MINUTES

TOTAL TIME: 5 MINUTES

EQUIPMENT: BLENDER

This refreshing smoothie is high in carbohydrate and protein, which is the perfect combination to have after exercise to kick-start your recovery. It contains over 20g of protein in total, which is bang on for recovery and muscle repair For a vegan-friendly smoothie, use vegan protein powder and replace the honey with maple syrup.

1   Place all of the ingredients in the blender and blitz until completely smooth. For a thicker or thinner smoothie, adjust the amount of milk and ice cubes to suit your preference.

Each portion provides:
- **vitamin C 207%** RI (165mg)
- **potassium 48%** RI (952mg)
- **chloride 85%** RI (680mg)

Potassium and chloride are two of the main electrolytes needed by the body for proper nerve and muscle function.

TITAN SHOT

CALORIES PER SERVING	CARBS (G)	PROTEIN (G)	FAT (G)	FIBRE (G)
123KCAL	28	1	1	3

>> EXERCISE DAY

⊙ IMMUNE SUPPORT

INGREDIENTS

½ tbsp turmeric (fresh or
    powdered)
½ thumb-sized piece of ginger
100ml freshly squeezed orange
    juice
100ml pineapple juice
100ml coconut water
¼ tsp black pepper
1 tsp honey
handful of ice cubes (for serving)

SERVES: 1

PREPARATION TIME: 3 MINUTES

TOTAL TIME: 3 MINUTES

EQUIPMENT: FOOD PROCESSOR

Use fresh or powdered turmeric to make this almighty
powerful shot of pure goodness! The fruit juice and honey
add another level of nutrition to the drink while disguising
the peppery spice of the turmeric.

1 Blitz all of the ingredients together in a food processor for
   2 minutes until completely smooth.
2 Serve in a small glass over ice.

GINGER ZINGER SHOT

CALORIES PER SERVING	CARBS (G)	PROTEIN (G)	FAT (G)	FIBRE (G)
140KCAL	19	1	7	2

» EXERCISE DAY

✓ IMMUNE SUPPORT

INGREDIENTS

150g pineapple
1 thumb-sized piece ginger
200ml light coconut milk
1 tbsp honey
handful of ice cubes

SERVES: 2
PREPARATION TIME: 3 MINUTES
TOTAL TIME: 3 MINUTES
EQUIPMENT: FOOD PROCESSOR

This is a refreshing drink yet the fresh ginger gives it a lovely warming kick at the same time. It's so simple to make, and a little like the Puerto Rican piña colada – sort of!

1 Blitz all of the ingredients together in a food processor for 2 minutes until completely smooth. You can blitz the ice cubes with the drink, or serve it over ice instead.

Each portion provides:
- **vitamin C 16%** RI (13mg)
- **copper 16%** RI (0.16mg)
- **manganese 34%** RI (0.68mg)

Pineapple and ginger are good sources of vitamin C, which is an antioxidant that aids the production of white blood cells, helping to defend the body in times of stress.

TROPICAL REFRESH

CALORIES PER SERVING	CARBS (G)	PROTEIN (G)	FAT (G)	FIBRE (G)
204KCAL	47	2	1	6

⋙ INTENSE EXERCISE DAY

⟳ IMMUNE SUPPORT

INGREDIENTS

200ml coconut water

200ml orange juice

100ml cranberry juice

1 tsp honey

¼ tsp salt

SERVES: 1

PREPARATION TIME: 1 MINUTE

TOTAL TIME: 1 MINUTE

EQUIPMENT: BOTTLE

A homemade sports drink is easy to put together and effective for rehydration during exercise. It sounds so simple but when you enjoy the taste of a drink you tend to drink more of it. This is easy to make and perfect for on-the-go around training and competition.

1 Add the ingredients to a bottle and shake well before drinking.

Each portion provides:
- **sodium 33%** RI (798mg)
- **vitamin C 149%** RI (119mg)

This recipe is a good source of vitamin C and electrolytes and can be used in recovery from performance by replenishing energy stores and electrolyte balance.

DIPS AND
SPREADS

CHIA SEED BERRY JAM

CALORIES PER SERVING	CARBS (G)	PROTEIN (G)	FAT (G)	FIBRE (G)
19KCAL	3.4	0.4	0.5	0.9

>> **EXERCISE DAY**

INGREDIENTS

300g mixed berries (fresh or
    frozen)
2 tbsp honey
2 tbsp chia seeds
zest of ½ a lemon

MAKES: APPROX. 350G

PREPARATION TIME: 2 MINUTES

COOKING TIME: 20 MINUTES

TOTAL TIME: 25 MINUTES, PLUS COOLING TIME

EQUIPMENT: LARGE POT, JAM JAR OR STORAGE CONTAINER

This chia seed berry jam is a beauty. Once you make it you will find yourself going through it in a flash. It goes well with your overnight oats, toast, natural yoghurt and protein pudding.

1 Pour the berries into a pot with 2 tbsp water and simmer, stirring regularly, for about 20 minutes until the liquid is reduced.
2 Next add in the honey, lemon zest and chia seeds and mix well.
3 Remove from the heat and allow to cool.
4 When the mixture is cool, pour into an air-tight container or jar. You can store the jam in the fridge and it will keep for a week.

ROASTED BELL PEPPER HUMMUS

CALORIES PER SERVING	CARBS (G)	PROTEIN (G)	FAT (G)	FIBRE (G)
163KCAL	12	6	10	4

» EXERCISE DAY

◔ IMMUNE SUPPORT

INGREDIENTS

400g tinned chickpeas

3 tbsp aquafaba (chickpea water)

2 roasted red peppers

1 clove garlic

2 tbsp tahini

1 tbsp lemon juice

2 tbsp olive oil

¼ tsp cumin

½ tsp cayenne pepper

¼ tsp salt

SERVES: 6

PREPARATION TIME: 2 MINUTES

TOTAL TIME: 5 MINUTES

EQUIPMENT: FOOD PROCESSOR

This super-quick hummus made with roasted red peppers is simple to make and vegan friendly. It works great served with crackers, roasted vegetables or a fresh salad.

1 Drain the chickpeas, reserving 3 tbsp of the liquid.
2 Blitz all of the ingredients, including the 3 tbsp liquid from the chickpeas, in a food processor for 2 minutes, until completely smooth.
3 You may need to stop the food processor, scrape the sides and blitz again to ensure all of the chickpeas are blitzed.
4 Remove from the food processor and serve.

Each portion provides:
- **vitamin C 47%** RI (40mg)
- **manganese 35%** RI (0.7mg)
- **phosphorus 16%** (114mg)

Manganese is an essential trace mineral that plays a role in blood clotting.

PART FOUR: FAQ

HEALTH-RELATED FAQ

1 An egg a day?

The average-sized egg provides an attractive blend of highly bio-available protein, essential fats, vitamins and minerals. According to the World Health Organization (WHO) eggs are a 'very good source of selenium, iodine, and vitamin B, protein, molybdenum, phosphorus, vitamin B5, vitamin B12 and vitamin D'. This illustrates just how nutritious eggs are and how much they can contribute to a varied and balanced diet. Although there is no clear consensus on how many eggs you can or should consume daily, I would suggest that up to two eggs daily is a safe guideline.

2 Does drinking tea or coffee result in dehydration?

If you are a habitual tea or coffee drinker, then drinking tea or coffee does not lead to dehydration. In fact, it will add to your fluid intake and help you to meet your daily fluid needs.

3 Is adding salt to your food as bad as people are led to believe?

If you are regularly physically active, eat a balanced diet and do not suffer from high blood pressure, normal salt intake is unlikely to be a risk for your health. Adding salt to your food for taste and flavour is not a health risk once you are not regularly exceeding intake guidelines. Athletes or those who regularly exercise can have a slightly higher intake of sodium or salt, as sodium is lost through sweating

4 How many cups of coffee can I drink daily?

Three to four cups of organic, freshly brewed coffee seems to be the number that offers health benefits without negative side effects. For someone who metabolises caffeine efficiently and doesn't suffer strong side effects, a cup or two in the morning and a cup in the early afternoon seems to be about right.

5 Is food enough or do I need to supplement?

A supplement is 'a food, food component, nutrient, or non-food compound that is purposefully ingested in addition to the habitually consumed diet with the aim of achieving a specific health and/ or performance benefit' (Maughan et al., 2018). In general, you shouldn't need to take a supplement if you are consuming a balanced diet. Vitamin D during the winter months is probably the exception. If you're concerned about potential deficiencies, it's worth attending your GP for a blood test to determine if any supplements are needed.

Commonly used supplements include vitamins, minerals, dairy protein, caffeine and creatine. All of these products either claim to, or will, add something to your nutrition, depending on the evidence to support their use and your current lifestyle and nutrition.

Supplements are used for:

- Micronutrient deficiencies
- Convenient consumption of energy and macronutrients

6 How do I know how much protein I need?

The International Society of Sports Nutrition (ISSN) recommends that protein intakes for people who regularly engage in physical activity should be between 1.4g and 2g per kg of bodyweight per day (g/kg/day). For people who are involved in regular physical training or resistance training, a figure closer to 2g/kg/day is recommended.

7 What is omega-3?

Omega-3 fatty acids come in three main forms: alpha-linolenic acid (ALA), eicosapentaenoic acid (EPA) and docosahexaenoic acid (DHA).

ALA is an essential fatty acid, meaning that the body cannot make it, so we must consume it through our foods (and/or supplements) if necessary.

When ALA is consumed, our body can convert it to EPA and then a small amount may be converted into DHA. It is, therefore, important to consume other foods containing EPA and DHA in addition to ensure that we meet our requirements of all these omega-3 fatty acids.

8 How can I add more fibre to my diet?

There are many simple ways to increase fibre intake in your diet that can lead to long-lasting benefits for your digestion and gut health. The focus should be on a variety of vegetables, whole grains and fruits but there are also practical changes you can make.

Some simple examples are as follows:

- Add more fruits or vegetables to your meals.
- Include plenty of vegetables with your meals – a salad or roast veg are both good options.
- Add pulses and vegetables where possible, such as to your curries, salads and sandwiches.
- Choose whole, fresh fruits over fruit juices or smoothies.
- Choose whole-grain options – wholewheat pasta, brown rice, brown bread and so on.
- Prepare your own homemade granola and protein bars to get you through the week.
- Replace processed foods like chocolate and crisps with homemade alternatives such as chocolate nut bars or popcorn.
- Leave the skin on fruit and vegetables where possible – for example, kiwis, apples, plums, potatoes, courgettes, aubergines.
- Include a hearty soup or stew packed with vegetables and pulses (beans, peas, lentils) in your meal plan.
- Add porridge oats instead of flour to your recipes where possible – for example, in pancakes, bread or burgers.
- Snack on nuts and seeds or add them to meals such as yoghurts and salads.

9 What is intermittent fasting?

Intermittent fasting involves eating within a certain time frame, such as 8 hours, and fasting for the remaining 16 hours of the day. For this reason, intermittent fasting is often referred to as 'time-restricted eating'. It may be beneficial for those pursuing weight loss but more research is needed regarding any other potential benefits, especially among athletes. Applying a 12-hour eating window and a 12-hour fasting window may be a more practical and sustainable approach to your eating routine.

10 Are there health risks associated with consuming whey protein powder?

People with a dairy protein allergy or lactose intolerance or those who experience digestive problems from dairy products should avoid consuming whey protein. There is no evidence to suggest that there are any other health risks from consuming whey protein within the recommended daily guidelines.

SPORTS NUTRITION FAQ

1 What is meal timing and is it important?

Meal timing is the timing of any meals or nutrients across the day to provide a benefit for performance, recovery and/or adaptation. Meeting your total daily intake for calories and nutrients is the priority, but when a person is training most days or twice a day, the timing of the intake of nutrients for recovery is an important nutrition strategy.

2 What is a recovery meal?

A recovery meal is a meal eaten after exercise to help our body replenish energy stores and repair muscle. A recovery meal will usually contain a source of carbohydrate and some protein.

3 Why is protein important after exercise?

Athletes take protein (in whatever form) after exercise to promote recovery by helping to repair damaged muscle fibres, but protein is also involved in countless other functions, such as reducing muscle protein breakdown and facilitating hormone production and immune support, all vital for recovery.

4 What happens if I eat more protein than I need in one sitting?

Research done on different patterns of protein consumption suggests that the body can manage more protein than is commonly believed. Protein usage will depend on total daily protein consumption, but it seems the body is capable of 'slowing' protein digestion to create an amino acid pool to draw from when needed. The small intestine is where the majority of protein in the form of amino acids is absorbed by the body. Protein that is not absorbed is transported to the colon where it is fermented by bacteria. Consistent excessive protein intake will lead to an increased protein excretion in faecal matter, and a bad smell!

5 Should I use a protein supplement?

Numerous whole food options can provide nutrient-rich sources of protein as quick snacks around sessions – milk, yoghurt, boiled eggs, cold meats, pulses and nuts. But a protein powder supplement (particularly whey or casein protein) can offer a practical, time-efficient and convenient method of meeting protein needs if you are time poor or just don't have high-protein foods to hand. This is particularly true for athletes who regularly train to a high intensity.

6 Does taking the supplement creatine benefit performance?

Creatine is a popular nutritional supplement, commonly used as an ergogenic aid by athletes and gym goers. Creatine supplementation gives rise to intramuscular creatine, which may lead to improved performance and adaptations to training. Some of the benefits to supplementing with creatine include improved power output, increases in anaerobic running capacity, enhanced recovery and greater training tolerance.

7 What causes stomach cramps or bloating during intense exercise?

There are a number of potential reasons for gut issues during exercise, including stress, meal timing and certain foods. Specific nutrients can cause gut issues if consumed too close to training and/or an event. These include protein, fibre, fat, fructose (a type of carbohydrate) and dairy products. However, this varies hugely between athletes.

8 How much carbohydrate do I need before a game or competition?

The amount of carbohydrate required in the 36-hour lead-up to a game or competition will depend on the length and intensity of the competition. For team-sport athletes, in a competition for >70 minutes, the requirement may be >8g of carbohydrate per kg of body mass for carbohydrate loading. This equates to 640–800g per day for an 80kg athlete. A simple way of doing this would be to add two extra carbohydrate meals on top of your typical food intake (usually six meals, as outlined on page 44). You could also use fruit juices to add carbohydrate to your meal plan – apple juice often works effectively here.

9 When should I have my last meal before a competition?

Your stomach should be more or less empty at the start of a competition, or indeed any intense exercise. For this reason, your last meal should be three to four hours pre-competition. The meal should be high in carbohydrate, easy to digest, with small to moderate amounts of protein, fat and fibre. Pasta and chicken are common choices but rice, noodles, potatoes and even something like pancakes can also work well.

MICRONUTRIENT INDEX

VITAMIN A THE SCIENCE

- Vitamin A protects our cells from damage caused by free radicals (Food and Nutrition Board, 2001).

RECIPES

Lunches and Dinners:
- Lentil Curry with Roasted Balsamic Potatoes **pg 144**
- Prawn and Sweet Potato Salad **pg 141**
- Half 'n' Half Aubergine Lasagne **pg 228**
- Coddin' Me Curry **pg 218**

Drinks and Smoothies:
- Mango Split Smoothie **pg 260**

VITAMIN C THE SCIENCE

- High doses of vitamin C supplementation can reduce eccentric exercise-induced muscle soreness and damage following high-intensity exercise engagement (Bryer et al., 2006).

- Vitamin C decreases oxidative stress when taken in doses of 200–1000mg. A small dose of vitamin C (200–1000mg), provided by five servings of fruit and vegetables daily, is believed to be sufficient to reduce oxidative stress (Braakhuis et al., 2012).

- Short-term intakes (1 to 2 weeks) of >0.2 g of vitamin C daily may benefit athletes during times of increased stress. Further research is required to clarify a dose-response and nutrient timing protocols on vitamin C (Braakhuis et al., 2012).

- Vitamin C supplements do not seem to have an ergogenic effect in athletes where their diet provides adequate amounts. As strenuous and prolonged exercise has been shown to increase the need for vitamin C, physical performance can be compromised with marginal vitamin C status or deficiency (Lukaski, 2004).

RECIPES

VITAMIN D THE SCIENCE

- There are no specific dietary vitamin D recommendations for athletes; however, research indicates that for muscle function, bone health, and avoidance of respiratory infections, maintenance concentrations between 80–100 nmol/L of serum 25-hydroxyvitamin D (circulating form of vitamin D) are required (von Hurst et al., 2015).

- It is well established that many athletes are vitamin D deficient due to a lack of sunlight exposure. Emerging evidence suggests that being deficient in vitamin D can impair muscle regeneration following damaging exercise (Owens et al., 2015, 2018).

- In a randomised, double-blind, placebo-controlled study, active adults who supplemented with vitamin D for 35 days had reduced inflammation immediately and improved recovery and power output compared to a placebo group (Barker et al., 2013).

- Athletes who live at northern latitudes or who train primarily indoors throughout the year, including gymnasts and combat sports people, are at risk for poor vitamin D status, especially if they do not monitor their dietary intake of vitamin D (Meier et al., 2004).

RECIPES

Breakfasts:
- Baked Egg Shakshuka **pg 78**
- Black Pudding Avocado Toast **pg 80**
- Black Pudding Frittata **pg 82**
- French Toast with Greek Yoghurt **pg 94**

Lunches and Dinners:
- Salmon Hash **pg 158**
- MD's Bulgur Wheat Salmon **pg 146**
- Cajun Salmon Burrito Bowl **pg 122**
- Claudia's Potato Salad with Boiled Eggs **pg 128**
- Creamy Salmon Mega Mix **pg 134**
- Get Shaky Salmon Pasta Bake **pg 226**

VITAMIN K THE SCIENCE

- A recent study showed that 4 weeks of vitamin K supplementation increased aerobically trained athletes' maximal cardiac output by 12%, with additional benefits to heart rate and lactate levels (McFarlin et al., 2017).

- As a fat-soluble vitamin, vitamin K is important in both blood clotting and bone metabolism. It is believed that low vitamin K intake may relate to a high bone turnover in athletes (Volpe, 2016).

- Some studies have shown that higher vitamin K intakes are associated with a lower incidence of hip fractures and low bone density. In addition, low blood levels of vitamin K have been linked with low bone density (Weber, 2001).

- Vitamin K supplementation has not been shown to improve athletic performance; however, researchers have evaluated the relationship between vitamin K status in athletes and bone and physical function. Sumida et al. examined 16 collegiate athletes who suffered from sports-related fractures. With respect to nutritional status and, in particular, vitamin K intake, they reported that 15 of 16 athletes had a lower than required vitamin K intake, as well as low intakes of calcium and vitamin D (Sumida et al., 2012).

RECIPES

Lunches and Dinners:
- Roast Vegetable and BBQ Chicken Salad with Peri-Peri Dressing **pg 150**
- Bulgur Broccoli Salad with Toasted Pumpkin Seeds **pg 120**
- Citrus Quinoa Avocado Salad **pg 126**
- Jerk Chicken Burger **pg 140**
- Prawn and Sweet Potato Salad **pg 141**
- Kimchi Toastie **pg 142**
- Smoky Chicken Pasta Salad **pg 152**
- Spanish-Style Fish **pg 154**
- Half 'n' Half Aubergine Lasagne **pg 228**
- Harissa Chicken Burger **pg 230**

- Including vitamin E in the diet of athletes has been shown to help protect against oxidative stress and muscle damage resulting from high-intensity exercise training (Itoh et al., 2000).

- As vitamin E concentrations in the body are typically relatively low in most dietary conditions and there is an association between low vitamin E stores and increased muscular fatigue, increasing vitamin E concentrations has the potential to be beneficial to athletes (Powers et al., 2014).

- The vast majority of benefits seen from vitamin E supplementation in athletes are seen when reaching the recommended daily intake. Some researchers have indicated that exceeding these limits has the potential to impair rather than improve some acute and chronic adaptive responses to exercise (Morrison et al., 2015).

- An adequate antioxidant status may be important to maintain healthy muscle function, especially during the recovery phase after acute exercise and endurance exercise activities (Broome et al., 2018).

- The evidence that a combination of antioxidants or single antioxidants including vitamin E may be helpful in reducing inflammation and muscle soreness during recovery from intense exercise or competition remains unclear but potential benefits are speculated (Van Essen et al., 2006; Takanami et al., 2000).

Breakfasts:
- Power-Up Mocha Shake **pg 104**
- Almond Breakfast Smoothie **pg 76**
- Cranberry and Pecan Granola **pg 90**

Lunches and Dinners:
- Creamy Garden-Pea Chicken Pasta **pg 132**
- Spicy Almond Hemp Fried Chicken **pg 156**
- Chicken Korma **pg 212**
- Enchiladas with Guacamole **pg 224**

Snacks:
- Almond Butter Toast **pg 164**
- Protein Boosted Battle Bars **pg 194**
- Puddle Bars **pg 196**

Drinks and Smoothies:
- Berry Happy Kefir Smoothie **pg 248**

VITAMIN B12 THE SCIENCE

- Our bodies are unable to synthesise vitamin B12, so we depend on intake from food sources to maintain healthy levels. Vitamin B12 is also involved in repairing cell damage following activities such as high-intensity exercise.

- Research indicates that athletes should regularly monitor their blood vitamin B12 concentration and, if necessary, adjust the oral supplementation individually to achieve the zone of 400–700 pg/mL as it may improve red blood cell parameters (Krzywański et al., 2020).

- Female athletes have been found to be at increased risk of vitamin B12 deficiency, and therefore may benefit from monitoring and supplementation of vitamin B12 to maintain sufficient levels (Thomas et al., 2016).

- Athletes who are strict vegans are at increased risk for vitamin B12 deficiency, mainly caused by avoidance of foods derived from animal origin, which are the only good dietary sources of vitamin B12 (Ryan-Harshman et al., 2008).

RECIPES

Breakfasts:
- Baked Egg Shakshuka **pg 78**
- Yuggy Berry **pg 112**
- Chia Protein Pudding **pg 86**
- Warming Caramelised Banana Porridge **pg 110**

Lunches and Dinners:
- Bacon, Egg and Avocado Bagel **pg 118**
- Cajun Salmon Burrito Bowl **pg 122**
- Chorizo Beef Burgers **pg 222**
- Chorizo Tuna Steaks **pg 124**
- Go Fish Yummy Spaghetti **pg 138**
- Potato Steak Bowl **pg 240**
- Meatballs and Chips **pg 236**
- Lemon Curry Trout **pg 234**
- Lamb Chilli Con Carne **pg 232**
- Salmon Spaghetti **pg 242**
- Get Shaky Salmon Pasta Bake **pg 226**
- Energise Prawn Quinoa Salad **pg 136**
- MD's Bulgur Wheat Salmon **pg 146**

Snacks:
- Affogato **pg 162**
- Lean Queen Yoghurt and Berries **pg 178**
- Chocolate Mousse **pg 170**

Drinks and Smoothies:
- Fresh Mint Banana Smoothie **pg 254**
- Hot Chocolate **pg 258**

- Iron is required for the formation of oxygen-carrying proteins, haemoglobin and myoglobin, and for enzymes involved in energy production. Oxygen-carrying capacity is essential for endurance exercise as well as normal function of the nervous, behavioural, and immune systems (Gleeson et al., 2004).

- Iron depletion is one of the most prevalent nutrient deficiencies observed among athletes, especially females. Iron deficiency, with or without anaemia, can impair muscle function and limit work capacity (Haymes et al., 2006).

- Iron deficiency negatively impacts athletic performance due to reduced oxygen transport to the exercising skeletal muscle placing higher demands on anaerobic metabolism, which could negatively influence performance (e.g. lower blood pH, depletion of muscle glycogen) (Rubeor et al. 2018).

- Despite the important role of iron for performance, research has reported that iron deficiency in athlete populations is at 15–35% of female and 3–11% of male athletes (Parks et al., 2017).

- To date, research indicates that there is no benefit to supplementation with iron beyond recommended daily allowance levels for athletes with normal iron status. However, regular monitoring and assessment of iron status during intense training periods is advised to ensure athletes do not become deficient (Sim et al., 2019).

Breakfasts:
- The Tofu Porridge Queen **pg 106**
- Black Pudding Avocado Toast **pg 80**
- Black Pudding Frittata **pg 82**
- Chocolate Puddle Pancakes **pg 88**
- French Toast with Greek Yoghurt **pg 94**

Lunches and Dinners:
- Potato Steak Bowl **pg 240**
- Lentil Curry with Roasted Balsamic Potatoes **pg 144**
- Citrus Quinoa Avocado Salad **pg 126**
- Meatballs and Chips **pg 236**
- Lamb Chilli Con Carne **pg 232**
- Bold Chorizo and Black Pudding Chicken with Spiced Wedges **pg 210**
- Chorizo Beef Burgers **pg 222**

Snacks:
- Protein Boosted Battle Bars **pg 194**

PHOSPHORUS THE SCIENCE

- Phosphorus is an essential structural component of cell membranes and nucleic acids but is also involved in several biological processes, including bone mineralisation, energy production and cell signalling. It is important to note that dietary phosphorus deficiency is very uncommon, and most individuals attain their recommended daily allowances through their everyday diet (Higdon, 2014).

- Phosphorus provides the phosphate for ATP (adenosine triphosphate) generation. ATP provides energy to drive processes in living cells in the body, including muscle contraction (Mattar et al., 2010).

- Maintaining sufficient dietary intake of phosphorus is believed to increase aerobic capacity, increase peak power output, increase anaerobic threshold and improve myocardial and cardiovascular responses to exercise. However, research does not provide evidence for enhanced performance benefits from phosphorus supplementation; simply consuming foods rich in phosphorus is maintaining sufficient levels that are beneficial to athletes (West et al., 2012).

- Elliot and colleagues have shown that an increase in dietary phosphorus has the potential to lower blood pressure as part of the recommendations for healthier eating patterns for the prevention and control of prehypertension and hypertension (Elliot et al., 2008).

RECIPES

Breakfasts:
- Cranberry and Pecan Granola **pg 90**
- Mangoloco Oats **pg 96**

Lunches and Dinners:
- Harissa Chicken Burger **pg 230**
- Cheat's Risotto **pg 206**
- Chicken Pie with Garlic Potatoes **pg 214**
- Half 'n' Half Aubergine Lasagne **pg 228**

Snacks:
- Porridge Bread with Mixed Seeds **pg 190**
- Eileen's Buns **pg 174**
- Banana Blueberry Pecan Bread **pg 166**
- Berry Bars **pg 168**
- Banana Chia Oat Bread **pg 176**
- Munchy Muesli Bars **pg 180**
- No-Bake Chocolate Protein Balls **pg 182**
- Protein Bombs Away **pg 192**
- Supercharger Rice Cakes **pg 202**
- Chocolate Mousse **pg 170**
- Banana Chia Oat Bread **pg 176**
- Peanut Butter and Berry Flapjacks **pg 186**

Drinks and Smoothies:
- Hot Chocolate **pg 258**

Dips and Spreads:
- Roasted Bell Pepper Hummus **pg 274**

POTASSIUM THE SCIENCE

- Potassium is one of the most important electrolytes in the body. Electrolytes are the minerals that ionise when dissolved in water and can conduct an electric current. Potassium is the major cation (positive ion) within the cells (intracellular) and has several important roles, including regulating blood pressure, controlling water and acid–base balances, conducting nerve impulses, controlling muscle contraction, and maintaining normal heart function (Von Duvillard et al., 2004).

- There is evidence to support that the participation of sodium and potassium in maintaining the normal activity of nervous and muscular systems is important for endurance athletes to sustain performance (Rechkalov et al., 2011).

- Potassium is important in skeletal muscle vasodilation, being responsible for hyperpolarisation of endothelial and smooth muscle cells and an essential component of conducted vasodilation for muscle contraction (Lindinger et al., 1991).

- The maintenance of fluid and electrolyte balance (sodium and potassium) is a key issue for the performance of athletes, especially when training or competing in a hot environment due to significant dehydration, which poses a challenge to both the health and performance of the athlete (Singh, 2005).

RECIPES

Breakfasts:
- Peanut Butter Yoghurt Toast **pg 100**
- Bluespresso **pg 84**
- Mixed Berry Smoothie Bowl **pg 98**

Lunches and Dinners:
- Paul Mannion's Smoked Tofu Satay **pg 148**
- Enchiladas with Guacamole **pg 224**
- Crispy Balsamic Tofu and Roast Veg with Chickpea Pasta **pg 220**
- Chicken Pie with Garlic Potatoes **pg 214**
- Bulgur Broccoli Salad with Toasted Pumpkin Seeds **pg 120**
- Spanish-Style Fish **pg 154**

Snacks:
- Crispy Homemade Chips **pg 172**
- Peanut Butter and Banana Cookies **pg 188**
- Raspberry Jelly Delight **pg 198**
- Supercharger Rice Cakes **pg 202**

Drinks and Smoothies:
- Booster C Juice **pg 250**
- Drop a Beet 'Shot' **pg 252**
- Fresh Mint Banana Smoothie **pg 254**
- Hot Chocolate **pg 258**
- Speedy Recovery Smoothie **pg 262**
- Titan Shot **pg 264**

CALCIUM THE SCIENCE

- Calcium is part of the mineralised matrix that gives bone its strength, and bone serves as the primary reservoir of calcium in the human body. Therefore, there is strong reason to believe that calcium plays an important role in bone density and fracture prevention in athletes (Kunstel, 2005).

- Findings in some studies have identified a link between calcium intake and either bone density or fracture risk in athletes (Nieves et al., 2010).

- Evidence indicates that those who consume a poorly constructed vegan diet are more likely to under-consume micronutrients, including calcium. Therefore, greater monitoring and management of calcium levels are required in vegan athletes (Davey et al., 2003).

- Many of the minerals found in chia seeds are known to be beneficial to bone health, including calcium, magnesium and phosphorus. One tablespoon of chia seeds (aprox. 12g) contains 79mg calcium, making them a significant non-dairy source of calcium.

- Female athletes are at greatest risk for low bone mineral density if energy intakes are low, dairy products and other calcium-rich foods are inadequate or eliminated from the diet, and menstrual dysfunction is present. Therefore, female athletes may need to give greater consideration to calcium intake and maintenance of sufficient levels (IOC).

RECIPES

- Like vitamin C deficiency, copper deficiency leads to impaired mechanical function of collagen-containing tissues, such as bone, resulting in an increased risk of fractures in those deficient in copper. The primary beneficial effects of copper are seen in the transition from deficiency to sufficiency (Close et al., 2018).

- As copper deficiency has been found to negatively impact immune function, athletes who restrict total energy and nutrient intake for long periods to reduce their body mass may be at greater risk of copper deficiency and its associated immunological effects (Lewis, 2010).

- In two separate studies that evaluated the copper and iron intake and status of 70 female athletes across different sports, copper intake ranged from 41% to 118% of the RDA. Of the athletes, 41% did not consume two-thirds of the RDA for copper. However, serum copper concentrations were within normal limits for all athletes (Gropper et al., 2003; 2006).

- The antioxidant function that is associated with copper reduces the oxidative damage caused by free radicals, which are thought to induce fatigue and to delay muscle recovery (Steinbacher et al., 2015).

Lunches and Dinners:

Snacks:

Drinks and Smoothies:

MAGNESIUM THE SCIENCE

- Magnesium helps maintain normal nerve and muscle function, heart rhythm (cardiac excitability), vasomotor tone, blood pressure, immune system, bone integrity and blood glucose levels, and promotes calcium absorption (Volpe et al., 2015).

- Magnesium deficiency impairs endurance performance by increasing oxygen requirements to complete submaximal exercise (Lukaski, 2000).

- Athletes in weight-class and body-conscious sports, such as wrestling, ballet, gymnastics and tennis, have been reported to consume inadequate dietary magnesium. Athletes should be educated about good food sources of magnesium. In athletes with low magnesium status, supplementation might be beneficial (Lukaski, 2004).

- Many studies support the role of magnesium in athletic performance and show that magnesium increases physical endurance and improves the force indices and muscle metabolism in athletes who have a diet rich in magnesium or receive magnesium supplements (Nielsen et al., 2006).

RECIPES

Breakfasts:
- Almond Breakfast Smoothie **pg 76**
- Bluespresso **pg 84**
- Warming Caramelised Banana Porridge **pg 110**
- Power-Up Mocha Shake **pg 104**
- Chocolate Puddle Pancakes **pg 88**
- Mixed Berry Smoothie Bowl **pg 98**
- Peanut Butter Yoghurt Toast **pg 100**
- Yummy Overnight Vegan Oats **pg 114**

Lunches and Dinners:
- Spicy Almond Hemp Fried Chicken **pg 156**

Snacks:
- Protein Bombs Away **pg 192**
- Protein Boosted Battle Bars **pg 194**
- Raspberry-Roons **pg 200**

- Many studies have investigated the effects of n-3 PUFA supplementation on the loss of muscle function and inflammation following exercise-induced muscle damage, with the balance of the literature suggesting some degree of benefit (DiLorenzo et al., 2014; Marques et al., 2015).

- Oily fish are brilliant sources of omega-3, a type of polyunsaturated fatty acid. Including foods containing omega-3s in your diet has a multitude of benefits as they have been shown to be a natural anti-inflammatory which may help improve joint pain caused by inflammation (Goldberg & Katz, 2007).

- A study on athletes from 2015 reported that a 3-week omega-3 fatty acid supplementation had a beneficial effect on exercise performance and cardiovascular adaptation to exercise (Żebrowska et al., 2015).

- There is strong evidence suggesting that dietary supplementation with omega-3 polyunsaturated fatty acids (n-3 PUFA) had a positive impact on vascular function in healthy subjects (Anderson et al., 2010; Khan et al., 2003) and patients with metabolic (Juturu, 2008) and cardiovascular disease (Lovegrove & Griffin, 2013).

- Omega-3 fatty acids are perceived as a potential supplement that may beneficially affect performance, recovery and the risk for illness/injury (Simopoulos, 2007).

Breakfasts:
- The Tofu Porridge Queen **pg 106**
- Yummy Overnight Vegan Oats **pg 114**
- Yuggy Berry **pg 112**
- Tummy-Loving Chia Pudding **pg 108**
- Chia Protein Pudding **pg 86**

Lunches and Dinners:
- Cheat's Risotto **pg 206**
- Spicy Almond Hemp Fried Chicken **pg 156**
- Go Fish Yummy Spaghetti **pg 138**
- Salmon Hash **pg 158**
- MD's Bulgur Wheat Salmon **pg 146**
- Cajun Salmon Burrito Bowl **pg 122**
- Creamy Salmon Mega Mix **pg 134**
- Salmon Spaghetti **pg 242**
- Lemon Curry Trout **pg 234**
- Get Shaky Salmon Pasta Bake **pg 226**
- Chia Base Pizza **pg 208**

Snacks:
- Porridge Bread with Mixed Seeds **pg 190**
- Banana Blueberry Pecan Bread **pg 166**
- Banana Chia Oat Bread **pg 176**
- Peanut Butter and Berry Flapjacks **pg 186**
- Peanut Butter and Banana Cookies **pg 188**

Dips and Spreads:
- Chia Seed Berry Jam **pg 272**

SELENIUM THE SCIENCE

- Current research indicates that there is no reason to suspect selenium deficiency in athletes. However, as there is a noted low intake of chromium in the general population, there is a possibility that athletes may be deficient (Clarkson, 1991).

- The relationship between selenium status and performance has not been established, but selenium may play a role as an antioxidant.

- Findings from one study indicated that athletes who engage in regular high volumes of exercise do not demonstrate a linear increase of dietary selenium requirements. Typically, athletes adopted a high-selenium diet naturally, which does not require additional supplementation (Margaritis et al., 2005).

- Findings reported in the *Lancet* highlight that the important concept of selenium effects with regard to health is the complicated U-shaped link with status. This indicated that additional selenium intake may benefit people with low status; however, those with adequate-to-high status might be affected adversely and should not take selenium supplements (Rayman, 2012).

RECIPES

Breakfasts:
- French Toast with Greek Yoghurt **pg 94**
- Yuggy Berry **pg 112**
- Peter's Quesadilla **pg 102**

Lunches and Dinners:
- Creamy Chorizo Pasta **pg 130**
- Creamy Garden-Pea Chicken Pasta **pg 132**
- Creamy Salmon Mega Mix **pg 134**
- Energise Prawn Quinoa Salad **pg 136**
- Smoky Chicken Pasta Salad **pg 152**
- Claudia's Potato Salad with Boiled Eggs **pg 128**
- Jerk Chicken Burger **pg 140**
- Nanny D's Fried Potato with Bacon and Veggies **pg 238**
- Bold Chorizo and Black Pudding Chicken with Spiced Wedges **pg 210**
- Chicken and Bacon Tagliatelle in Tomato Sauce **pg 211**
- Chicken Korma **pg 212**
- Coddin' Me Curry **pg 218**
- Chorizo Tuna Steaks **pg 124**

Snacks:
- Affogato **pg 162**

- Zinc status has been shown to directly affect thyroid hormone levels, basal metabolic rate, and protein use, which in turn can negatively affect health and physical performance (Volpe, 2006).

- Athletes should apply caution when it comes to using single-dose zinc supplements as they often exceed RDA levels, and unnecessary zinc supplementation may lead to low HDL cholesterol and nutrient imbalances by interfering with absorption of other nutrients such as iron and copper (Lukaski, 2004).

- This mineral aids in post-exertion tissue repair and in the conversion of food to fuel. Both male and female athletes have lower serum zinc levels compared with sedentary individuals. Studies correlate endurance exercise with periods of compromised immunity – zinc depletion may be one reason (Cordova, 1995).

- Athletes can often be deficient in zinc as it is lost through sweat. Therefore, it is important that athletes replace these stores to enable greater muscle recovery following exercise and in the lead-up to competition (Kiełczykowska et al., 2018).

RECIPES

Breakfasts:
- Chocolate Puddle Pancakes **pg 88**

Lunches and Dinners:
- Creamy Chorizo Pasta **pg 130**
- Nanny D's Fried Potato with Bacon and Veggies **pg 238**
- Meatballs and Chips **pg 236**
- Bacon, Egg and Avocado Bagel **pg 118**
- Cheat's Risotto **pg 206**
- Chicken Pie with Garlic Potatoes **pg 214**
- Chorizo Beef Burgers **pg 222**

FIBRE THE SCIENCE

- A diet high in fibre is associated with overall metabolic health, colonic health, and gut health while functioning as an important mediator for the regulation of appetite, metabolic processes, mental health and chronic inflammatory pathways (Anderson et al., 2009).

- Dietary fibre is the main nutrient that increases the diversity of gut microbiota. Therefore, inadequate intake of dietary fibre and carbohydrates by athletes can counteract the benefits of exercise and a high-protein diet that tend to increase gut microbiota diversity (Hawley et al., 2014).

- It has been recommended that athletes consume a high amount of monosaccharides and dietary fibre to maximise glycogen storage and sustain blood glucose during training and competition, as well as minimising intake of dietary fibre and resistant starch to prevent gastrointestinal disturbances. Low intake of dietary fibre and resistant starch may lead to decreased bowel movements, resulting in decreased bowel function, and also decrease the diversity of gut microbiota (Rodriguez et al., 2009).

RECIPES

Breakfasts:
- Yummy Overnight Vegan Oats **pg 114**
- Yuggy Berry **pg 112**
- Tummy-Loving Chia Pudding **pg 108**
- Chocolate Puddle Pancakes **pg 88**
- Chia Protein Pudding **pg 86**

Lunches and Dinners:
- Paul Mannion's Smoked Tofu Satay **pg 148**
- Coconut Dahl and Easy Naan **pg 216**
- Potato Steak Bowl **pg 240**
- Chicken Korma **pg 212**
- Creamy Garden-Pea Chicken Pasta **pg 132**
- Creamy Chorizo Pasta **pg 130**
- Bacon, Egg and Avocado Bagel **pg 118**
- Bulgur Broccoli Salad with Toasted Pumpkin Seeds **pg 120**
- Citrus Quinoa Avocado Salad **pg 126**
- Lentil Curry with Roasted Balsamic Potatoes **pg 144**
- Roast Vegetable and BBQ Chicken Salad with Peri-Peri Dressing **pg 150**
- Smoky Chicken Pasta Salad **pg 152**
- Crispy Balsamic Tofu and Roast Veg with Chickpea Pasta **pg 220**

CHLORIDE THE SCIENCE

- Chloride is an anion in intracellular fluid and one of the most important extracellular anions. It contributes to many body functions including the maintenance of blood pressure, hydration and muscle function. Electrolytes have many important roles, including regulation of nerve and muscle function, balancing blood pressure and acidity, maintaining hydration of the body and the movement of water and solutes between fluid compartments (Turck et al., 2019).

- Chloride is one of two main electrolytes needed by the body to maintain healthy function. Muscles and neurons are often referred to as the 'electrical tissues' of the body and rely on the movement of electrolytes through the fluid inside, between and outside the cells (Turck et al., 2019).

RECIPES

Breakfasts:
- Peanut Butter Yoghurt Toast **pg 100**
- Black Pudding Avocado Toast **pg 80**

Lunches and Dinners:
- Claudia's Potato Salad with Boiled Eggs **pg 128**
- Cheat's Risotto **pg 206**
- Chicken and Bacon Tagliatelle in Tomato Sauce **pg 211**
- Coconut Dahl and Easy Naan **pg 216**

Snacks:
- Crispy Homemade Chips **pg 172**
- Eileen's Buns **pg 174**
- Munchy Muesli Bars **pg 180**
- Orange Split Jellies **pg 184**
- Peanut Butter and Berry Flapjacks **pg 186**
- Supercharger Rice Cakes **pg 202**

Drinks and Smoothies:
- Speedy Recovery Smoothie **pg 262**

FOLATES THE SCIENCE

- Folate is critical for numerous biological functions, and inadequate intake, especially classified as deficiency, has been implicated in several adverse health conditions including congenital heart disease, pregnancy-related complications, various psychiatric diseases, osteoporosis and cancer (Shane, 1995).

- Folate is the natural form of vitamin B9 in food, while folic acid is a synthetic form. Folic acid is an important co-factor in the methionine pathway. Low folic acid intake is known to contribute to increased levels of homocysteine (Hcy) as a result of its interrelation with methionine metabolism (König et al., 2003; Hermann et al., 2005).

- Research indicates that the prevalence of moderate folic acid deficiency (folate <5.9 ng/ml) is an average of 15% in recreational and competitive athletes (Hermann et al., 2005).

- A group of 14 high-performance handball players were routinely assessed following dietary supplementation with 200µg folic acid for months. Findings indicated that folic acid supplementation may protect athletes against alterations that can lead to cardiovascular events related to exertion during competition (Molina-Lopez et al., 2013).

RECIPES

Drinks and Smoothies:
- Drop a Beet 'Shot' **pg 252**

GUT HEALTH THE SCIENCE

- Gut health is now considered one of the most important contributors to overall health and fermented foods have been shown to have a positive impact on the gut microbiome as well as decreasing markers of inflammation in the body (de Vos et al., 2022).

RECIPES

Lunches and Dinners:
- Kimchi Toastie **pg 142**

Drinks and Smoothies:
- Berry Happy Kefir Smoothie **pg 248**

- A systematic review indicates that caffeine supplementation produces a similar ergogenic benefit for aerobic performance and fatigue index in male and female athletes. The ability of caffeine to produce increased power, total weight lifted and to improve sprint performance with respect to a placebo was higher in men than women athletes despite the same dose of caffeine being administered. Thus, the ergogenic effect of acute caffeine intake on anaerobic performance is potentially higher in men than in women (Mielgo-Ayuso et al., 2019).

- The current guidelines for caffeine intake for athletes recommend the ingestion of low-to-moderate doses of caffeine, ranging from 3 to 6mg/kg, approximately 60 minutes prior to exercise to experience performance improvements. Higher doses of caffeine (9–13mg/kg) do not result in an additional improvement in physical performance and potentially increase the incidence and magnitude of main caffeine-related side effects (Goldstein et al., 2010; Pasman et al., 1995).

- The central and peripheral effects of caffeine supplementation influence its observed benefits in improving psychomotor function manifested as improved agility and decision making. These factors are required during the intermittent high-intensity efforts needed for velocity and precision in rugby or football players (Stuart et al., 2005; Foskett et al., 2009).

- The coffee bean is also rich in many bioactive compounds and antioxidants and may support performance by reducing central fatigue and increasing blood pressure, heart rate and adrenaline levels (Erikson & Aschner, 2019).

Breakfasts:
- Bluespresso **pg 84**

Snacks:
- Affogato **pg 162**

MANGANESE THE SCIENCE

- Manganese is an essential trace element that plays a role in many biological processes in the body such as metabolism, bone formation, brain function and blood clotting. It is found in all tissues in the body and can be obtained from foods such as whole grains, nuts, green leafy vegetables and red meat. Manganese is also involved in the formation of cartilage and bones.

- Athletes who undertake a diet high in protein can benefit from ensuring sufficient levels of manganese due to proneness to muscular strains and increased possibility of inflammation (Food and Nutrition Board, 2001).

RECIPES

Breakfasts:
- Cranberry and Pecan Granola **pg 90**
- Espresso Oats **pg 92**
- Mangoloco Oats **pg 96**

Lunches and Dinners:
- Tangy Tasty Prawn Curry **pg 244**
- Chia Base Pizza **pg 208**
- Creamy Chorizo Pasta **pg 130**

Snacks:
- Porridge Bread with Mixed Seeds **pg 190**
- Eileen's Buns **pg 174**
- Almond Butter Toast **pg 164**
- Banana Blueberry Pecan Bread **pg 166**
- Berry Bars **pg 168**
- Chocolate Mousse **pg 170**
- Banana Chia Oat Bread **pg 176**
- Munchy Muesli Bars **pg 180**
- No-Bake Chocolate Protein Balls **pg 182**
- Peanut Butter and Berry Flapjacks **pg 186**
- Peanut Butter and Banana Cookies **pg 188**
- Protein Bombs Away **pg 192**
- Puddle Bars **pg 196**
- Raspberry-Roons **pg 200**

Drinks and Smoothies:
- Titan Shot **pg 264**
- Ginger Zinger Shot **pg 266**

Dips and Spreads:
- Roasted Bell Pepper Hummus **pg 274**

COLLAGEN THE SCIENCE

- Collagen has been shown to support the repair of bones, tendons, connective tissues and muscles. Research has shown that consuming 50 mg of vitamin C with 10–15g of gelatin prior to physical activity promotes improved collagen synthesis in tissue injuries (Lis & Baar, 2019).

RECIPES

Snacks:
- Orange Split Jellies **pg 184**
- Raspberry Jelly Delight **pg 198**

REFERENCES

Abdulghani, H.M., Al-Drees, A.A., Khalil, M.S., Ahmad, F., Ponnamperuma, G.G. and Amin, Z., 2014. What factors determine academic achievement in high achieving undergraduate medical students? A qualitative study. *Medical Teacher, 36*(sup1), pp.S43–S48.

Braakhuis, A.J. and Hopkins, W.G., 2015. Impact of dietary antioxidants on sport performance: a review. *Sports Medicine, 45*(7), pp.939–955.

Brown, D.J., Arnold, R., Reid, T. and Roberts, G., 2018. A qualitative exploration of thriving in elite sport. *Journal of Applied Sport Psychology, 30*(2), pp.129–149.

Bucher, A. and White, N., 2016. Vitamin C in the prevention and treatment of the common cold. *American Journal of Lifestyle Medicine, 10*(3), pp.181–183.

Beswick, Bill. *Changing Your Story: 20 Life Lessons Drawn From Elite Sport.*

Cohen, S., Doyle, W.J., Alper, C.M., Janicki-Deverts, D. and Turner, R.B., 2009. Sleep habits and susceptibility to the common cold. *Archives of Internal Medicine, 169*(1), pp.62–67.

Collins, J., Maughan, R.J., Gleeson, M., Bilsborough, J., Jeukendrup, A., Morton, J.P., Phillips, S.M., Armstrong, L., Burke, L.M., Close, G.L. and Duffield, R., 2021. UEFA expert group statement on nutrition in elite football. Current evidence to inform practical recommendations and guide future research. *British Journal of Sports Medicine, 55*(8), pp.416–416.

Duhigg, C., 2012. *The Power of Habit: Why We Do What We Do in Life and Business.* Random House.

Gleeson, M., Nieman, D.C. and Pedersen, B.K., 2004. Exercise, nutrition and immune function. *Journal of Sports Sciences, 22*(1), pp.115–125.

Griffiths, C., Harnack, L. and Pereira, M.A., 2018. Assessment of the accuracy of nutrient calculations of five popular nutrition tracking applications. *Public Health Nutrition, 21*(8), pp.1495–1502.

Hammarström, A., Wiklund, A.F., Lindahl, B., Larsson, C. and Ahlgren, C., 2014. Experiences of barriers and facilitators to weight-loss in a diet intervention: a qualitative study of women in Northern Sweden. *BMC Women's Health, 14*(1), pp.1–10.

Hemilä, H. and Chalker, E., 2013. Vitamin C for preventing and treating the common cold. *Cochrane Database of Systematic Reviews,* (1).

Hemilä, H., Petrus, E.J., Fitzgerald, J.T. and Prasad, A., 2016. Zinc acetate lozenges for treating the common cold: an individual patient data meta-analysis. *British Journal of Clinical Pharmacology, 82*(5), pp.1393–1398.

Impey, S.G., Hammond, K.M., Shepherd, S.O., Sharples, A.P., Stewart, C., Limb, M., Smith, K., Philp, A., Jeromson, S., Hamilton, D.L. and Close, G.L., 2016. Fuel for the work required: a practical approach to amalgamating train-low paradigms for endurance athletes. *Physiological Reports, 4*(10).

Jasper, M., 2003. *Beginning Reflective Practice.* Nelson Thornes.

Jones, G., Hanton, S. and Connaughton, D., 2002. What is this thing called mental toughness? An investigation of elite sport performers. *Journal of Applied Sport Psychology, 14,* pp.205–218.

Kahneman, D., 2011. *Thinking, Fast and Slow.* Macmillan.

Katz, D.L., Frates, E.P., Bonnet, J.P., Gupta, S.K., Vartiainen, E. and Carmona, R.H., 2018. Lifestyle as medicine: the case for a true health initiative. *American Journal of Health Promotion, 32*(6), pp.1452–1458.

Kerksick, C.M., Arent, S., Schoenfeld, B.J., Stout, J.R., Campbell, B., Wilborn, C.D., Taylor, L., Kalman, D., Smith-Ryan, A.E., Kreider, R.B. and Willoughby, D., 2017. International society of sports nutrition position stand: nutrient timing. *Journal of the International Society of Sports Nutrition, 14*(1), pp.1–21.

Kerksick, C.M., Wilborn, C.D., Roberts, M.D., Smith-Ryan, A., Kleiner, S.M., Jäger, R., Collins, R., Cooke, M., Davis, J.N., Galvan, E. and Greenwood, M., 2018. ISSN exercise & sports nutrition review update: research & recommendations. *Journal of the International Society of Sports Nutrition, 15*(1), p.38.

Khatri, M., Naughton, R.J., Clifford, T., Harper, L.D. and Corr, L., 2021. The effects of collagen peptide supplementation on body composition, collagen synthesis, and recovery from joint injury and exercise: a systematic review. *Amino Acids,* pp.1–14.

Knowles, Z., Gilbourne, D., Cropley, B. and Dugdill, L. (eds.), 2014. *Reflective Practice in the Sport and Exercise Sciences: Contemporary Issues.* Routledge.

Krebs, P. and Duncan, D.T., 2015. Health app use among US mobile phone owners: a national survey. *JMIR mHealth and uHealth, 3*(4), p.e4924.

Laird, E., Rhodes, J. and Kenny, R.A., 2020. Vitamin D and inflammation: potential implications for severity of Covid-19. *Irish Medical Journal, 113*(5), p.81.

Liu, Y. and Wang, Z., 2014. Positive affect and cognitive control: approach-motivation intensity influences the balance between cognitive flexibility and stability. *Psychological Science, 25*(5), pp.1116–1123.

Ljungqvist O., Soreide E., 2003. Preoperative fasting. *British Journal of Surgery, 90*(4), pp.400–406.

Metzgar, C.J., Preston, A.G., Miller, D.L. and Nickols-Richardson, S.M., 2015. Facilitators and barriers to weight loss and weight loss maintenance: a qualitative exploration. *Journal of Human Nutrition and Dietetics, 28*(6), pp.593–603.

'Mindset', *Cambridge Dictionary,* dictionary.cambridge.org. Retrieved 10 December 2019.

Owens, D.J., Allison, R. and Close, G.L., 2018. Vitamin D and the athlete: current perspectives and new challenges. *Sports Medicine, 48*(1), pp.3–16.

Potgieter, S., 2013. Sport nutrition: a review of the latest guidelines for exercise and sport nutrition from the American College of Sport Nutrition, the International Olympic Committee and the International Society for Sports Nutrition. *South African Journal of Clinical Nutrition, 26*(1), pp.6–16.

Quintero, K.J., de Sá Resende, A., Leite, G.S.F. and Junior, A.H.L., 2018. An overview of nutritional strategies for the recovery process in sports-related muscle injuries. *Nutrire, 43*(1), p.27.

Rao, G. and Rowland, K., 2011. Zinc for the common cold – not if, but when. *The Journal of Family Practice, 60*(11), p.669.

Rooks, J.D., Morrison, A.B., Goolsarran, M., Rogers, S.L. and Jha, A.P., 2017. 'We are talking about practice': the influence of mindfulness vs. relaxation training on athletes' attention and well-being over high-demand intervals. *Journal of Cognitive Enhancement, 1*(2), pp.141–153.

Shaw, G., Lee-Barthel, A., Ross, M.L., Wang, B. and Baar, K., 2017. Vitamin C–enriched gelatin supplementation before intermittent activity augments collagen synthesis. *The American Journal of Clinical Nutrition, 105*(1), pp.136–143.

Smith-Ryan, A.E., Hirsch, K.R., Saylor, H.E., Gould, L.M. and Blue, M.N., 2020. Nutritional considerations and strategies to facilitate injury recovery and rehabilitation. *Journal of Athletic Training, 55*(9), pp.918–930.

Thomas, D.T., Erdman, K.A. and Burke, L.M., 2016. American College of Sports Medicine joint position statement. Nutrition and athletic performance. *Medicine and Science in Sports and Exercise, 48*(3), pp.543–568.

Tipton, K.D., 2015. Nutritional support for exercise-induced injuries. *Sports Medicine, 45*(1), pp.93–104.

Velten, J., Bieda, A., Scholten, S., Wannemüller, A. and Margraf, J., 2018. Lifestyle choices and mental health: a longitudinal survey with German and Chinese students. *BMC Public Health, 18*(1), pp.1–15.

Waldinger, R., 2015. What makes a good life? Lessons from the longest study on happiness. *The Harvard Study of Adult Development, 28*(8), p.2017.

Wall, B.T., Morton, J.P. and Van Loon, L.J., 2015. Strategies to maintain skeletal muscle mass in the injured athlete: nutritional considerations and exercise mimetics. *European Journal of Sport Science, 15*(1), pp.53–62.

Walsh, N.P., 2019. Nutrition and athlete immune health: new perspectives on an old paradigm. *Sports Medicine, 49*(2), pp.153–168.

World Health Organization. *Constitution of the World Health Organization.* Basic documents, forty-fifth edition, supplement.

MICRONUTRIENT INDEX REFERENCES

Abbaspour, N., Hurrell, R., Kelishadi, R., 2014. Review on iron and its importance for human health. *Journal of Research in Medical Sciences: The Official Journal of Isfahan University of Medical Sciences, 19*(2), p. 164.

Abdul Rahim, N., Mohamad Shalan, N.A.A., 2018. The potential effects of vitamin E in sport performance, *International Journal of Current Research in Biosciences and Plant Biology, 5*, pp. 17–27.

Anderson, J.S., Nettleton, J.A., Herrington, D.M., Johnson, W.C., Tsai, M.Y., & Siscovick, D., 2010. Relation of omega-3 fatty acid and dietary fish intake with brachial artery flow-mediated vasodilatation in the multi-ethnic study of atherosclerosis. *The American Journal of Clinical Nutrition, 92*, pp. 1204–1213.

Barker, T., Schneider, E.D., Dixon, B.M., Henriksen, V.T., Weaver, L.K., 2013. Supplemental vitamin D enhances the recovery in peak isometric force shortly after intense exercise. *Nutrition and Metabolism, 10*, pp.69.

Bergeron, M.F., 2008. Muscle cramps during exercise – is it fatigue or electrolyte deficit? *Current Sports Medicine Reports 7*, S50–5.

Braakhuis, A.J., 2012. Effect of vitamin C supplements on physical performance. *Current sports medicine reports 11*(4), pp.180–4.

Bryer, S.C., Goldfarb, A.H., 2006. Effect of high dose vitamin C supplementation on muscle soreness, damage, function, and oxidative stress to eccentric exercise. *International Journal of Sport Nutrition and Exercise Metabolism, 16*, pp.270–80.

Clarkson, P.M., 1991. Minerals: exercise performance and supplementation in athletes. *Journal of Sports Sciences, 9*(S1), pp.91–116.

Cordova, A., 1995. Behaviour of zinc in physical exercise: a special reference to immunity and fatigue. *Neuroscience & Biobehavioral Reviews 19*(3), pp. 439–45.

Davey, G.K., Spencer, E.A., Appleby, P.N., Allen, N.E., Knox, K.H., Key, T.J., 2003. EPIC-Oxford: lifestyle characteristics and nutrient intakes in a cohort of 33 883 meat-eaters and 31 546 non meat-eaters in the UK. *Public Health Nutrition 6*(3), pp.259–68.

de Vos, W.M., Tilg, H., Van Hul, M., & Cani, P.D., 2022. Gut microbiome and health: mechanistic insights. *Gut*. Advance online publication. https://doi.org/10.1136/gutjnl-2021-326789.

Elliott, P., Kesteloot, H., Appel, L.J., Dyer, A.R., Ueshima, H., Chan, Q., Brown, I.J., Zhao, L., Stamler, J., 2008. Dietary phosphorus and blood pressure: international study of macro-and micro-nutrients and blood pressure. *Hypertension 51*(3), pp.669–75.

Food and Nutrition Board, Institute of Medicine, 2001. *Dietary reference intakes for vitamin A, Vitamin K, Boron, Chromium, Copper, Iodine, Iron, Manganese, Molybdenum, Nickel, Silicon, Vanadium, and Zinc.* National Academies Press, pp.394–419.

Foskett, A., Ali, A., & Gant, N., 2009. Caffeine enhances cognitive function and skill performance during simulated soccer activity. *International Journal of Sport Nutrition and Exercise Metabolism 19*(4), pp.410–23.

Gleeson, M., Nieman, D.C., Pedersen, B.K., 2004. Exercise, nutrition and immune function. *Journal of Sports Sciences, 22*, pp.115–25.

Goldstein, E.R., Ziegenfuss, T., Kalman, D., Kreider, R., Campbell, B., Wilborn, C., Taylor, L., Willoughby, D., Stout, J., Graves, B.S. et al., 2010. International Society of Sports Nutrition position stand: caffeine and performance. *Journal of the International Society of Sports Nutrition, 7*, p.5.

Gropper, S.S., Blessing, D., Dunham, K., et al., 2006. Iron status of female collegiate athletes involved in different sports. *Biological Trace Element Research, 109*(1), pp.1–14.

Gropper, S.S., Sorrels, L.M., Blessing, D, 2003. Copper status of collegiate female athletes involved in different sports. *International Journal of Sport Nutrition and Exercise Metabolism, 13*(3), pp.343–57.

Hawley, J.A., Hargreaves, M., Joyner, M.J., Zierath, J.R., 2014. Integrative biology of exercise. *Cell, 159*(4), pp.738–49.

Haymes, E. Iron. In: Driskell, J., Wolinsky, I. (editors), 2006. *Sports Nutrition: Vitamins and Trace Elements.* CRC/Taylor & Francis, pp.203–16.

Herrmann, M., Obeid, R., Scharhag, J., Kindermann, W., Herrmann, W., 2005. Altered vitamin B_{12} status in recreational endurance athletes. *International Journal of Sport Nutrition and Exercise Metabolism, 15*, pp.433–41.

Higdon, J., 2014. Phosphorus. https://lpi.oregonstate.edu/mic/minerals/phosphorus.

Institute of Medicine, 1997. *Dietary Reference Intakes for Calcium, Phosphorous, Magnesium, Vitamin D, and Fluoride.* The National Academies Press.

International Olympic Committee (IOC) Consensus Statement on Relative Energy Deficiency in Sport (RED-S): 2018 Update.

Itoh, H., Ohkuwa, T., Yamazaki, Y., Shimoda, T., Wakayama, A., Tamura, S. et al., 2000. Vitamin E supplementation attenuates leakage of enzymes following 6 successive days of running training. *International Journal of Sports Medicine*, 21, pp.369–74.

Juturu, V., 2008. Omega-3 fatty acids and the cardiometabolic syndrome. *Journal of the Cardiometabolic Syndrome*, 3, pp.244–253.

König, D., Bissé, E., Deibert, P., Deibert, P., Müller, H.M., Wieland, H., Berg, A., 2003. Influence of training volume and acute physical exercise on the homocysteine levels in endurance-trained men: interactions with plasma folate and vitamin B12. *Annals of Nutrition and Metabolism*, 47, pp.114–118.

Krzywański, J., Mikulski, T., Pokrywka, A., Młyńczak, M., Krysztofiak, H., Frączek, B., Ziemba, A., 2020. Vitamin B12 status and optimal range for hemoglobin formation in elite athletes. *Nutrients*, 12(4), pp.1038.

Kunstel, K., 2005. Calcium requirements for the athlete. *Current Sports Medicine Reports*, 4(4), pp.203-6.

Lewis, N.A., Moore, P., Cunningham, P., 2010. Serum copper and neutropenia in elite athletes. *Medicine and Science in Sports and Exercise*, 42, p.1137.

Lindinger, M.I., Sjøgaard, G., 1991. Potassium regulation during exercise and recovery. *Sports Medicine*, 11(6), pp.382–401.

Lis, D. M., Baar, K., 2019. Effects of different vitamin C-enriched collagen derivatives on collagen synthesis. *International Journal of Sport Nutrition and Exercise Metabolism*, 29(5), pp.526–531. https://doi.org/10.1123/ijsnem.2018-0385.

Lovegrove, J. A., Griffin, B. A., 2013. The acute and longterm effects of dietary fatty acids on vascular function in health and disease. *Current Opinion in Clinical Nutrition & Metabolic care*, 16, pp.162–167.

Lukaski, H.C., 2004. Vitamin and mineral status: effects on physical performance. *Nutrition*, 20, pp.632–44.

Lukaski, H.C., 2000. Magnesium, zinc, and chromium nutriture and physical activity. *The American Journal of Clinical Nutrition*, 72(2 Suppl.), pp. 585S–593S.

Margaritis, I., Rousseau, A.S., Hininger, I., Palazzetti, S., Arnaud, J., Roussel, A.M., 2005. Increase in selenium requirements with physical activity loads in well-trained athletes is not linear. *Biofactors*, 23(1), pp.45–55.

Mattar, L.E., Mattar, M.A., Batal, M., et al., 2010. Stimulation of postprandial in vivo glycogenesis and lipogenesis of rats fed high fructose diet with varied phosphate content. *Nutrition Research*, 30, pp.151–155.

McFarlin, B.K., Henning, A.L., Venable, A.S., 2017. Oral consumption of vitamin K2 for 8 weeks associated with increased maximal cardiac output during exercise. *Alternative Therapies in Health & Medicine*, 23(4).

Meier, C., Woitge, H.W., Witte, K., Lemmer, B., Seibel, M.J., 2004. Supplementation with oral vitamin D3 and calcium during winter prevents seasonal bone loss: a randomized controlled open-label prospective trial. *Journal of Bone and Mineral Research*, 19, pp.1221–1230.

Mielgo-Ayuso, J., Marques-Jiménez, D., Refoyo, I., Del Coso, J., León-Guereño, P., Calleja-González, J., 2019. Effect of caffeine supplementation on sports performance based on differences between sexes: a systematic review. *Nutrients*, 11(10), p.2313.

Molina-López, J., Planells, E., 2013. Nutrition and hydration for handball. In: *Handball Sports Medicine*. Springer, pp.81–101.

Morrison, D., Hughes, J., Della Gatta, P.A., Mason, S., Lamon, S., Russell, A.P., Wadley, G.D., 2015. Vitamin C and E supplementation prevents some of the cellular adaptations to endurance-training in humans. *Free Radical Biology and Medicine*, 89, pp.852–862.

Nielsen, F.H., Lukaski, H.C., 2006. Update on the relationship between magnesium and exercise. *Magnesium Research*, 19(3), pp.180–189.

Nieves, J.W., Melsop, K., Curtis, M., Kelsey, J.L., Bachrach, L.K., Greendale, G., Sowers, M.F., Sainani, K.L., 2010. Nutritional factors that influence change in bone density and stress fracture risk among young female crosscountry runners. *Physical Medicine and Rehabilitation*, 2, pp.740–750.

Ottoboni, F., Ottoboni, A., 2005. Ascorbic acid and the immune system. *Journal of Orthomolecular Medicine*, 20, pp.179–183.

Parks, R.B., Hetzel, S.J., Brooks, M.A., 2017. Iron deficiency and anemia among collegiate athletes: a retrospective chart review. *Medicine and Science in*

Sports and Exercise, 49(8), pp.1711–1715.

Pasman, W.J., van Baak, M.A., Jeukendrup, A.E., de Haan, A., 1995. The effect of different dosages of caffeine on endurance performance time. *International Journal of Sports Medicine, 16*, pp.225–230.

Powers, S.K., Sollanek, K.J., Wiggs, M.P., 2014. Endurance exercise and antioxidant supplementation: sense or nonsense? – part 2. *Sports Science, 27*, pp.1–4.

Rayman, M.P., 2012. Selenium and human health. *The Lancet, 379*(9822), pp.1256–1268.

Rechkalov, A.V., Gorshkova, N.E., 2011. Blood biochemical parameters in athletes after combined muscular exercise and food loading. *Human Physiology, 37*(4), pp.449–454.

Rodriguez, N.R., DiMarco, N.M., Langley, S., 2009. Position of the American Dietetic Association, Dietitians of Canada, and the American College of Sports Medicine: nutrition and athletic performance. *Journal of the American Dietetic Association, 109*(3), pp.509–527.

Rubeor, A., Goojha, C., Manning, J., White, J., 2018. Does iron supplementation improve performance in iron-deficient nonanemic athletes? *Sports Health, 10*(5), pp.400–405.

Ryan-Harshman, M., Aldoori, W., 2008. Vitamin B12 and health. *Canadian Family Physician, 54*(4), pp.536–541.

Shane, B., 1995. Folate chemistry and metabolism. In: Bailey, L.B. (ed.), *Folate in Health and Disease.* Marcel Dekker Inc., pp.1–22.

Sim, M., Garvican-Lewis, L.A., Cox, G.R., Govus, A., McKay, A.K., Stellingwerff, T., Peeling, P., 2019. Iron considerations for the athlete: a narrative review. *European Journal of Applied Physiology, 119*(7), pp.1463–1478.

Steinbacher, P., Eckl, P., 2015. Impact of oxidative stress on exercising skeletal muscle. *Biomolecules, 5*, pp.356–377.

Stuart, G.R., Hopkins, W.G., Cook, C., Cairns, S.P., 2005. Multiple effects of caffeine on simulated high-intensity team-sport performance. *Medicine and Science in Sports and Exercise, 37*(11), pp.1998–2005.

Takanami, Y., Iwane, H., Kawai, Y., Shimomitsu, T., 2000. Vitamin E supplementation and endurance exercise: are there benefits? *Sports Medicine, 29*, pp.73–83.

Thomas, D.T., Erdman, K.A., Burke, L.M., 2016. Position of the Academy of Nutrition and Dietetics, Dietitians of Canada, and the American College of Sports Medicine: Nutrition and athletic performance. *Journal of the Academy of Nutrition and Dietetics, 116*, pp.501–528. doi: 10.1016/j.jand.2015.12.006.

Van Essen, M., Gibala, M.J., 2006. Failure of protein to improve time trial performance when added to a sports drink. *Medicine and Science in Sports and Exercise, 38*, pp.1476–1483.

Volpe, S., 2006. Vitamins, minerals and exercise. In: Dunford, M (ed.), *Sports Nutrition: a Practice Manual for Professionals.* American Dietetic Association, pp.61–63.

Volpe, S.L., 2016. Vitamin K, osteoarthritis, and athletic performance. *ACSM's Health & Fitness Journal, 20*(1), pp.32–33.

Von Duvillard, S.P., Braun, W.A., Markofski, M., Beneke, R., Leithäuser, R., 2004. Fluids and hydration in prolonged endurance performance. *Nutrition, 20*(7–8), pp.651–656.

Von Hurst, P.R., Beck, K.L., 2014. Vitamin D and skeletal muscle function in athletes. *Current Opinion in Clinical Nutrition and Metabolic Care, 17*(6), pp.539–545.

Wastyk, H.C., Fragiadakis, G.K., Perelman, D., Dahan, D., Merrill, B.D., Yu, F.B., Topf, M., Gonzalez, C.G., Van Treuren, W., Han, S., Robinson, J.L., Elias, J.E., Sonnenburg, E.D., Gardner, C.D., Sonnenburg, J.L., 2021. Gut-microbiota-targeted diets modulate human immune status. *Cell, 184*(16), pp.4137–4153. https://doi.org/10.1016/j.cell.2021.06.019

West, Ayton, Wallman & Guelfi, 2012. The effect of 6 days of sodium phosphate supplementation on appetite, energy intake, and aerobic capacity in trained men and women. *International Journal of Sport Nutrition and Exercise Metabolism, 22*, pp.422–429.

Żebrowska, A., Mizia-Stec, K., Mizia, M., Gąsior, Z., Poprzęcki, S., 2015. Omega-3 fatty acids supplementation improves endothelial function and maximal oxygen uptake in endurance-trained athletes. *European Journal of Sport Science, 15*(4), pp.305–314.

INDEX